About Pearson

Pearson is the world's learning company, with presence across 70 countries worldwide. Our unique insights and world-class expertise comes from a long history of working closely with renowned teachers, authors and thought leaders, as a result of which, we have emerged as the preferred choice for millions of teachers and learners across the world.

We believe learning opens up opportunities, creates fulfilling careers and hence better lives. We hence collaborate with the best of minds to deliver you class-leading products, spread across the Higher Education and K12 spectrum.

Superior learning experience and improved outcomes are at the heart of everything we do. This product is the result of one such effort.

Your feedback plays a critical role in the evolution of our products and you can contact us at reachus@pearson.com. *We look forward to it.*

The Self-destructive Habits of Good Companies

...great to gone

Jagdish N. Sheth
Charles H. Kellstadt Professor of Business,
Goizueta Business School, Emory University

Pearson

ISBN 9789390531318
First Impression, 2021
Second Impression, 2025

Published by Pearson India Education Services Pvt. Ltd, CIN: U72200TN2005PTC057128.

Head Office: 1st Floor, Berger Tower, Plot No. C-001A/2, Sector 16B, Noida - 201 301, Uttar Pradesh, India.
Registered Office: Featherlite, 'The Address' 5th Floor, Survey No 203/10B, 200 Ft MMRD Road, Zamin Pallavaram, Chennai – 600 044.
Website: in.pearson.com; Email: companysecretary.india@pearson.com

Printed in India at: Manipal Technologies Limited, Manipal

BRIEF CONTENTS

CONTENTS

PROLOGUE

Jagdish N. Sheth

INTRODUCTION

The first edition of the book, *Self-Destructive Habits of Good Companies*, was well received. The book was the outcome of a very insightful question asked by the former Chairman of Bellsouth, Duane Ackerman: "Why good companies fail?" This prompted further research in an attempt to answer that question and the findings led to the conclusion that most good companies fail because they are either unable to or unwilling to adapt to the changing ecosystem in which they succeeded and thrived earlier. And their failure or inability to adapt to changing circumstances is a direct result of the *seven* bad habits they acquire and nurture over time. The seven bad habits of good companies are (1) denial of new realities, (2) arrogance, (3) complacency, (4) overdependence on competence, (5) myopic views about competition, (6) territorial impulse (turf wars), and (7) obsession over business volume.

The book was published in April 2007, just before the Great Recession of 2008-2009. It struck a chord and was translated in more than a dozen languages. The seven bad habits of good companies have become indeed become a go-to checklist for companies that look inward to assess their shortcomings or failures. I was asked to write separate books on why good universities, hospitals, and even nations fail. Also, several friends have encouraged me to write about how good individuals also fail due to self-destructive habits. While specific bad habits vary from one institution to another and between the institution and the individual, the underlying message is the same: We all fail because we are either unable or unwilling to change with the changes that surface dramatically in the ecosystem that has been supporting us all along.

Need for Resilience

I also found that institutions that survive in disruptive times have both emotional and physical resilience. In other words, they have the *courage* and the *resources* to transform themselves dramatically to become more adept at dealing with a hostile or unfriendly ecosystem. Generally, the resilience of the institution reduces over time. It seems only natural. Just as young stem cells are more resilient and regenerative than old stem cells, so are organizations that were once young and full of ambitions. But having earned their money, all that the organizations want to do is to metaphorically sit on the beach, sipping Pina Colada and enjoying life, spending the interest earned. In other words, this affliction has a specific name—taking success for granted or complacency borne out of falsely thinking we are too big to go down.

As institutions grow, they develop a strong work culture (identity), procedures and processes (bureaucracy), systems (technology, finance, compliance), and structure (organization) in order to scale up and deliver efficiently through economies of scale. However, though this guarantees success in some measure, it does make the organization less resilient and rigid over time. Compare the time it takes in the Big Three (GM, Ford, and Chrysler) for the concept vehicle to travel from the drawing board to the actual pilot production with time taken by a Japanese automaker or, even better, a nimble-footed Korean automobile manufacturer like Hyundai. It is not just speed but instituting dramatic changes within the organization work culture that helps organizations survive amidst fierce completion at the global marketplace. While it is easy to believe that the company's culture is the hardest to change, my experience is just the opposite: Among all the resources (land, capital, and people), I find that people can change more easily than processes or the work culture instituted, at times forcibly, by the organization. It is easy to blame it on work culture. What is more difficult to change are, however, the processes and systems within the organization. Therefore, one needs to focus on bringing transformation to processes and systems or even replacing them with new, radically different processes and systems that infuse fresh blood into ailing organizations. For example, I find that most big companies lag in IT systems and order processing.

The typical characteristics constituting organizational inability or unwillingness to adapt are presented in the following table:

Typology of Organizations

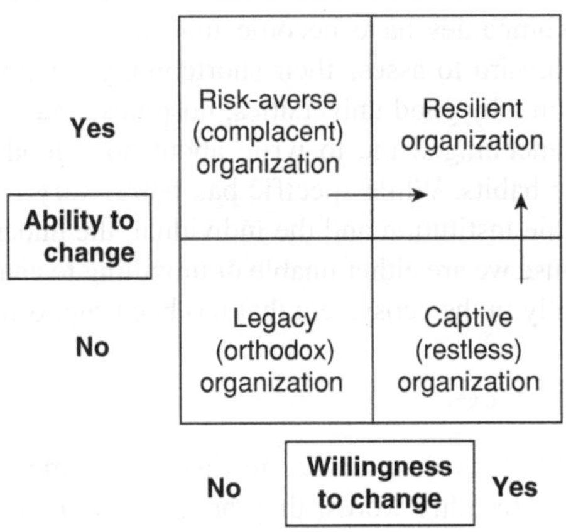

Thus, a resilient organization is both willing to change (emotionally ready) and able to change (physically ready).

The best example of a non-resilient industry is the brick-and-mortar retailers. In 2019 alone, more than 9,300 retail outlets closed shop in America. Large retail chains such as Payless Shoes, Radio Shack, Toys R Us, and Sears, all declared bankruptcy recently. Most of them had legacy systems that became bottlenecks when consumers shifted to online shopping and buying from online B2C sellers like Amazon. Similarly, shopping malls are increasingly becoming service malls (restaurants and movie theaters). Some are also specializing in providing indoor recreation and entertainment.

THE CHANGING ECOSYSTEM OF BUSINESS

Since 2007, the changes in external drivers (ecosystem) have been happening at a more rapid pace. This has generated a greater sense of urgency. It implies that unless the company is resilient in its culture, processes, systems, and structure, it will have a hard time surviving. In my view, most good companies are a victim of a sense of comfort in the scale and scope of operations and steady inflow of profits that they think will go on forever. They believe that their sheer size will keep them alive (too big to fail). Unfortunately, that has never been the case if the government's bailout of Big Three time and again. Other examples include General Electric, DuPont, and Kraft Foods. In fact, the most admired companies in the consumer packaged good industry such as Heinz, Anheuser-Busch (Beer), Procter and Gamble, Unilever, and Nestle are today struggling to grow.

The seven drivers of change in the ecosystem we need to watch are illustrated in the following chart:

Seven Drivers of Change in the Ecosystem

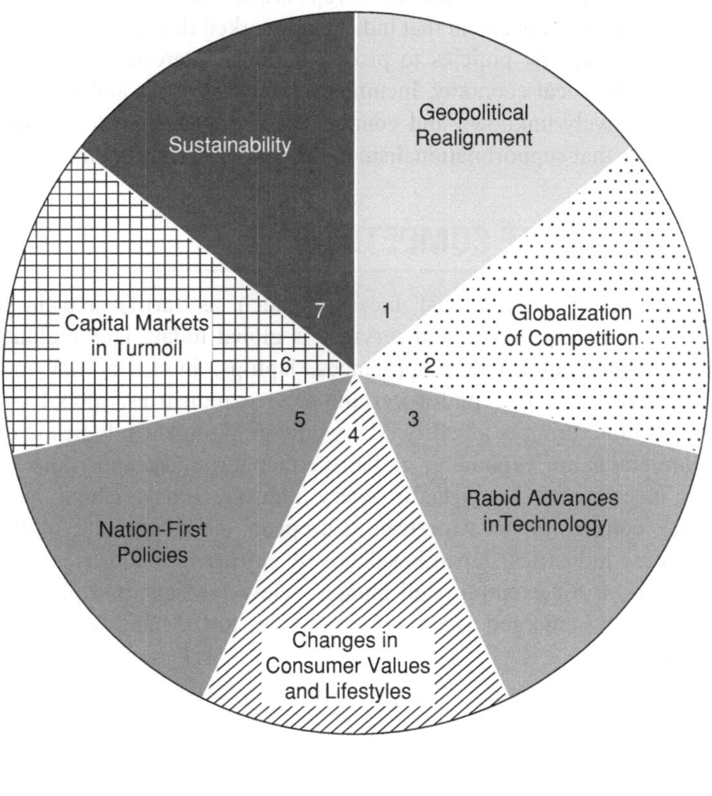

GEOPOLITICAL REALIGNMENT

There is a tectonic shift in the geopolitical alignment of nations (Sheth 2004). The economic power of the old triad of giants consisting North America (Canada and America), Western Europe, and Japan (the 12 common market countries), which controlled 70 percent of the world GDP and 45 percent of the world trade has decisively shifted to a new triad of power consisting of United States, China, and India. Today, the largest consumer markets are China and India for most household products, including automobiles, luxury goods, cell phones, and consumer electronics. This was unimaginable in the past as recent as the 1990s. At the same time, the Middle East is going through constant political unrest and calamities, and no superpower such as the United States or Russia can or wants to control it because of their own internal problems, unlike the Cold War or post–Second World War periods. Finally, collapse of the Soviet Union in 1989 led to the emergence of new powers-that-be such as China in addition to existing power centers such as the United States, with Russia (or the former USSR) no longer in the race for world supremacy. It seems that every nation wants to shift its past allegiance to the United States now to China as the latter seems to be all set to emerge as the number one economy in the world backed by a strong military. China's Belt and Road Initiative (BRI) is a multi-trillion-dollar investment in global infrastructure for trade between China and the rest of the world and especially with Africa and Southeast Asia. Finally, the old alliances between the United States and Europe are in a limbo. On top of this, there is a worldwide populism movement that indicates a marked rise in nationalist sentiments that insist on nation-first policies to protect national interests from FDI even if it means well for the local economy. Incumbent political parties and leaders are being replaced by relatively unknown and younger leaders who seem to support hawkish populist agendas that support nationalism at the cost of even economic growth.

GLOBALIZATION OF COMPETITION

Despite the use of protectionist measures such as tariffs and import bans, competition for most products and services is global today. This includes a range of products, from automobiles, appliances, laptops, industrial raw materials to agricultural fertilizers. Except for certain service industries, global competition with local manufacturing is a reality. Many emerging market's domestic enterprises and conglomerates are expanding globally either through acquisitions or through greenfield investments. In virtually every industry today, China has emerged as a global competitor to American, European, and Japanese multinationals. Indeed, in some industries, Japan is selectively exiting the industries due to higher price competition, for example, cell phones, television sets, and pharmaceuticals. Similarly, India has emerged as a major competitor to IBM and Accenture in the IT services industry.

TECHNOLOGY ADVANCES

Rapid change in technology is another driver of change. This includes not only cell phones, cloud computing, artificial intelligence, and 5G networks but also the exponential growth and popularity of social media. In less than 20 years, social media companies such as Facebook, WhatsApp, Instagram, and Google have truly emerged as global enterprises for information, influence, and transactions. In fact, the two social media platforms with user count bigger than the population of China and India combined are Facebook and WhatsApp. Each has more than two billion subscribers. Today, Ali Baba and Ten Cents in China seem to be ahead of Amazon in e-commerce and online payment platforms. And all of this is not limited to digital technology. There are dramatic discoveries in biological sciences, including DNA-based therapies.

We have seen the disruptive power of Amazon on retailing; Uber in ridesharing; Moocs in education; and Airbnb in the hospitality industry. And the disruptive journey has just begun with unicorn startups in fintech, health tech, agro tech, and any other kind of social networking tech, including those offering online dating and virtual matrimony.

CONSUMER VALUES AND LIFESTYLES

Perhaps the biggest driver of change is consumer values and lifestyles. If the transition of the family from the agriculture age to the industrial age was transformative, it will be even more dramatic and rapid as we transition from the industrial age to the knowledge age. First, in the industrial age, most factory workers were men and most women were homemakers (except teachers, nurses, or some professionals). Today, there is greater gender inclusion in the workforce. More than 60 percent of women work today. There are more women in the workforce than men. This has resulted in a majority of two-wage earner families. This, in turn, has resulted in time shortage and time shift. Today's family needs more conveniences that ever before. There is also a role blurring and role reversal in the family, where husband helps in domestic chores and, in some instances, he is a full-time homemaker.

Second, biggest outsourcing today is not IT services to India, but the family outsourcing the entire gamut of domestic chores such as cooking, cleaning, and childcare to commercial enterprises. In the United States today, 1.5 meals per day are eaten out (breakfast and lunch) and more than 50 percent of the meals eaten at home are ready-to-serve meals home-delivered or picked up from drive-thru food delivery outlets.

Finally, the generation gap is getting shorter and shorter between generations. It is now down to less than 10 years. Often the younger sibling is unable to relate to the older sibling in lifestyles and values. The changing consumer values and lifestyles seem to be more universal and globally enabled by social media, online shopping, and home deliveries.

NATION-FIRST POLICIES

There is a growing trend toward protectionism and nation-first sentiments. What was true for defense and homeland security is now also true for economic policies of countries. The quarter century of liberalization of trade and establishment of the World Trade Organization (WTO) has now taken a backseat to make-in-India, China, or America. What matters most is domestic employment and slowing down cross-border labor mobility between nations and even within regional trade blocks. The BREXIT decision in the United Kingdom was partly due to the free movement of labor in the European Union. The recent trade wars using tariffs as a mechanism are just the tip of the iceberg. Fortunately, unlike the colonial era, today it matters less if the domestic manufacturers are global multinationals. In other words, who owns the business is less relevant so long as they invest locally and employ large number of workers.

CAPITAL MARKETS IN TURMOIL

Since the book's publication in 2007, capital markets have been in turmoil. The great bailout of many iconic companies such as General Motors, Chrysler, and large banks during the great economic recession has shifted capital markets (equity as well as debt) to private capital. Some of the largest corporates today with several trillion dollars of assets under management are companies such as Blackstone and Black Rock, and they are investing everywhere, ranging from venture capital to large infrastructure projects. This is further complemented by national sovereign funds of countries like Norway, Singapore, China, and Saudi Arabia.

In some sense, today's private capital markets remind us what happened in the 1980s following the first energy crisis of 1974-1976. Private capital bought out some of the largest conglomerates and broke them up to create value for investors. Today, it is the activist investors who are forcing mergers, demergers, and breakup of enterprises. Examples include Kraft Foods, DuPont-Dow Chemicals, General Electric, and the health care industry in general.

SUSTAINABILITY MANDATE

There is no greater existential threat than environmental sustainability. With the growing middle-class population in China and India, and recently in Africa, all of whom want to buy and consume branded products, it is inevitable that the environment will be the showstopper (Sheth 2014, Chindia Rising). Denying climate change is probably the biggest risk that no company can afford to ignore. And it will be especially true for fossil fuel energy and its derivatives such as petrochemicals. It will also have an enormous impact on the agriculture sector, especially as it relates to water pollution and deforestation.

In addition to these seven drivers of the changing ecosystem, there are of course, several "Black Swan" events, which are unpredictable and spread rapidly like wildfires. These include the "Me too" movement and the coronavirus. The "Black Swan" events are difficult to forecast and plan. What a company needs to do is to be totally prepared and keep resource stockpile ready for survival in the short-term as well as to prepare for the long-term transformation.

A large number of "good to great" companies today are "great to gone." In the United States, these include Sears, General Electric, Research in Motion (Blackberry), Motorola, Lucent, Chrysler, Merrill Lynch, and numerous hospitality brands. In many cases, their core competency has in fact become their liability. In other cases, their myopic view of competition prevented them from identifying or recognizing the presence of nontraditional competitors. Finally, some of them suffered from turf wars between functional disciplines such as engineering, sales, finance, R&D, and marketing.

The decade of the 2020s will experience greater turbulence due to political uncertainty and declining confidence in the stock markets. This will result in more consolidation within the industry and globally. A good proactive diagnosis of the organization on the seven bad habits and especially the denial of new realities (competition, technology, and emerging markets) may go a long way in assuring survival and resilience.

While most businesses succeed by accident, they don't decline accidentally. There is no inevitability of birth and death or even the survival of the fittest. The stories are different today as compared to the first edition that came out more than a decade ago. However, the message is the same. If you don't want to be "great to gone," you must engage in preventive diagnosis, regular checkups, and audit of the company's health. It will be also necessary to do forensic tests periodically and enact downside risk simulations and stress tests to measure company's preparedness.

Despite all this, you will need luck and divine intervention. As they say in Star Wars, "may the force be with you."

PREFACE

I trace this book's origins to one of the most insightful questions I have ever been asked by a corporate executive: ***Why do good companies fail***? The CEO who posed this riddle had been a great fan of the 1980s business best seller ***In Search of Excellence*** by Tom Peters and Robert Waterman. However, as time went by, he was struek by how many of the companies cited as exemplars of world-class corporations were either struggling or no longer in existence. This included such icons of U.S. business as Sears, Dana Corporation, AT&T, Xerox, IBM, and Kodak.

The more I pondered the CEO's question, the more curious I became as to why companies that seem to be doing so well and that are at the top of their industry can almost overnight spiral downward into survival mode. The eompanies I'm talking about are not government-protected monopolies that have suddenly been cast into the churning seas of competition. I'm referring to world-class businesses that appear to have top managers, a proven track record of success, inventive products, and a seemingly unassailable competitive position. Why do these companies go bad?

My journey toward an answer began with archival research to identify companies that were great in their time and that had subsequently faded away. During this proeess I tried to understand the reasons for their downfall. The message that came out of the research was simple: Good companies fail when they are unable or, more curiously, unwilling to change when their external environment changes significantly.

Underlying this inability or unwilhngness to change, I discovered the self-destructive habits successful companies acquire on their way to greatness. As my research progressed, I began to give presentations to professional managers and MBA students on my findings, and I would talk about self-destructive habits such as denial, complaeency, or cost-ineffieieney. I would often joke that I should write a book called ***The Self-Destructive Habits of Good Companies***. Instead of making a joke of it, more and more people suggested that I write the book.

I have written about seven self-destructive habits in this book. Although I could have included an eighth or ninth habit, my purpose is not to present an exhaustive list of self-destructive habits but to identify those that are the most crucial to avoid. And if forced to narrow down this list even further, 1 would have to say that denial of the new reality (Chapter 2) and the territorial impulse, or internal turf wars (Chapter 8), are the two most dangerous habits.

There are three conflicting theories as to why companies die. One is population ecology or "survival of the fittest" theory: Companies die because bigger and better companies will come along and take away their business. In other words, you die by being systemically weeded out by the competition.

The second is the inevitability or "birth and death" theory. Just like the human life cycle, this theory suggests that a cycle of birth and death is inevitable for all companies. There is nothing you can do about your company's eventual demise—it's just a matter of time before fate runs its course.

My view, however, is that most companies can survive forever if they recognize and take steps to counter self-destructive habits or set up processes to keep them from arising in the first place. I felt this was possible because habits are learned behaviors, not inevitabilities. Therefore, it is important that I not only show you how to identify self-destructive habits but also suggest prescriptive measures for curing them, and I have done so in each chapter. And while curing self-destructive habits is an admirable achievement for the afflicted, an even more sound approach is to devise preventive programs to avoid them in the first place (Chapter 9).

An underlying theme of this book is that great leadership is crucial for helping a company avoid or break self-destructive habits. Good leaders provide vision for the company. However, great leaders, in addition to being visionaries, must be grounded in the reality of current and potential vulnerabilities posed by a hostile and constantly changing external environment. Great leaders are constantly looking out for self-destructive habits that will get in the way of the exciting vision.

I hope to generate dialog from the readers oi this book. I encourage you to provide stories you have encountered about any of the self-destructive habits. The website www.destructivehabits.com has been set up for you to post examples of companies that have been afflicted with self-destructive habits, as well as companies that have done a good job of correcting or avoiding them. I also plan to have a blog that will provide updates and commentary about the companies mentioned in this book and the companies suggested by readers. With your help, I might be able to offer a revised version of this book in the near future.

Jagdish N. Sheth

ACKNOWLEDGMENTS

This book's thoroughness and readability would not have been possible without the assistance of John Yow. This is the second book he has helped me complete, and again his in-depth research and uncanny knack for shaping ideas and concepts into a highly readable and entertaining tome were an important element of the final manuscript. John is the consummate Southern gentleman. Working with him was a pleasure both professionally and personally.

I look forward to collaborating with him on future books.

Mark Hutcheson also provided key assistance in moving this book to a final manuscript. He provided additional research on companies, offered editorial comments and suggestions, and contributed to a number of passages. He also worked diligently to manage the manuscript process and to coordinate efforts with the publisher.

I would also like to thank my longtime assistant, Beth Robinson, for her devotion and for keeping me on track during the hectic times that surrounded the writing of this book. Not only does she manage a constant flood of e-mails, phone calls, appointments, and business travel planning with professionalism and calm, she is also a great sounding board.

This book would not have been written, or at least would not have been written as quickly, without enthusiastic encouragement from Yoram (Jerry) Wind, coeditor of Wharton School Publishing. As soon as 1 explained to him how these self-destructive habits destroy great companies, he was insistent that I move forward with a manuscript and bring the project to Wharton School Publishing. His enthusiasm and excitement were infectious and were a major reason why you're reading this book. 1 also received similar enthusiastic support from Wharton's executive editor, Tim Moore.

And finally, I would like to express my gratitude to everyone at Wharton School Publishing who was involved with this book's review and production. This goes especially to Paula Sinnott, who was a pleasure to work with and who kept the publication process on track, and to Russ Hall, who provided valuable editorial polish to the final manuscript.

Jagdish N. Sheth

ABOUT THE AUTHOR

Dr. Jagdish (Jag) N. Sheth is the Charles H. Kellstadt Professor of Marketing in the Goizueta Business School at Emory University. Prior to his present position, he was at the University of Southern California (7 years); at the University of Illinois (15 years); and on the faculty of Columbia University (5 years) as well as the Massachusetts Institute of Technology (2 years). Dr. Sheth is well known for his scholarly contributions in consumer behavior, relationship marketing, competitive strategy, and geopolitical analysis.

Professor Sheth is highly sought out as a keynote speaker at many industry, academic, and public forums. He has worked for numerous industries and companies in the United States, Europe, and Asia, both as an advisor and as a seminar leader. His clients include AT&T, BellSouth, Cox Communications, Delta, Ernst & Young, Ford, GE, Lucent Technologies, Motorola, Nortel, Pillsbury, Sprint, Square D, 3M, Whirlpool, Wipro, Alcatel, Ericsson, Siemens, General Foods, Unilever, Philips, Thysson-Krupp, ABG, Tata Group, Marico, General Mills, and many more. He has offered more than a thousand presentations in at least twenty countries. Dr. Sheth is frequently quoted and interviewed by the ***Wall Street Journal, New York Times, Fortune, Financial Times, Economic Times***, and radio shows and television networks such as CNN, CNBC (India), and BBC. He is also on the board of directors of several public companies, including Cryo Cell International (NASDAQ), Wipro Limited (NYSE), and Shasun Chemicals.

In 1989, Dr. Sheth was given the Outstanding Marketing Educator award by the Academy of Marketing Science. In 1991 and again in 1999, he was given the Outstanding Educator Award by the Sales and Marketing Executives International (SMEI). Dr. Sheth was also awarded the P.D. Converse Award for his outstanding contributions to theory in marketing in 1992 by the American Marketing Association. In 1996, Dr. Sheth was selected as the Distinguished Fellow of the Academy of Marketing Science. In 1997, Dr. Sheth was awarded the Distinguished Fellow award from the International Engineering Consortium. Dr. Sheth is also a Fellow of the American Psychological Association (APA). The year 2004 marked a stellar year for Dr. Sheth as he was awarded both the Richard D. Irwin Distinguished Marketing Educator and the Charles Coolidge Parlin Awards, which are the two highest awards given by the American Marketing Association. In 2005, he was recognized as the Society for Marketing Advances's 2005 Elsevier Distinguished Professor, and in 2006 he received the RHR International Award for Excellence in Consultation from the American Psychological Association. Dr. Sheth was named the Emory University Faculty Lecturer for 2007, the first time a business school professor has been given this honor.

A prolific author, in 2000 Dr. Sheth and Andrew Sobel published a best seller. ***Clients for Life*** (Simon & Schuster). His book, ***The Rule of Three*** (Free Press), coauthored with Dr. Rajendra Sisodia, altered the current notions on competition in business. It was published in 2002 and has been translated into German, Italian, Polish, Japanese, and Chinese. It was the subject of a seven-part television series by CNBC (India) and was a finalist for the 2004 Best Marketing Book Award from the American Marketing Association. His most recent book, ***Firms of Endearment: How World-Class Companies Profit from Passion and Purpose***, was published in 2007 by Wharton School Publishing.

FOREWORD

I am surprised and flattered that my close friend and distinguished colleague chose to dedicate his new book to me. I am especially pleased that my question to Dr. Jagdish Sheth all those years ago proved to be the impetus for ***The Self-Destructive Habits of Good Companies***—one of the most insightful business books to appear in some time.

My friendship with Jag (as he is known to all) goes back many years, as does my debt to his wise counsel. Jag was a trusted confidant of mine, and of BellSouth's, during years of considerable turmoil in the telecommunications industry, and he helped us challenge the status quo business beliefs that followed our company as we exited our monopoly ancestry. Jag helped us challenge the thinking of senior leaders as well as middle managers and that work influenced the culture that emerged in a competitive BellSouth.

Of course, BellSouth is but one of many companies for whom Jag has provided his invaluable expertise. The list of distinguished companies that have called upon his help is a long one and spans three continents—North America, Europe, and Asia. I'm constantly amazed at his frenetic consulting and speaking schedule, yet he still finds time to teach some of the most popular courses at Emory University's Goizueta Business School, where he holds the Charles H. Kellstadt chair. The university and the community were fortunate when Jag decided to make Atlanta his home.

This new book (the latest of several, by the way) quickly reveals the breadth of Jag's expertise and the depth of his insights. For obvious reasons, I was particularly interested in the chapter entitled "Complacency: Success Breeds Failure," especially about the complacency that results "when your past success came via a regulated monopoly." Reading again about the forced breakup of AT&T in 1984 reminded me of the painful lessons that companies in many industries were forced to learn thanks to deregulation—lessons that Jag spells out in no uncertain terms. I must say I had to laugh when Jag's account reminded me that, after the breakup, AT&T at first wanted to rename itself American Bell International, until Judge Harold Greene intervened. Jag writes that he still has the tie that Randall Tobias gave him with the new ABI logo on it. "Hold onto it," Tobias told Jag. "It'll be a keepsake one day."

I also particularly enjoyed the chapter, "The Territorial Impulse: Culture Conflicts and Turf Wars." It's no secret that teamwork has always been a mantra of mine, and Jag's metaphor of the company structured as "a complex of 50-story office towers, connected only by common areas at the bottom and the top" speaks volumes about the way many businesses are run today.

So it is in chapter after chapter that Jag analyzes companies like Digital Equipment, CM, Firestone, and Zenith. Jag's dozens of illustrations are always incisive, but the book wouldn't be complete without, at the end of each chapter, his "warning signs" of each bad habit and, most helpful, his step-by-step approach to breaking each habit before it does its damage.

The Self-Destructive Habits of Good Companies is entertaining, instructive, and tremendously valuable. I could not recommend it more strongly.

—F. Duane Ackerman, Chairman Emeritus, BellSouth Corporation

CHAPTER 1

WHY DO GOOD COMPANIES GO BAD?

Why do good companies go bad? Honestly, I hadn't thought too much about this question. Then a CEO friend of mine brought up the 62 "excellent" companies praised by Tom Peters and Robert Waterman in their early 1980s bestseller ***In Search of Excellence.*** A great many of them—including such stalwarts as Sears, Xerox, IBM, and Kodak—had faced serious hardships in the 20-odd years since. Some of them recovered. Some, as I write, are struggling mightily to recover. Some are dead or, in all likelihood, soon will be.

So why do good companies go bad? This heartfelt and insightful question launched me on a journey of discovery. I started by conducting archival research on companies that had failed during the past several decades, interviewed people from some of the failed companies, and eventually came to the conclusions presented here. Although it is commonly believed that institutions are (at least potentially) immortal and humans are mortal, I found that the average life span of corporations is declining, even as that of humans is rising. Others have come to similar conclusions. In the best-known work in this area, ***The Living Company,*** Arie de Geus found that one-third of the companies listed in the 1970 Fortune 500 had vanished by 1983, either through acquisition, merger, or being broken up. De Geus quoted a Dutch survey showing that the average corporate life expectancy in Japan and Europe was 12.5 years. Another study found declining corporate life expectancy across the major European economies: from 45 to 18 years in Germany, from 13 to nine years in France, and from ten to four years in Great Britain.

Much of the decline in corporate life expectancy is the result of a heightened level of merger and acquisition activity in recent decades. However, most of this activity is due to distress selling rather than strategic buying because so many companies are in trouble.

Let me say at once that I have no intention of discounting the need to learn the underlying causes of success—the "good habits" of good companies. Nor will I second-guess de Geus or Peters and Waterman or others, like Jim Collins. For very good reasons, they singled out certain companies as models of success—companies that, for very different reasons, have since fallen on hard times. My purpose is not to reexamine why these companies were considered "excellent" or "visionary" in the first place. I am interested in what happened to them afterward—why they fell, why they failed, why they lost the magic touch. What happened?

In my view, when companies rise to excellence, they often unwittingly develop self-destructive habits that eventually undermine their success. As with people, these self-destructive habits are learned, not innate, and we can watch as companies adopt patterns of behavior that are self-destructive. Sometimes these habits get worse over time and become, in effect, addictions. But self-destructive habits can also be broken and overcome, and companies can be put back on the road to improved health.

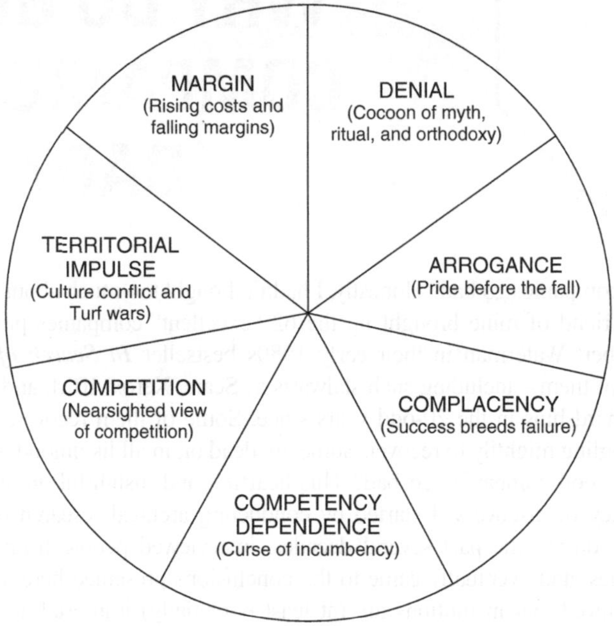

Figure 1-1 Self-destructive habits of good companies

Often the turnaround is precipitated by a crisis. Our self-destructive habits creep up on us, if you will. We overeat, fail to exercise, maybe even smoke, but we think we're still doing okay—until we have that major heart attack, that—potent reminder of mortality. Suddenly our self-destructive habits are gone, and we're eating salads and walking five miles a day. In the case of corporations, the crisis might take the form of an emerging competitor, a sudden erosion of market share, or a technological advance that threatens to leave the company behind. Such developments can spell doom, or they can serve to shake companies out of their destructive behavior patterns.

We'll see plenty of examples of companies that are actively working to curb their self-destructive habits, to change their behavior, as well as companies that have already done so and are "in recovery." Our message is positive: if you're willing to examine yourself honestly enough to discover your weaknesses, you can ultimately transform yourself.

So what are these self-destructive habits? We'll enumerate them one by one in the following chapters (and they're summarized in Figure 1-1). But first, let's see them in action by examining three companies in the technology sector.

DIGITAL

It's one of the great success stories in the annals of American business. In 1957 Kenneth Olsen, a 31-year-old engineer at MIT's Lincoln Laboratory, asked for $70,000 from American Research & Development to start a new firm he wanted to call Digital Computer Corp. He got the money, but the venture capitalists made him change the name. They pointed out that too many big companies, like RCA and General Electric, were losing money in the computer business.

So Digital Equipment Corporation set up shop in an old wool mill in Maynard, Massachusetts, and Ken Olsen set about to pursue his dream: to revolutionize the computer industry with the introduction of the "minicomputer"—a smaller, simpler, more useful, and far cheaper device than the bulky mainframes that were the industry standard.

In its first year. Digital had sales of $94,000. Five years later that number reached ***$6.5*** million. In 1977, the company hit the ***$1*** billion mark. Digital found itself leading an industry boom rippling from the Boston area that created so many high-paying jobs and thus came to be called the Massachusetts Miracle. At the same time, the reputation of its founder grew. He was brilliant and eccentric. He protected his innovative engineers. He instituted a no-layoff policy. Digital was known as "a fun place to work."

No wonder that when Tom Peters and Bob Waterman went "in search of excellence" for what became their 1982 bestseller. Digital not only made the list of excellent companies but was also considered one of the 15 "exemplars" that basically did everything right. It was one of the companies that represented "especially well both sound performance and the eight traits [of excellence]" the authors identified. Such high accolades appeared to be borne out when ***Fortune*** magazine, in 1986, declared Olsen "arguably the most successful entrepreneur in the history of American business."

Let's jump ahead to the end of that decade. In January 1989, Digital announced it would introduce a range of personal computers, along with their more powerful cousins, workstations. The question was, had Olsen already waited too long? One thing was certain: the stock was trading at ***$98,*** down from ***$199*** just a year and a half earlier. Another certainty was that the minicomputer, the radical innovation on which Olsen had staked his company, was rapidly becoming a high-tech dinosaur. Today it's clear that the writing was on the wall. But Olsen had erased it and scrawled his own message; "The personal computer will fall flat on its face in business." Now his company appeared to be acknowledging its failure to see the future.

Despite the eleventh-hour about-face, the hemorrhaging at Digital continued through 1991. Top executives were fleeing, and the company that abhorred layoffs was in the process of cutting 10,000 employees from the payroll. By then, Olsen had been in charge for 34 years and still entertained no thoughts of retirement. Instead, he used the annual shareholders' meeting that year to introduce the company's next-generation "Alpha" computer chip, which Olsen claimed was four times faster than the top-of-the-line chip from Intel. But the shareholders probably weren't heartened because the stock was now trading at $59 a share.

In the spring of 1992, the company flabbergasted Wall Street with the news that it had lost 294 million in the quarter that had just ended, only the second time in its history that Digital had reported a loss. Olsen responded with a massive restructuring of top-level management. It didn't help. By the end of April, the stock had fallen to $46, its lowest price since 1985, and takeover rumors were circulating.

That same spring, the ***Wall Street Journal*** seemed to be working on its first draft of Olsen's obituary. The journal noted that a secret meeting between Olsen and Apple's John Sculley—a meeting that might have produced an alliance with much potential for Digital—had come to nothing. Instead, Apple had shocked the industry by inking a broad technology-sharing agreement with archenemy IBM.

The journal described this as another opportunity apparently lost to Digital and Olsen. His persistent doubts about the PC—"he used to call it a 'toy'"—had crippled the nation's second-largest computer maker when the market turned to PCs. The journal also noted that Olsen's resistance to another major trend of the last decade—so-called open systems that use standard operating software—had similarly impeded the company's performance.

Digital was now faced with the danger of being left behind by the industry it was instrumental in creating. As it struggled with huge losses on declining sales, repeated restructurings, and the exodus of key executives who questioned Olsen's decisions, the company watched its value plummet, with shares trading at one-fourth of their 1987 high.

At the same time, Olsen's autocratic style was drawing widespread criticism. John Rose, who a month earlier had resigned as manager of Digital's PC unit, told the journal that the company "has everything it needs to turn around—good people, good products and great service—but it won't happen while he's still in charge." And one of Digital's former computer designers described Olsen as the Fidel Castro of the computer industry, adding that he's "out of touch, and anyone who disagrees with him is sent into exile."

One who had fallen into disfavor amid the recent turmoil was Digital's chief engineer William Strecker, who had opposed a mainframe project that Olsen backed, despite the fact that it was proving a costly failure. The disbanding of Strecker's group was viewed as an especially strong signal of disarray in the executive suite. A former Digital manager told the journal that it was a "criminal shame," because Strecker was the only member of the inner circle who could develop a coherent product strategy.

The journal suggested that Olsen's support of the ill-fated VAX 9000 mainframe, which cost ***$1*** billion to bring to market but attracted few buyers, was partly responsible for Olsen's failure to work out a deal with Apple. Roger Heinen, an Apple senior vice president who was privy to the meeting, blamed the stalemate on Olsen's disinterest and lack of understanding of the importance of the personal computer industry. The journal concluded that Olsen's vision of the computer industry was lacking and that his choices were leaving the company at a disadvantage in a market that was rapidly transforming.

Just two months later, in July 1992, Digital announced that Olsen would retire as president and CEO, effective October 1. Olsen quickly followed with his own announcement that he would also vacate his seat on the board at that time, thus severing all formal ties to the company he had led since its inception. His resignation would also give a free hand to his successor, Robert Palmer, who faced the unenviable task of rescuing a company that had reported a loss of ***$2.79*** billion in fiscal 1992.

Would the seven-year Digital veteran prove up to the challenge? He certainly seemed to be giving it his best shot. After six months on the job. Palmer had reorganized, slashed costs as well as jobs, recruited a new management team from outside, changed the color of the Digital logo, and, most radically, sold the old mill, the company's first and only home base. Palmer also announced a fundamental change in philosophy: a 19% spending cut on product development and engineering. No longer would Digital put competing teams to work on the same or similar problems (a practice highly praised in ***In Search of Excellence***). "We have to rationalize our spending, have less redundancy in hardware and software design," Palmer told the business press.

Early results were promising. In July 1993, the company announced quarterly earnings of 113 million. The stock price was rising back into the mid-40s. Even more important in many analysts' minds, wrote the ***Washington Post,*** was that "under Palmer the company is no longer in denial."

Too little, too late. Ultimately, Palmer couldn't stop the bleeding. In January 1998, the crippled giant was acquired by Compaq—ironically, the world's largest maker of PCs—for 9.15 billion. The great Digital was dead.

All the postmortems agreed that, in the last analysis, the visionary's vision had failed: the company blinked and missed the PC revolution; blinked again and missed the change to open, rather than proprietary, systems; and, in classic denial, continued through the early 1990s to pour money into developing a new mainframe.

As C. Gordon Bell, one of the chief engineers in Digital's early days, told the ***Boston Globe,*** the company's success bred its failure. "The VAX [minicomputer] took over the company, and what it allowed them to do was not think. No one had to think from 1981 until 1987 or '88 because the VAX was so dominant."

Digital was not the only giant computer company that found itself struggling in the early 1990s. Big Blue, IBM itself, was also on the ropes. What happened there makes for an interesting contrast. But first let's back up.

IBM's roots go back to 1911, when two small companies specializing in measuring scales, time clocks, and tabulating machines for clerks and accountants merged to form the Computing, Tabulating, and Recording Company. The new company floundered for three years, and its board seriously discussed liquidation. Instead, they hired Tom Watson Sr. away from National Cash Register in 1914. Under Watson's leadership, the company's health gradually improved, and by 1930 it had become the market leader in tabulating machines. Watson's far-reaching vision for the company was in evidence when in 1925 he changed the company's name to International Business Machines.

Watson Sr.'s success, and that of his company, is often attributed to his fierce adherence to what he called his "three basic beliefs": give full consideration to the individual employee, spend a lot of time making customers happy, and go the last mile to do things right and seek superiority in all that we undertake. Watson Sr. also consciously created a culture to embody and promulgate these beliefs—"an organization of dedicated zealots," as Jim Collins and Jerry Porras called it in ***Built to Last.*** IBM's process of institutionalization and indoctrination encompassed appearance (dark suits), behavior (no drinking), and attitudes (high and mighty). In the words of Watson Sr., "You cannot be a success in any business without believing that it is the greatest business in the world."

Guided by its core beliefs and proud of its unique culture, IBM evolved from the leader in tabulating machines to the dominant player in the computer industry, a position it has held for decades. Not surprisingly, IBM was not only hailed as one of the 15 "exemplars" in ***In Search of Excellence***, it was also one of the 18 "visionary" companies profiled in Collins and Porras's influential study, published in 1994.

To attain "visionary" status, say Collins and Porras, a company must be willing to take the big risk (much as Digital did by developing the minicomputer). A company must be willing to pursue what the authors call a "Big Hairy Ambitious Goal." In IBM's case, the BHAG was to reshape the computer industry in the early 1960s with an all-or-nothing investment in a new computer—the IBM 360. According to the authors, when IBM rolled the dice on the 360, it was the largest privately financed commercial project ever attempted, and it used more resources than the United States did to develop the first atomic bomb. Tom Watson Jr., who succeeded his father as CEO, described it as the biggest and riskiest decision he had ever made.

The gamble paid off, to say the least. The company soared on the success of the 360, and its position of industry leader was further solidified—that is, until the company began to slip in the late 1980s and early 1990s. In 1992 IBM suffered its worst year in history, posting a nearly $5 billion net loss. Its stock was down 70% from its all-time high, wiping out more than 70 billion in shareholder value. What had happened?

In the case of Digital, Ken Olsen was in denial; he refused to change. In contrast, IBM knew it needed to change but simply couldn't. Presiding CEO John Akers was no Ken Olsen, and he lamented his inability to bring about the necessary transformation. He couldn't make the ocean liner change direction. IBM's culture was too ingrained, and its DNA seemed inalterable. The company was trapped by its own competency, victimized by what I call the "expertise paradox." Plus, it had been doing so well for so long that it had become complacent. Ironically, IBM had originated the concept of the home computer in the early 1980s. But its position in mainframes was so dominant and so secure that it continued to set the eompany's direction while the PC market was inundated by less expensive IBM clones. Lou Gerstner, former CEO at IBM, hit on an appropriate metaphor in the title of his autobiography: ***Who Says Elephants Can't Dance?***

Collins and Porras say that IBM began to lose its stature as a visionary company in the late 1980s and early 1990s because it lost sight of Watson Sr.'s core beliefs. There was too much emphasis on the ***trappings*** of its vaunted culture—blue suits, white shirts, and even computers—and not enough on real core values. "IBM should have much more vigorously changed ***everything*** about itself ***except*** its core values," write the authors. "Instead, it stuck too long to strategic and operating practices and cultural manifestations of the core values."

Collins and Porras go on to say that visionary companies have an extraordinary resiliency and the ability to rebound from adversity. However, interestingly, they looked with disapproval at IBM's overtures toward Lou Gerstner, who was being offered IBM's top post even as they were writing. "What should one make of IBM's 1993 decision to replace its internally grown CEO with Gerstner—an outsider from R.J. Reynolds with no industry experience? How does this massive anomaly fit with what we've seen in our other visionary companies? It doesn't fit. IBM's decision simply doesn't make any sense to us—at least not in the context of the seventeen hundred cumulative years of history we examined in the visionary companies."

If the IBM board was looking for drastic change, the authors write, "With Mr. Gerstner, they'll probably get it. But the real question for IBM—indeed, the pivotal issue over the next decade—is: Can Gerstner preserve the core ideals of IBM while simultaneously bringing about this momentous change?"

They were not the only ones asking such questions in 1993. Before Gerstner's ascension, IBM had had only six chief executives in its long history—all career Big Blue men. The new chief would not only have to master a new industry, he would somehow have to transform an entrenched corporate culture. At the same time, he had to tackle the fundamental task of rebuilding shareholder value and reenergizing IBM's huge workforce. Frankly, there weren't many believers. As soon as word of Gerstner's selection got out, the company's stock fell more than three dollars.

But within just a few months, the doomsayers were recanting. Gerstner was being widely praised for listening to and acting on the recommendations of his 200 top customers, rather than on the advice of his internal management team. It seemed he had stifled the turf wars among competing functions and product lines by going straight to customers and finding out what ***their*** needs were. Collins and Porras, no doubt, would have also applauded because in so doing Gerstner was surely getting back to Watson Sr.'s basic beliefs—particularly number 2: "Spend a lot of time making customers happy."

In two short years, the Gerstner turnaround was well under way. He had cut the workforce; sold assets, including real estate and a 300-piece art collection; and cut the dividend on the company's common stock. Costs were down, and profit margins were **rising**. The company was already back on the block by 1994; then it reported record profits in the first quarter of 1995, far exceeding analyst forecasts. Shares were back up to $90, more than double their 1993 low. The company even began to act like its old "imperial" self again—moving to acquire Lotus Corp. for ***$3.5*** billion.

By 1998, Gerstner's work was complete. As the ***San Francisco Chronicle*** rhapsodized, "Given up for dead by many people just five years ago. Big Blue has enjoyed under Lou Gerstner one of the great turnarounds in the annals of U.S. business." IBM's record sales and profits in 1997 and soaring stock price were signs that IBM had regained its throne atop the computing world.

But it's not enough to say that IBM had returned to its old self; more accurately, the company, under Gerstner, had managed to reinvent itself. The ***Chronicle*** noted that what had really driven IBM's prosperity was its ability to help businesses enter the Internet age by working with them to develop, implement, and maintain their computer systems. This included their networks, intranets, and electronic commerce websites. IBM not only supplied the equipment—whether its own or other companies'—it also serviced the systems. Such services now account for more than 50% of IBM's sales.

The transformation has been quite remarkable. Golf fans watching the 2005 Masters Tournament, for example, saw dozens of commercials touting "IBM Global Services," which basically continues the "Solutions for a Small Planet" and "e-business" campaigns that began back in 1997 and 1998. With the help of those ads, IBM was trying to acquire a reputation as the company that others turn to for their technology needs. It was much more successful in promoting that image than its nearest competitor, Hewlett-Packard (HP).

In the last analysis, Gerstner not only changed the fortunes of IBM; he changed its image. The focus on services and the advertising supporting it gave the company a new personality. "Five years ago, people would say that IBM has an incredible brain, but not a heart," says Ogilvy Mather's Shelly Lazarus, whose company created the "Solutions" campaign. "Today, it...also has a heart and a soul and a sense of humor."

INTEL

In 1968, Andy Grove and Gordon Moore built a factory to manufacture chips for video game makers such as Atari. It was a good idea, and their company, Intel Gorp., had promise—until the video game industry was overwhelmed by Nintendo, which preferred to buy chips made in Japan. Suddenly Intel had more chips than buyers. About that time, though, IBM began to develop the PC, for which it would need just the sort of microchips that Intel was producing in abundance. It was a match made in high-tech heaven. Intel quickly became the world's number-one chip maker, a position it has maintained ever since.

But technology, as we have seen, continues to develop. What happened to the mainframe, and what subsequently happened to the minicomputer, is now happening to the PC. Cell phones, handheld computers, and other gadgets are eroding the demand for PCs. Now it is Intel's turn to adjust to a changing marketplace. Let's take a quick look at how the company has been doing.

At the end of 2000, Intel announced that its two-year partnership with Analog Devices was about to yield fruit. The company was ready to bring to market a new chip—the high-performance digital signal processor (DSP) for use in "third-generation" wireless devices such as advanced cell phones and palm-size computers. The problem, though, as we saw with Digital, was that Intel was following, not leading, the market. Indispensable components of electronic gadgets like modems, CD players, and cell phones, DSPs had for some time been the fastest-growing segment of the microchip market.

Intel's job, then, was not only to produce the DSP but also to oust the market leader, Texas Instruments. (It's worth noting that TI showed considerable prescience in making the leap to DSP. It could have continued to make PG chips, but, realizing that Intel had already won that battle, it looked over the horizon. There it saw the future in "best-access" gadgets like the then-emerging cell phone, and it concluded that the DSP was the direction to take.) For its part, Intel realized, correctly, that its PC chip business was tied to slowing growth in PC sales, but the realization came later rather than sooner. TI had already tied up a 60% share of the digital wireless phone business, and Mike McMahan, the company's head of R&D, told the ***Boston Globe*** that he was confident of their position in the market.

Like Digital and IBM, Intel's story illustrates that when you're totally dominant in your chosen arena, it's hard to pay much attention to what's happening outside that arena. It's too easy, also, to ignore competition. If that was the case with the DSP in 2000, it happened to Intel again in 2003, when Advanced Micro Devices (AMD) beat Intel to the market with a product it called Opteron—a chip that offered advanced 64-bit computing power while retaining the ability to run thousands of 32-bit Windows-compatible programs. According to one account, Intel and others inside the industry scoffed at the new chip from AMD, but within a year its customer list included IBM, Sun Microsystems, and HP. Then Intel had to play catch-up again. In early 2004, the company announced that it would add 64-bit capacity to its 32-bit Xeon server chips.

The story's amusing twist is that, a decade earlier, Intel's then CEO Andy Grove had derided AMD as "the Milli Vanilli of semiconductors," taunting the smaller company for mimicking Intel chip designs rather than creating its own processors from scratch. Fred Weber, AMD's chief technology officer, admitted to feeling "some emotional satisfaction" from seeing the tables turned. He credited AMD's success not to chance but to a five-to-seven-year strategy of "innovating in places where they were not."

Has Intel's dominant position also allowed it to take its customers for granted? An executive at Boxx Technologies, an AMD customer, points out that AMD keeps Intel honest and that competition is critical. "If you took AMD out of the picture," he says, "Intel would really slow down to maximize its return on investment." AMD's Weber puts it more forcefully: "Intel has an arrogance out of being a near monopolist.... Its respect for the customer is created by customers yelling at it."

Whether Intel will be able to shed its perceived arrogance and complacency, stay abreast of its competitors, and respond to the evolving demands of the marketplace is a question now facing its newly appointed CEO, Paul Otellini, a company veteran who ascended through the marketing, rather than engineering, ranks. Will Otellini be able to reinvent Intel as Gerstner reinvented IBM and find a new direction for the company in the face of a largely saturated PC market? Based on his advocacy of the "right-hand turn"—a sharp break from the "cherished belief' that nothing matters more than ever-faster, more powerful computer chips—Otellini may be the right man for the job. He appears to be pushing the company toward the realization that, in addition to speed, customers now want things like built-in security features, wireless connectivity to the Internet, and better graphics and audio. With his marketing background, maybe he'll be able to shake up the company's elitist, high-tech engineering culture.

IT'S ALL ABOUT LEADERSHIP

So what "self-destructive habits" do you find in the interconnected stories of these three companies? Denial? Arrogance? Complacency? Check. Check. Check. How about "competency dependence" and "competitive myopia"? Check, check. Given a slightly different slant, these stories could also illustrate our final two self-destructive habits, "territoriality" (internal turf wars) and "volume obsession" (too-high cost structures). But I have lots more stories to tell. The following chapters spell out, define, and illustrate all seven of the self-destructive habits, examine other companies that have exhibited them, and look at how they corrected them—or failed to. The discussion, I hope, will show you ways to identify such behavior in your own business and ultimately point the way back toward health and longevity.

First, though, let's define our terms a little further. For our purposes, let's consider two aspects, or connotations, of "bad." The first is the more obvious and direct: bad means unhealthy, not good for you, contrary to your self-interest, or destructive. Behavior that makes your customers or suppliers resent you, that makes them seek out other business partners, seems clearly "bad" in this sense. Arrogance or abuse of stakeholders would seem to be good examples. But "bad" in the business arena can also suggest "lost opportunity." Here, perhaps complacency, or underestimation of the competition, causes you to fail to maximize your potential. Your behavior may not be "actively" bad, nor are you reviled by others in your community. But your vision has failed, and you have lost, or are about to lose, your chance.

Finally, a word about leadership. Sometimes CEOs are directly responsible for the self-destructive habits their companies develop. This is most likely to be the case with founding CEOs, or CEOs who refuse to retire, or who "clone" their successor, or whose directors have been handpicked. Family-run businesses, where the "genetic influence" is strong, are similarly likely to fall into self-destructive habits.

However, whether or not the CEO is responsible for the company's self-destructive habits, it is definitely his or her job to break them. When proactive intervention is necessary, it can only come from the top. Sometimes, especially when the crisis is severe, when the habits have become addictions, a new leader must be brought in. We saw this in the case of IBM, and you will see other examples in the chapters to come.

Consider the performance of GE under Jack Welch. When Welch became CEO in the early 1980s, analysts regarded the company as a solid but staid performer, growing at the same rate as the gross national product. Welch disagreed, and he soon threw GE into turmoil by declaring it had to radically transform itself. He launched a major restructuring under a strategy called "No. 1, No. 2," which mandated "fixing, closing, or selling" every business that was not first or second in worldwide market share and that did not offer major global growth opportunities. In implementing this strategy, GE eventually sold 400 businesses and product lines—including housewares and mining operations—worth $15 billion and acquired 600 others worth ***$26*** billion. By 1988, GE was organized into 14 major high-tech or service businesses that Welch believed had tremendous global growth potential.

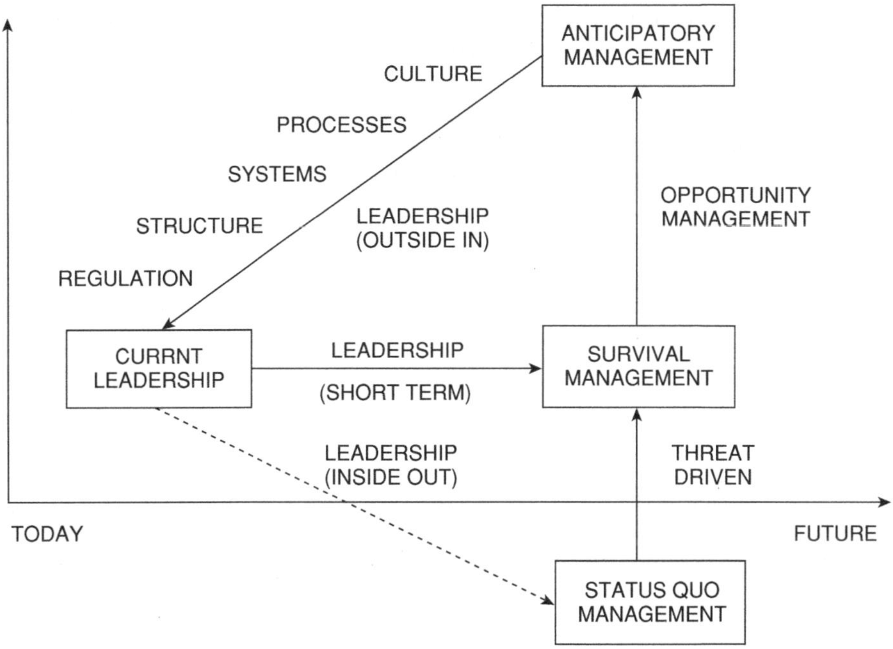

Figure 1-2 Leadership styles

GE is a prime practitioner of anticipatory management, a proactive approach to controlling one's destiny in a changing market.

Anticipatory management is most needed and works best when the external environment is undergoing rapid and discontinuous change. Anticipatory management gives organizations a major competitive advantage. Trends that are anticipated can be planned for, and competitive advantage accrues for firms that do so better and earlier than their competitors.

As shown in the following figure, when a company continues to practice "status quo" management and look inside-out rather than outside-in when the environment is changing, it begins a slippery downward spiral. These companies die a slow death, as if inflicted with a chronic disease.

If the company confronts a sudden threat, it goes into crisis management as a survival necessity. For example, if an investment bank suddenly loses important customers because it has taken them for granted, it can immediately undertake a campaign to assess how its remaining customers view the company and focus more attention on relationship management. Such threat-driven changes can prolong survival, but they don't ensure growth or prosperity in the long run.

Leaders must anticipate environmental changes and proactively position their companies to be even more successful than they were under the status quo. They must intervene and transform the company's culture, processes, structure, and systems internally. They also must alter the regulation externally to safely position the company's future in a changing world of technology, competition, capital markets, regulation, globalization, and market needs.

Leadership is about shaping expectations; management is about delivering expectations. Management is perfectly capable of sustaining habits, whether good or bad. Real change is likely to come only from an executive with the power to initiate it.

Now, let's look at those self-destructive habits.

CHAPTER 2

DENIAL: THE COCOON OF MYTH, RITUAL, AND ORTHODOXY

The dictionary's primary definition of denial is accurate enough: "disbelief in the existence of reality of a thing" or "refusal to recognize or acknowledge that reality." No better example could be imagined than Ken Olsen's refusal to acknowledge the arrival of the PC. But there are many others.

The field of psychology has refined the definition of denial, as follows: "an unconscious defense mechanism used to reduce anxiety by denying thoughts, feelings, or facts that are consciously intolerable." For our purposes, the "thoughts, feelings, or facts that are consciously intolerable" may be those that seek to remind high-flying companies that they arrived at their success through good fortune as much as through their own brilliance and that they may prove to be fallible after all.

BEING THERE

In many companies I've looked at, it seems that the process of denial begins when a company leaves behind its humble beginnings and begins to create a mythology about its greatness. This pattern is particularly striking (and humorous) when you consider how many companies succeeded by accident and how many companies that became icons had the good fortune to be in the right place at the right time. Like a struggling young actor or musician, they were lucky enough to be "discovered"—not by a talent scout, but by a single important customer. In fact, most companies are made by one customer, and half the time the customer discovers them. (These stories always remind me of the novel by Jerzy Kosinski, ***Being There,*** which was made into a great movie starring Peter Sellers in 1979. It's the story of Chance the Gardener, who, by doing nothing except "being there," allows society's myth-making machinery to elevate him—temporarily—to an almost godlike status.)

Consider, for example, the story of Daimler-Benz (now Daimler-Chrysler). The company's roots go back to the late 1880s, when a couple of Germans, Carl Benz and Gottlieb Daimler, independent of one another, began developing internal combustion–powered automobiles. Fortunate break No. 1 occurred in the early 1900s, when an Austrian dealer named Emil Jellinek won a race in a Daimler car and then proceeded to place the first substantial order for Daimler's automobiles. Jellinek did have two conditions for the bonanza order. First, he would be granted the exclusive Daimler concession for Austria-Hungary, France, and Belgium. Second, he would be allowed to call the cars "Mercedes," his daughter's name.

Lucky accident No. 2 occurred after Daimler-Motoren-Gesellschaft merged with its rival, Benz & Cie. to become Daimler-Benz AG in 1926. (It is unlikely that the two founders ever met, by the way.) Some ten years later, a Mercedes was involved in a head-on collision. The car's owner, who, typical of the time, was riding in the back, escaped unharmed—and was duly impressed by the safety of his vehicle. His name was Adolf Hitler. He decided at once that the Mercedes-Benz would become the official automobile of the German government and that Daimler-Benz would manufacture all military and state vehicles. In short order, Daimler-Benz became the largest corporation in Germany.

Another interesting example is the Upton Machine Company. Who? Well, the Upton Machine Company dates from 1911, when brothers Fred and Lou Upton started manufacturing electric motor–driven washing machines. They weren't making much headway, though, until five years later when they were discovered by the nation's leading retailer, Sears, Roebuck & Co. By 1925 they were supplying all of Sears' washers, under the brand name Kenmore. In 1950, the company changed its name to Whirlpool, and the rest is history.

Not that there's anything wrong with succeeding by accident. Success is good, however it happens. The problem arises when the company forgets its scruffy origins, forgets those lucky accidents, and begins to take all the credit for its good fortune. I find that in most cases (but not all) it isn't the founders who make this mistake, but the second and succeeding generations. With the founders gone, the myths seem to arise, coloring the facts of the company's history. Initially, they are good stories that give employees a connection—if somewhat romanticized—to the corporate past and to the company's core values. But over time myths become orthodoxies, they become rituals, they ossify. Still, even rituals can work as long as the environment doesn't change. But when the waves of change lap against the company's foundations, rigid orthodoxies tend to respond with denial.

The kind of change that inspires denial may take many forms, but one of its likeliest forms is the emergence of new technology. Think of the transportation or communications or information industries. Old ways of doing things are suddenly gone forever, and if you don't jump on the bus, you get run over. This is the "creative destruction" that economist Joseph Schumpeter believed lay at the heart of capitalism. It's the "paradigm shift" that Don Tapscott and Art Gaston wrote about more than a decade ago. More recently, it's the idea of "disruptive technology" in Clay Christensen's ***The Innovator's Dilemma***.

I've already noted Ken Olsen's infamous declaration that the PC would "never make it" in the business world. Here's another good one. Shortly after the telephone was invented in 1876, one of Alexander Graham Bell's business partners offered to sell the rights to the telephone patents to Western Union for $100,000. The president of Western Union, William Orton, passed on the deal. "What use could this company make of an electrical toy?" sniffed Orton. A dozen years later, American Telephone and Telegraph bought controlling interest in Western Union.

We chuckle at these guys, but it's not easy to see the future, especially when you have a good thing going in the present. What's more, it's not just individuals or individual companies that fall into denial and suffer the consequences. Technological change creates whole new industries—and wipes out old ones.

How many pocket watches do you see these days? The watch industry blossomed in Europe with the elegant craftsmanship of the Swiss and Germans. Watches, often tucked into a vest pocket, were hand-built, with intricate jeweled workings. Making them was labor-intensive, and volume was low, but that didn't matter because a single watch might last a generation—or more, if it was passed down as an heirloom. But then, in 1950, came mechanical, pin-levered watch manufacturing, led by Timex (which actually had its own ancient history as the Waterbury Clock Company). It was the world's first inexpensive watch, and suddenly the great Swiss and German makers were niche players.

The "paradigm shift" was not simply mechanization; it also lay in the revolutionary idea that a watch could be disposable. Timex was quite brilliant in destroying the notion of "a watch for a lifetime." A hundred watches in a lifetime meant serious volume. A watch (maybe with a Mickey Mouse face) could be given to a child as soon as he or she learned how to tell time. If the child lost or broke it, well, buy another one. Thus an industry was transformed, and the old players were left gasping on the sidelines.

The wristwatch industry continues to be fun to watch, by the way. Timex, in turn, didn't foresee the change from analog to digital technology, and, as with so many other consumer gadgets, the Japanese stormed into the market in the early 1970s with the Pulsar digital. The Timex hegemony was broken, and soon everyone (even Texas Instruments) was making digital wristwatches with their super-accurate liquid crystal readouts. By the late 1970s, the digital boom was such that the old analog watch (with hands, powered by a mainspring) seemed to be headed to the techno-graveyard.

That didn't happen largely because digital watches gained a reputation for being cheap and ugly. They weren't fashionable, which didn't appeal to the predominant buyers of watches: women. Enter the Japanese again, led by Seiko, with the introduction of an analog watch powered by a quartz crystal—a prettier watch that could compete in accuracy (and price, if you wanted it to).

Now it seemed like digital was dead. That didn't happen either, thanks to the arrival of the multimode sports watch in the late 1980s. These watches not only told you the time; they also kept your calendar, timed your laps around the track, and woke you up in the morning. The Japanese (Seiko, Casio, Citizen) still led the way, but Timex was back in the game with the Ironman Triathlon popularized by President Clinton. Even more surprising, plodding Timex got the jump on its rivals with the 1992 introduction of its glow-in-the-dark Indiglo brand, which within a little over a year had pumped the company's sales 30%. Casio and Seiko rushed to the market with clones.

(In the interest of full disclosure, I guess we have to admit that the Swiss watchmakers didn't completely die out. With Rolex, Cartier, Movado, and others selling individual watches for a 100,000 dollars or so, maybe volume isn't so important after all.)

As we know, much the same thing happened in the television industry. The U.S. created it, nurtured it, developed the market for it—and then lost it. Our vacuum tube–based technology was wiped out by the solid-state technology used by the Japanese. And now here comes the flat screen.

Since our primary focus here is on individual companies, let's look at a few, representing a variety of industries. We'll focus first on the ***ever-changing*** technology sector. Then we'll move to other kinds of "new realities" to which companies have responded by turning out the light and pulling the covers over their heads.

DENIAL OF EMERGING TECHNOLOGIES

If asked to give an example of a company that transformed the landscape of American business with the development of a single new technology, you couldn't go wrong with the tale of Xerox. It's quite a story—the stuff of myth and legend.

XEROX: TRYING TO COPY ITS OWN SUCCESS

The technology of xerography took shape in 1937 in the mind of one Chester Carlson, a barber's son who pulled himself out of poverty to become a patent attorney—and patent holder. For ten frustrating years Carlson must have felt like an obscure author trying to sell a first manuscript. According to David Owen, author of a history of the Xerox machine called ***Copies in Seconds,*** Carlson shopped his idea to IBM, RCA, Bell & Howell, GE, and Kodak, among many others, all of whom responded with what he would later describe as "an enthusiastic lack of interest."

In 1947, Carlson found the partner he was looking for: Joe Wilson, entrepreneurial head of Haloid Co., a photographic paper supplier based in Rochester, New York, home of Kodak. Wilson embraced the opportunity to put Carlson's patents on xerography to work, and Haloid was reborn as Xerox. It took 12 years for the company to produce the first practical "dry" copier, but when it did, the young company had the business world at its feet.

Through the 1960s, shielded by its patents, the company enjoyed a virtual monopoly on copiers, and earnings rose at a heady 20% a year. The stock hit an all-time high of 171 in August 1972. Moreover, at Xerox PARC, its famous research headquarters in Palo Alto, California, in-house wizards were developing the graphical user interface, the Ethernet LAN for connecting computers and printers, the laser printer, and even the first personal computer. But here, in the story of PARC's Alan Kay, we see the first symptoms of denial; we see a company denying the future its own engineers were creating.

Charged with developing "the office of the future," Alan Kay and his Learning Research Group built the prototype of the personal computer. Named the Alto, it had sophisticated graphics, overlapping windows, even a mouse to point and click. In 1977, however, after pondering for several months whether to introduce the Alto to the world as the first sophisticated word processor for the office typing market, Xerox opted instead for a "glorified electric typewriter" called the Xerox 850. Obsolete the day it was introduced, the 850 failed utterly. Alan Kay eventually departed to pursue other interests.

Meanwhile, the eompany was squandering its dominant position in copiers. The Japanese were invading with better and cheaper models, and Xerox's margins and profit share plummeted. It diversified—first into computers, and then into financial services. Both were disasters. Throughout the 1980s and into the 1990s, as the business world underwent the transition from copiers to computer-powered printers. Xerox wandered in the darkness. After all, it was ***the*** copier company, and it seemed unable to acknowledge that the world had shifted beneath its feet.

Toward the end of 1997, Chairman Paul Allaire appeared to see the light. He hired Rick Thoman away from IBM and installed him as Xerox's new president, with a clear mission to bring Xerox into the present day. Thoman quickly announced the launch of the company's powerful digital network laser printers—the opening salvo of an assault on printer giant Hewlett-Packard. The new DocuPrint N32, with a 32-page-per-minute capacity, was priced less than HP's comparable LaserJet 5Si, the industry leader. Both products were designed to make multiple copies of computer-created documents at prices comparable to regular copiers. Thoman's willingness to incite a price war was a sign of his "aggressiveness"—presumably just what Xerox needed. The stock price was on the rise.

Thoman's next move was his purchase of Tektronix Inc.'s color printing unit for 950 million, the largest deal of its kind in Xerox's 103-year history. This was clearly another foray into HP territory. As Thoman told the business press, "This helps us become more printer-centric and less copier-centric." He said he expected the acquisition to result in more than 30% market share in office color printing, second only to HP.

Then the worm turned. Just six months later, in April 2000, Xerox announced that it would be cutting 5,200 jobs and taking a restructuring charge of ***$625*** million in the first quarter. Everybody agreed on the reason for the company's ongoing difficulties. It was still struggling to adjust to the growing shift of business customers from copying to computer printing, where it was a "newcomer" and faced stiff competition. But that begs the question: Why was this longtime technology leader a "newcomer" in computer printing? Answer: denial.

In just one more month, Thoman was gone. According to Robert Alexander and Douglas K. Smith, authors of ***Fumbling the Future; How Xerox Invented, Then Ignored, the First Personal Computer,*** his departure confirms the adage about managing change: "Culture wins." Thoman was an outsider brought in to manage Xerox's transition from the old economy to the new, but three years was insufficient. "After he had served just two years as president and hardly one as CEO, the Xerox culture rejected him like a bad transplant."

That culture, say the authors, was shaped in the 1950s by Joe Wilson, the man who seized upon Chester Carlson's invention and created the juggernaut of the 1960s and 1970s called Xerox. But in a familiar story, with the founder gone the culture became rigid, tightly knit, insular, and hostile to outsiders. Wilson's successor, Peter McCullough, paid lip service to R&D, while giving real focus to "old-economy imperatives" like sales and finance. "Rewind to the mid-1980s," suggest Alexander and Smith. "Having blindly ignored new ideas from outside (small copiers, liquid toner, indirect sales) and inside (networked personal computing and laser printers), and while the functional chiefs bloodied one another, Xerox suffered a meltdown in market share and profits." The company's board turned to David Kearns, who, "unsurprisingly, focused on recapturing the glories of the copier past and abandoned all effort to commercialize the digital future that then still remained within Xerox's grasp."

Before the difficult year 2000 was over. Xerox had exhausted two-thirds of its 7 billion revolving credit agreement and was announcing "nonstrategic asset sales" along with further operational improvements. One of those asset sales sounded pretty drastic: half of its 50% stake in Fuji Xerox to Fuji Photo Film, the first change in the ownership structure of the joint venture since it was launched in 1962. More remarkable, Xerox was also contemplating bringing outside partners into the famous PARC.

In the last analysis. Xerox, in denial, had waited too late to meet the challenge of digital technology. When Thoman tried to pursue a strategy of refocusing on high-technology networking, printing, and copying services rather than just the sale of beige copier boxes, the stolid Xerox culture, which had further ossified under Kearns, proved unable to execute Thoman's strategy, and the profit warnings began. Chairman Allaire, who had brought in Thoman, returned to his old job of CEO and elevated Anne Mulcahy to president and COO. But investors were dumping the stock, and Moody's was reviewing the company's credit ratings for a downgrade.

At about the same time, November 2000, noted professor and commentator Paul Kedrosky summed up the company's decline this way: "Xerox had no second act. After photocopiers, the company never really found another market to dominate. And now, low-margin offshore products are squeezing Xerox at the low end of the copier business, and the high-end market is saturated." On top of that, the market itself was in decline because computer-related communications technology was making photocopiers look "like buggy whips." In Kedrosky's eyes. Xerox's decline had been in the making for quite some time, "arguably since it turned its back on its own stellar inventions."

In October 2004, federal prosecutors concluded a criminal investigation of Xerox without filing any charges, bringing closure to a long inquiry into the company's accounting and disclosure practices. That was the good news. The bad news was two years old. In 2002, Xerox agreed to pay a then-record 10 million in civil penalties and to restate its earnings to settle fraud charges brought by the SEG. Without admitting or denying guilt, the company restated its financials and conceded it had misbooked 6.4 billion of equipment revenue and overstated its pretax income by 36%, or, 1.4 billion, over the five years through 2001. In 2003, six former executives, including two ex-chief executive officers, paid 22 million in fines and penalties to settle related charges with the SEG. According to SEG officials, the executives had personally profited from bonuses and stock sales related to the false financial reports.

Nevertheless, Xerox spokeswoman Christa Garone told the ***Wall Street Journal,*** "We are a much stronger company today. We believe we are making significant progress in writing the next chapter about Xerox's return to greatness."

Maybe so. But at the end of 2005, 70% of the company's revenue was being generated from post-sale business like ink and toner cartridges, and its stock was trading at under K15. In the meantime, a different lesson is suggested: When self-destructive habits become addictions, radical intervention may be necessary.

Interestingly, Tektronix, the company that sold its color printing unit to Xerox in 1999, offers another example of denial. Founded in 1946 as an electronic testing company, Tektronix went public in 1963 and by the end of that decade controlled 75% of the world market in oscilloscopes. Like Xerox, however, Tektronix suffered in the 1980s as it failed to recognize the fundamental shift from analog to digital technology. Earnings fell sharply, and layoffs followed. In 1990, facing continued losses, the board seized control of the company.

But this story has a different ending—proof that self-destructive habits can be broken. Perhaps because the turnaround specialist the board brought in, Jerome Meyer, was given enough time to complete the job, or perhaps because Tektronix culture was not so resistant and unyielding, the overhaul of the company was ultimately successful. The spin-off of the color printing unit left a smaller and more focused Tektronix, which returned to its core business, moved back into the black in 2000 and enjoyed record sales and earnings in 2001. Under chairman and CEO Rick Wills, who succeeded Meyer, the company has prospered since.

DENIAL OF CHANGING CONSUMER TASTES

What could be more fickle than the tastes of the contemporary consumer? I'd hate to be the company that banked its future on lava lamps, or pet rocks, or Beanie Babies. Of course, we know fads don't last. But even iconic retailers have hurt themselves by refusing to acknowledge their customers' changing tastes, preferences, and buying patterns. As an example, consider the following.

A&P: RETAIL PIONEER IN PERIL

Talk about roots. The Great American Tea Company (later renamed the Great Atlantic and Pacific Tea Company) was founded in 1859 when George Hartford and his partner set up shop oh New York City's docks so that they could sell tea to the public at a 50% discount by buying directly from the cargo ships and eliminating the middleman. The young company advertised itself by drawing its signature red wagon through the city's streets.

By 1912, when Hartford's sons, George and John, were moving into the business, America's original retail chain store had 400 outlets, with its pioneering policy of house brands at discount prices. It was in that year that John Hartford added a new wrinkle to the business. He opened a store that dispensed with two of the hallmarks of retailing—customer credit and premium giveaways. It was strictly "cash and carry," which reduced prices even further; the concept took off like a brush fire. Between 1912 and 1915, A&P opened one of its "Economy Stores" every three days, and by 1930 there were more than 15,000 cash-and-carry outlets in 29 states.

The success of the billion-dollar enterprise delighted consumers but drew the wrath of independent retailers. By the 1930s, the government's displeasure resulted in chain-store taxes and a new antitrust law, the Robinson-Patman Act, aimed directly at chain-store pricing tactics. In fact, the Justice Department fought A&P for 12 years, questioning the legality of its fundamental strategy: subsidiaries supplying A&P stores with meat, dairy goods, produce, bakery, and canned items to be sold under the store's own label. But the litigation produced only a slap on the wrist, and A&P continued to do business as usual.

The company fought so hard not only because the formula had worked so well but because A&P's own labels were integral to its reputation. A&P represented quality at an affordable price. During two World Wars, with the Great Depression in between, this was what the American consumer wanted and needed. Throughout the 1950s and into the 1960s, A&P remained the bastion of the private label in U.S. retailing. Its label was its mantra. Its label became its orthodoxy. But patterns of consumption changed as the frugality of the war years gave way to growing affluence, and branded products became popular symbols of that new affluence. Despite this new reality, A&P stuck to its private label. As Ralph Burger, who succeeded John Hartford at the company's helm, liked to say, "You can't argue with a hundred years of success."

Denial? Clearly. But A&P's refusal to acknowledge the new reality of branded products is only half the story. The other half is detailed by Jim Collins in ***Good to Great.***

Collins points out that by the early 1950s, A&P had become the largest retailing organization in the world and one of the largest corporations in the United States. In the 1960s, however, as Kroger mounted a challenge, A&P began to falter. After 1973, the two companies' paths diverged, and over the next 25 years, Kroger generated cumulative returns ***ten times the market*** and ***80*** times better than A&P.

"How did such a dramatic reversal of fortunes happen?" Collins asks. "And how could a company as great as A&P become so awful?"

Collins agrees that A&P had a perfect model for the first half of the twentieth century—cheap, plentiful groceries sold in utilitarian stores. But it's his contention that in the second half of the century Americans began to want not just branded products but an entirely different kind of grocery store. American shoppers wanted nicer and bigger stores and a greater choice of products. They desired "fresh-baked bread, flowers, health foods, cold medicines, fresh produce, forty-five choices of cereal, and ten types of milk.... They wanted Superstores, with a big block "S" on the chest—offering almost everything under one roof with lots of parking, cheap prices, clean floors, and a gazillion checkout lines."

Collins notes that both A&P and Kroger knew the world around them was changing. However, their responses to the evolution of the industry were quite different. One faced "the brutal facts of reality head-on" by changing its entire system. The other one "stuck its head in the sand."

As an example of the "spirited defense" A&P mounted against the new reality confronting it, Collins relates the anecdote of The Golden Key, the new store A&P opened to experiment with some of the new ideas in grocery retailing. "It sold no A&P branded products," Collins writes, "it gave the store manager more freedom, it experimented with innovative new departments, and it began to evolve toward the modern superstore. Customers really liked it." A&P was well on its way to understanding why it had been losing market share, and in the process it was discovering the means by which it could reverse its fortunes.

"What did A&P executives do with The Golden Key? They didn't like the answers that it gave, so they closed it."

According to Collins, A&P tried to save itself by lurching from one strategy to another, including a "radical price-cutting strategy to build market share," overlooking the basic fact that customers wanted different stores, not just lower prices. Denial resulted in a downward spiral: "The price cutting led to cost cutting, which led to even drabber stores and poorer service, which in turn drove customers away, further driving down margins, resulting in even dirtier stores and worse service. 'After a while the crud kept mounting,' a former A&P manager told Collins. 'We not only had dirt, we had dirty dirt.'"

For the past decade, the A&P story has been one of declining profits, mounting debt, and closing stores. As a poignant sign of its retreat, in 2004 the once-mighty chain sold its famous Eight O'clock Coffee division to a San Francisco–based private equity firm.

DENIAL OF THE NEW GLOBAL ENVIRONMENT

It's not just technology, not just consumer tastes, not just new competition. Successful companies must face the truth that ***everything*** is changing. The world of yesterday is gone. Today's company must embrace new technologies, must not just acknowledge but outperform new competitors, must not only hold its old markets but actively court new ones. Some companies that have had success in the past find it difficult to leave that past behind. Their former glory is a shackle that impedes their movement into the future.

GENERAL MOTORS: AUTO GIANT IN THE (GAS) TANK

In a retrospective piece on General Motors that appeared in ***Fortune*** in 2004, Alex Taylor offers this telling anecdote: When Jack Smith was a fast-rising executive at GM in the early 1980s, he visited Japan to study Toyota's stamping and assembly operations, "something nobody at GM, amazingly, had done before." What he found was that GM needed more than twice as many people as Toyota to build the same number of cars. But when he presented his findings to GM's executive committee, they reacted with total disbelief and dismissed his report.

"GM was in denial," declared Taylor. GM was so deep in denial that a very simple explanation had been missed; GM's structure was entirely different from that of Toyota—"as well as from Ford, Volkswagen, and every other automaker." The reason lies in the company's early history, when it was assembled from independent automakers—Chevrolet, Oakland (later Pontiac), Oldsmobile, Buick, and Cadillac—all of which operated differently and which, 60 years later, were still competing against one another.

Even if nobody else did, writes Taylor, Smith realized that GM's decentralized structure was fundamentally flawed, and when the board of directors installed him as CEO in 1992, he set out to change the organization. As Smith told ***Fortune,*** "Frankly, at the time we weren't like any other auto company in the world."

Smith and his successor, Rick Wagoner, spent ten years making over GM in the image of its Japanese competitor, and the result is that "for the first time in its 96-year history, GM is running as one company."

Well, that's good. But how the company runs is only half the story. The other half is what it produces.

Especially today, with gas prices surging to unprecedented levels, it's instructive to look back to 1988, when, for the third year in a row, the Reagan administration excused Ford and GM from government-mandated fuel-economy standards. GM threatened to close an auto plant in Texas—29 key electoral votes—if the DOT did not reduce mileage requirements for 1989 cars.

To back up a little further, in 1975, as a result of the Arab oil embargo. Congress passed the Energy Policy and Conservation Act, which required automakers to work toward an average fleet mileage of 27.5 mpg. Gas hogs could still be produced, as long as the average was attained. By 1986, the corporate average fuel-economy minimum, or CAFE, had increased from 12 to 26 mpg with Detroit reluctantly complying. But oil prices were coming back down, and manufacturers lobbied for a rollback on the mileage requirements. Three times the Reagan administration capitulated.

"Detroit's operating maxim is that small cars produce small profits, and large cars produce large profits," the ***Seattle Times*** editorialized at the time. To conform to this view, U.S. automakers convinced themselves that American consumers were only interested in buying large cars. However, "the evidence argued otherwise; first the popular Volkswagen and later the flood of Japanese imports."

At first, the editorial continued, Detroit scoffed at the engineering economies and fuel economies of small cars as a way of defending its huge dinosaurs. Then, to reinforce its own bias, Detroit built crummy small cars. When nobody wanted them, the automakers could say, "We told you so."

The editorial asked prophetically, "How many Detroit workers will lose their jobs when oil prices soar again and gasoline rockets past a dollar a gallon?" It rebuked the Reagan administration for letting Detroit off the hook and thus rewarding its failure to develop and implement new technology. But my point is, why should GM need a government mandate to respond to the marketplace?

Let's back up a little further and look at GM's story as yet another illustration of how success itself can form the culture in which self-destructive habits take root.

GM passed Ford in car sales in 1931, and as demand mushroomed in the 1940s and 1950s, its position as world leader was solidified. In 1954, GM accounted for more than half the cars sold in the U.S. On the first Fortune 500 list in 1955, GM was No. 1, with registered sales of ***$9.8*** billion, 42% higher than runner-up Standard Oil. That same year, Harlow Curtis, who had recently taken the company's reins, was named ***Time*** magazine's Man of the Year. It did indeed seem true that what was good for General Motors was good for America.

Part of what made the system work was Alfred Sloan's "aspirational ladder," according to which customers would first buy a Chevy and then move up to a Pontiac, an Oldsmobile, a Buick, and finally a Cadillac. This was the rationale behind the company's decentralized structure, and it made sense as long as the car market kept exploding and the competition remained weak. But by the 1980s the automotive landscape had been transformed. While Japan flooded the American market with its better-made, less expensive cars, GM coasted on the strength of its famous brands and product lines like full-sized trucks, where imports didn't compete. At the same time, what had been the key strategy—maintaining the independence of the brands comprising the "aspirational ladder"—was now the source of huge inefficiencies. It was time for change, but decentralization had become GM's orthodoxy. In this way successful strategies quietly mutate into self-destructive habits such as denial—not to mention complacency and competitive myopia.

It should be noted that Jack Smith was not the first to recognize that GM was headed for trouble. In the mid-1980s, CEO Roger Smith tried—rather desperately—to shake up the company. He closed plants, made (now-questionable) acquisitions, and tried to streamline operations. As the ***Los Angeles Times*** noted at the end of his tenure, "the radical amputations and transplants he performed on the company finally led to the wrong sort of immortality for Smith as the involuntary star of the satirical film ***Roger and Me***." But Smith ultimately did not fix either of the two fundamental problems plaguing the company: the inefficiency of its operations and the deficiencies of its products. And when he handed over the company to his successor, Robert Stempel, in 1990, the hemorrhaging was only beginning.

GM lost ***$2*** billion in 1990, its worst performance ever. In 1991, it lost $4.5 billion, then an all-time record for a U.S. corporation. Before the 1992 numbers were in, Stempel had been ousted in a "boardroom revolt" thought to have been spearheaded by outside member John Smale, former head of P&G. Jack Smith was promoted to run the company, and Smale became the new chairman. At the same time, GM also announced a 50% cut in its dividend, from ***$1.60*** a year to 80 cents.

That was prudent because the company would need all the money it could hold on to. When the 1992 figures were released, it turned out that GM had lost an eye-popping 23 billion dollars.

The loss was so staggering, and its implications so huge that filmmaker Steve Talbot was hired to create a ***Frontline*** documentary to investigate what had happened to the mighty company. Not surprisingly, GM refused to cooperate, but knowledgeable people no longer affiliated with the company were willing to talk, including former board member Ross Perot. He told Talbot that his reward for consistently speaking out about GM's problems was to be ousted from the board. To Perot, there seemed to be little interest at GM in hearing the truth about the company's worsening situation. Ultimately, what Talbot found was the same thing Jack Smith admitted when he took the reins from Stempel: GM's resistance to change had been going on for a long time. In a world where an Arab oil embargo, energy crisis, gasoline lines, and a Japanese small car invasion had converged, big cars were a liability—and GM was all about big cars. However, even with the onset of hard times, GM continued to turn its face from reality.

Of course, it was too early for Talbot to gauge the effects of the massive restructuring Jack Smith was undertaking. Smith stopped the bleeding, and at the end of 1995, his efforts were rewarded when GM offered him the additional title of chairman of the board. In stepping down from the chair, John Smale declared confidently that "GM's management team under Jack Smith's leadership has turned GM around."

Had it? Again, the company was certainly running better, but questions about the product persisted, and a lot of second-guessing went on when, in 2000, the company announced that Oldsmobile, the oldest auto brand still in production, would be folded. Not that it was a bad decision. Nobody doubted that the company was still trying to support too many brands and, as a result, was still competing against itself. With market share at 27% and falling, drastic action was called for.

The question was, why had the company taken so long to act? Why had GM invested $3 billion in something called the Centennial Project, a plan to produce a lineup of all-new Olds models by the year 2000—models like the Bravada SUV and Aurora, which flopped? Where was the design genius that had created the Cutlass Supreme, which led Oldsmobile's charge in the late 1970s and early 1980s? Writing in ***USA TODAY,*** David Kiley recalls GM's laughable effort to change Olds' image in the late 1980s, when it launched the "It's Not Your Father's Oldsmobile" campaign. One of the ads featured former Beatles drummer Ringo Starr and his daughter. "The campaign," writes Kiley, "has become synonymous with advertising desperation."

Rick Wagoner was promoted to CEO in 2000, and in 2002 Jack Smith stepped aside so that Wagoner could be elevated to chairman of the board as well. Perhaps the most intractable problem facing the new chairman was GM's growing pension liability. Analysts noted that the health of the company's pension fund depended on a 10% annual return on its investments, and that, consequently, the continuing bear market had left the fund short by a whopping $20 billion. Wagoner would have to watch GM pump more than three billion into the pension fund in 2003, with no assurance that things would improve.

In fact, just a couple months later (June 2003), the financial press noted that GM's pension crisis was forcing it to offer huge rebates to stimulate sales, and the result was a price war among the Big Three (GM, Ford, and Chrysler) that threatened the health of the whole industry. The drain on profits precipitated by the pricing and incentive skirmish had enmeshed all three big carmakers in "a downward competitive spiral."

Since then, the situation has only deteriorated. "Once again," wrote ***The New York Times*** in the spring of 2005, "Detroit has resumed its long slide to automotive oblivion." GM and Ford "are rapidly losing customers at home and their debt is rated one notch above junk by Standard & Poor's."

In the 1990s, only the popularity of the high-margin SUVs allowed the Big Three to "skate past lagging reputations and terminally tacky design." Now, as the demand for SUVs stalls, GM's latent problems have become glaring: increasing foreign competition (including Hyundai from Korea and eventually car makers from China and India), those soaring pension costs (GM spends $12,000 per car on health care and pension benefits) and their impact on labor negotiations, and, most fundamentally, lack of design distinction.

GM is "stuck in the middle," BMW CEO Helmut Panke told the *Times* Cadillac has done better, thanks to refurbishing its image as "the American luxury brand," but how about Pontiac, Chevrolet, Buick, GMG, Saab, and Saturn? According to Panke, if you removed all their labels and badges, "you would have a hard time recognizing who's who, what is what."

The Times suggested that maybe GM should concentrate on making cars people want, instead of ones they're willing to tolerate in order to score a 5,000 rebate. In the late 1980s GM had avoided building more fuel-efficient-cars by convincing the Reagan administration to roll back fuel standards. Today, instead of making cars that customers will love, the company is trying to substitute with huge rebates and zero percent financing.

The ***Times'*** gloomy assessment was confirmed with the news that GM lost $1.3 billion in the first quarter of 2005—the company's first loss since 1992. First-quarter sales were down 5% from a year earlier, and GM's U.S. market share had fallen from 26.3% to 25.2% over the past 12 months.

GM blamed the depressing numbers on its huge "legacy costs," but people outside the company could readily see that those costs didn't explain why the company was not selling cars. Everybody except GM could see that with rising gas prices and heightened environmental concerns, buyers were moving away from all-wheel-drive SUVs and other gas guzzlers. Everybody outside GM could see that the car marketplace was changing to meet the demands of new generations of consumers. But GM wasn't changing, and the joke going around was that the only people buying its cars were employees, their families, and rental fleet operators.

In other words, we are back again to the problem of the product, a problem that got more than the usual coverage when, in April 2005, Dan Neil, the auto writer for the ***Los Angeles Times,*** gave a negative review to GM's new and much-hyped Pontiac G6.1 should back up and note that to address the problem of GM's lackluster designs, Rick Wagoner had, brought in former Chrysler vice chairman Bob Lutz, said to be a passionate car enthusiast, and that the G6 was among the first of the Lutz designs to hit the market. To say that the company hoped for good reviews would be an understatement.

Neil found little to like about the new car, inside or outside. He was particularly critical of its lackluster handling: "You want excitement from the 'Excitement' division? Try to get this thing to turn in a sharp corner." Ultimately, he dismissed it as product that wouldn't be able to compete in the marketplace.

While he was at it, Neil took a few broader swipes at GM's larger product strategy. Why have four nearly identical minivans, four nearly identical SUVs? Looking at all 11 brands (including those offshore), he concluded that GM's overall strategy must be to remove any unique characteristics in its automobiles for the sake of global efficiencies. He accused GM of completely missing out on hybrid gas-electric technology while rivals Toyota and Honda were selling hybrids as fast as they could build them. He questioned GM's decision to speed up development of new SUVs and trucks in the pipeline at a time when SUV sales were nose-diving. He found no mystery in GM's ever-declining market share: "The cars aren't selling."

"When ballclubs have losing records," Neil concluded, "players and coaches and managers get their walking papers. At GM, it's time to sweep the dugout."

GM's response to the article? The company pulled all its advertising from the ***Los Angeles Times*** until further notice.

At the end of ***that Fortune*** magazine retrospective from 2004, Rick Wagoner recalls that GM founder William Durant lost his fortune in the 1920s speculating in the stock market and at the end of his life was manning a bowling alley in Flint. Durant then jokes that GM's chairmen had apparently been haunted by Durant's fate since then. Writer Alex Taylor concludes the article by noting that Wagoner's willingness to relate such an anecdote was more evidence that GM had moved beyond its state of complete denial.

A year later, Taylor might still be willing to make that claim, but, then again, it might be too late. The company lost another ***$9*** billion in 2005, despite reducing its dividend, slashing executive salaries, and cutting health benefits for salaried workers. It also announced the elimination of 30,000 hourly jobs and the closing of 12 plants by 2008. Most recently, in a desperate effort to improve its balance sheet, GM announced the sale of 51% of GMAG— its profit-generating finance arm—for ***$14*** billion. The infusion, presumably, will help restore the company's debt rating so that it can borrow more money. The question remains: How wisely will it spend that money?

THE WARNING SIGNS OF DENIAL

Hindsight, as they say, is 20/20. It's quite simple for me to diagnose these failures and to isolate denial as an underlying cause. It's much more difficult for an institution to give itself the necessary psychological examination—especially before it's too late, especially before institutional health has deteriorated.

So, if I'm a CEO, how do I know my company is in denial? What do I look for? Here are three telltale signs.

THE "I AM DIFFERENT" SYNDROME

We are all familiar with this behavior pattern, from the self-destructive habits we and our friends cultivate in our personal or social lives. Maybe we smoke. Maybe we drink too much. But it's okay. Others might develop lung cancer. Others might become alcoholic. But we're different. Our bodies are stronger. Our genes are sturdier. It can't happen to us.

This syndrome must certainly have been at work in GM's culture. Sure, Chrysler went down, GM must have told itself. Yes, Chrysler suffered the ultimate indignity of the merger with Daimler-Benz. But it can't happen here at GM. We are too big, too strong, too powerful. We are different.

THE "NOT INVENTED HERE" SYNDROME

Are you too proud to admit that somebody else has come up with a better way? Are you reluctant to give your competitors the satisfaction of seeing you adopt their advanced technology? If so, you've got NIH syndrome. This form of denial is epidemic in the technology sector, as we saw in the case of Xerox. (In fact, Xerox's NIH syndrome reached such an advanced stage that it denied the worth of new technology coming out of ***its own*** research facility.) But note that non-technology companies suffer from this syndrome as well. A&P, for example, was so wedded to the store-brand strategy it pioneered that it could not see the rising tide of branded products that would eventually drown it.

When NIH mutates into NNH ("not nurtured here"), we have the related syndrome of inbreeding. Obviously, inbreeding is in evidence when companies have a strong preference for hiring from the same talent pool (university or graduate school) and promoting from within—even when things aren't going well. The syndrome is advanced when (as in the case of Xerox) outsiders who ***are*** recruited are doomed to failure by an inbred, close-knit culture of resistance. The syndrome is similarly advanced when (as in the case of GM's Jack Smith) the insider rises through the ranks to the leadership position and fails to address the fundamental problems facing the company but is nevertheless hailed upon his departure as the conquering hero.

By contrast, IBM's willingness to bring in Louis Gerstner ***and*** Gerstner's willingness to transform IBM into a services company suggests that the syndrome can be broken.

THE "LOOKING FOR ANSWERS IN ALL THE WRONG PLACES" SYNDROME

Something's wrong. Maybe several things are wrong. You see the signs; loss of market share, delayed product release, rising employee turnover, union animosity, the government looking over your shoulder. Just like with symptoms in the body, your initial response is to ignore them. When that fails, this third syndrome manifests itself as rationalization. You explain your problems away without fixing them. You spin them. You assign blame to any number of far-distant causes: the Asian meltdown, the war in Iraq, the dumping of Chinese products.

Managers are under pressure to come up with answers. "We're losing money because of our pension costs," says GM. "Shoppers aren't coming because Walmart is undercutting our prices," says A&P. "We can no longer compete because our patents have expired," says Xerox. But it's the responsibility of leaders to get to the ***right*** answers: "We're losing money because we're making the wrong cars." "Shoppers aren't coming because they don't like our stores." "We can't compete because we failed in our role as technology leaders."

HOW TO BREAK THE HABIT OF DENIAL

So you're thinking: Well, maybe I'm in denial. I'm not admitting it, but I guess it's possible. What should I do just in case? Here's a four-step program to put you on the road to recovery.

LOOK FOR IT

Look for the "I am different syndrome" by analyzing your response to the failures of other companies. Do you pat yourself on the back? Do you snicker smugly? Or do you dissect those failures like an anatomist, looking for any comparisons between those unhealthy corporate bodies and your own?

Look for the "not invented here" syndrome by examining your products, processes, and personnel. Do you find prejudices, unwarranted preferences, or pockets of resistance to change?

Look for the "rationalization" syndrome by listening carefully to your managers, by applying common sense and intellectual rigor. Are you getting the easy answers that get the company off the hook, or the hard ones that demand change? Recall that Louis Gerstner began the process of turning around IBM when he realized he was not getting the right information from his managers and, instead, listened closely to his top 200 customers.

ADMIT IT

When GM sent Jack Smith to Japan to study Toyota, it was looking for symptoms of denial. When he brought back the truth, GM refused to admit it. When it opened The Golden Key, A&P was looking for the same thing. When Golden Key delivered the answer, the company refused to admit it. It's not enough to look for the symptoms of denial. When you find them, you have to admit you have the disease.

ASSESS IT

You've admitted it. Now you have to measure it. How deeply are you in denial? It may be a superficial problem, fixed by replacing a manager or retiring a product line. Or it may be as deep as your entire culture. It's instructive that Jack Smith was perceptive enough to address decades of GM denial regarding the company's decentralized structure. But GM's denial goes even deeper than that—and still has not been entirely rooted out.

CHANGE IT

If your company has created a culture of deep denial—if you believe "it can't happen here," if you unreasonably protect your own people and processes, if rationalization is your preferred approach to problems—change will be difficult. It may be time for not only a new leader but for a "vision transplant." It may be time to rewrite the mission statement.

We've already seen examples of companies that have resisted change and remained in denial. But we've seen one example (Tektronix), and we'll look at many others that prove change is possible. It comes easier once we stop denying its inevitability.

In essence, denial is at the root of most of the self-destructive habits we'll discuss in the following chapters. After all, if it weren't for denial, a lot of problems would be addressed and corrected before they devolved into self-destructive habits. From arrogance (Chapter 3) to territorial impulses (Chapter 8), our first reaction, most likely, is to deny that we have such problems. It's always easier to look outside—to the weather, the war, the weak dollar—to find the source of our problems.

Based on the attention it gets from psychologists, it's clear that denial is a fundamental human response—a dependable defense mechanism used to avoid confronting painful truths. It may even be necessary to our survival, and like "functional alcoholics," there may be millions of "functional denialists" for whom facing reality is more destructive than evading it.

But make no mistake. The comforts of denial do not pertain to the corporate body. If the truth is painful, hiding from it means failure, not survival, in the unforgiving world of business.

DENIAL

Things that lead to denial:

- Denial of emerging technologies
- Denial of changing consumer tastes
- Denial of the new global environment

The warning signs of denial:

- **The "I am different" syndrome:** "We're different, so there is no way it can happen to us."
- **The "not invented here" syndrome:** You're too proud to admit that somebody else has come up with a better way.
- **The "looking for answers in all the wrong places" syndrome:** You ignore, rationalize, or blame others for your situation.

How to break the habit of denial:

- **Look for it:** Analyze your response to the failures of other companies. Examine your products, processes, and personnel for prejudices, unwarranted preferences, or pockets of resistance to change. Listen carefully to your managers.
- **Admit it:** When you find symptoms of denial, you must admit you have the disease.
- **Assess it:** Measure how deeply you are in denial.
- **Change it:** Change is harder the deeper you are in denial—but it is possible.

CHAPTER 3

ARROGANCE: PRIDE BEFORE THE FALL

The standard definition of arrogance goes something like this—an offensive display of superiority or self-importance, pride, haughtiness, insolence, or disdain. Arrogance has everything to do with an inflated sense of self; it's liking the sound of your own voice too much to listen to anybody else. Arrogance is an overblown self-image that just doesn't square with the facts. In ancient Greek drama, arrogance—or hubris—was the "tragic flaw" that led to the downfall of great heroes. In today's world, the same flaw has caused mighty companies to stumble. Let's consider a number of scenarios that are likely to give rise to arrogance.

WHEN EXCEPTIONAL ACHIEVEMENT IN THE PAST WARPS YOUR PERCEPTION OF PRESENT REALITY

Like several of the other self-destructive habits, arrogance can arise from exceptional achievement. One situation especially predictive of arrogance is when a company, through unexpected or stunning accomplishment, catapults to the position of industry leader and then goes on to successfully defend itself against wave after wave of competitive, regulatory, and even public opinion assault. Quite naturally, such a company comes to believe it is immune to external forces—a belief bolstered by the media and its stakeholders (suppliers, dealers, etc.)—and its reputation is blown out of proportion. To me, this is the real meaning of "good to great": The company doesn't change, but its accomplishments are exaggerated by a media overly fond of big words and big stories. Gradually, the arrogance-prone company comes to believe its own press clippings. Then we have the familiar story: Success courts its own demise. For a particularly good illustration, let's look again at...

GENERAL MOTORS

It was under Alfred P. Sloan, who ran GM as president and then chairman for 33 years, that GM rose to the apex of American business—and developed its culture of supreme arrogance. And why not? The company overwhelmed the competition, controlled its labor force, lobbied lawmakers, and won the hearts of consumers—and by the early 1930s was firmly entrenched as the world's leading carmaker. By 1941, its share of the U.S. market was more than 40% and growing, compared with just 12% 20 years earlier.

As for defeating the competition, Sloan's greatest—and most ruthless—victory was not over Ford, or over the foreign manufacturers he held at bay. Sloan paved the way for GM's hegemony, and for the American car culture more generally, by first utterly destroying the domestic streetcar industry. In the early 1920s, only 10% of the population owned an automobile, and Sloan saw very clearly where his real competition lay. While he was buying up and dismantling streetcar lines, he also orchestrated a massive campaign to convince American consumers that the automobile was the form of transportation they really wanted. It was truly an arrogance-inspiring performance.

GM's attitude toward its own lower-echelon workers came to light in 1937, when assembly-line employees staged violent sit-down strikes that stalled production in Flint. Sloan wanted the governor to send in troops, but the governor demanded negotiation instead.

Eventually, in 1940, a permanent agreement allowed GM workers to join the United Auto Workers, but relations "between GM and its workforce remained acrimonious. According to Irving Bluestone, who directed UAWs GM department from 1970 to 1980, the syndrome at GM was not unusual for big companies during that time: that management was there to make the decisions, and workers were there to obey the decisions. "The arrogance was typical," said Bluestone, "and very deeply resented."

Perhaps the final—and fatal—measure of GM's arrogance came in response to the "Japanese invasion" in the 1970s and 1980s. As consumer tastes seemed to change, and as American families wanted a second car for the commute to work, GM could have tried to manufacture smaller cars that would truly compete. Instead, it made the strategic blunder of allowing its own dealers—Pontiac, Buick, and Olds—to carry Honda, Toyota, and Nissan. Previously, European automakers had been niche players. Even Volkswagen never gained more than 2.5% of the market. Why? Because of the prohibitive expense of setting up a distribution pipeline. But GM was so little concerned with the Japanese threat that it essentially gave away this tremendous competitive asset. "Who cares?" said GM. "Americans won't go for these boxy little Toyota Corollas and Datsun 210s." In effect, GM helped create the monster that would come back to terrorize it.

The rise of Toyota is just one of many examples of how the most dangerous competition comes from low-quality/low-price competitors (see the following figure). Utilizing price as their most tantalizing selling point, they establish a presence in the marketplace. Their upstream competitors generally malign them as easily dismissed peddlers of "junk" or just ignore them. But if these "inferior" competitors improve quality while maintaining their relative cost advantage, they become irresistible value propositions to customers. Once they have elbowed their way into the value box, they are poised to further extend their reach into the top of the market by developing highly innovative or luxury products.

For example, Honda, which was known more for its motorcycles than its cars, entered the U.S. market with the diminutive and, by U.S. standards, quirkily engineered Civic. Even its low-expectations slogan, "It will get you where you're

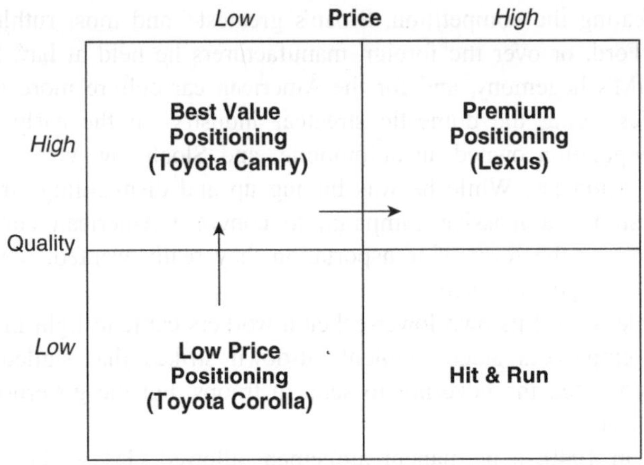

Figure 3-1 The move from the low end to the high end of the market

going," appeared questionable to most American consumers. But the car quickly improved and established a solid home in the lower end of the market. Building on the Civic's success, Honda introduced the Accord, which became the wildly successful standard for value. From there, the company moved into the luxury market under the Brand name Acura. Similarly, Toyota started with the Corolla, moved up to the Camry, and then took on the U.S. luxury car market with the successful entry of Lexus.

This story is repeated again and again, whether the industry is automobiles, marble and granite, leather goods, textiles, steel, semiconductors, or consumer electronics. The Korean companies Samsung and Hyundai are some of the most recent examples, and we are now beginning to hear the rumblings of multinationals in the making from emerging economies such as China, India, Brazil, Eastern Europe, and Russia.

BOEING

Boeing provides another example of how being the biggest and best produces a culture of arrogance. Founded in 1916, Bill Boeing's Boeing Airplane Company literally got off the ground with a World War I contract to build training planes for the U.S. Navy. After the war, Boeing partnered with Frederick Rentschler, developer of the air-cooled engine, to form United Aircraft and Transport, which both built and flew airplanes. The government's new antitrust rules broke the company apart in 1934, leaving Boeing Airplane with the manufacturing side of the business. But the government more than made up for that ruling by favoring Boeing with fabulously lucrative contracts during World War II—contracts that facilitated the development of legendary aircraft like the B-17 "Flying Fortress" and the B-29 bomber. At one point the company was producing 362 planes per month for the war effort.

Boeing parlayed this bonanza into a dominant position as No. 1 in the commercial aircraft industry. Its 307 Stratoliner was the first airliner with a pressurized cabin. In 1958, it revolutionized the industry with the introduction of the 707, the first successful jetliner. The 727 and 737 followed over the next decade, cementing

Boeing's position as worldwide industry leader. Indeed, no one else was really in the game. With its purchase of McDonnell Douglas in 1997 for ***B16*** billion, it became the No. 1 military aircraft maker as well—or, to put it more grandly, the world's largest aerospace company.

In case you're wondering, the Federal Trade Commission happily signed off on the deal, noting that McDonnell wasn't an effective competitor for commercial jet orders anymore. But opposition to the deal came from the European Commission, which threatened a trade war unless Boeing offered some concessions. The most important concession was the termination of the 20-year deals Boeing had just signed to be the exclusive provider for three major airlines: Delta, American, and Continental. A door was opened, but we'll come back to that.

As it tried to absorb McDonnell Douglas (and Rockwell, which it had bought in 1996), the giant company so accustomed to having its own way began to falter. In an agreement with the Department of Labor in 1999, Boeing acknowledged having underpaid women and minority executives and forfeited 4.5 million in back wages and raises to settle the claims. A year earlier, the company agreed to a **1 15** million settlement of two class-action lawsuits involving current and former African American employees. The company's hometown newspaper, the ***Seattle Times,*** speculated that Boeing was having difficulty changing a culture "that many employees regarded as intimidating." At the same time, a Boeing engineer and board member of the company's second-largest union told the ***Times*** that Boeing's luster was on the wane. "Attrition has reached historic highs, especially among experienced and valued employees. Morale survey scores have dropped precipitously. Layoffs and shifting work packages have instilled a pervasive sense of insecurity."

Boeing also stumbled financially after the merger, losing $***03*** billion in costs related to airliner production backlogs. Harry Stonecipher had been CEO of McDonnel Douglas and was named Boeing Vice Chairman after the merger. He was credited with the hard-nosed leadership necessary to clean up the mess and refocus the company on the bottom line. His work apparently completed, Stonecipher stepped down in 2002, leaving Chairman Phil Condit in sole control of the company. That arrangement didn't last long, however. The following year, allegations surfaced that Boeing tried to hire a Pentagon official before the official left office. It was also alleged that the same official may have provided Boeing inside information on a huge contract for 100 refueling tanker aircraft for the Air Force. Boeing fired its chief financial officer, Michael Sears, and Condit resigned from the company. Stonecipher, who had remained on the board, was named the new chief executive. This particular plotline ended with its own ironic twist in March 2005. Stonecipher was forced to resign when an internal investigation revealed that he had been having an extramarital affair with another Boeing executive.

Now let's go back to 1996, and even earlier, to examine the seeds of the dispute between Boeing and the European Commission. We need to begin with the history of Airbus Industrie because Boeing's arrogance has been most damaging in its competition with this European rival. Like the American automotive giants in the face of the Japanese invasion, Boeing couldn't believe that its utter dominance in aircraft manufacturing might be challenged.

The product of a French-German-Spanish-British conglomerate, Airbus was formed in 1970 with the clear intent of breaking Boeing's hegemony. With plenty of help from all four European governments. Airbus quickly began to develop into a competitor. Boeing opened its sleepy eyes in 1992, when it petitioned the European Union to set restraints on its lavish subsidies to Airbus. Europe agreed to limit the subsidies, but the agreement stipulated that Airbus would still receive generous government loans to launch new aircraft.

We begin to see Airbus's strategy in protesting the Boeing–McDonnell Douglas merger in 1996. It claimed the deal would give Boeing an unfair monopoly, but Airbus's share of the world market was already 35%, and the 5% that McDonnell Douglas represented would not really make Boeing significantly bigger. Airbus wanted other concessions. It wanted out of the 1992 agreement. More urgently, it wanted to overturn Boeing's 20-year contracts with Delta, American, and Continental. In the meantime, it began to work its way into the U.S. market by offering sweet deals to carriers in financial trouble. United, America West, and Northwest all came under contract to buy Airbus planes.

In Europe, government support made certain that Airbus's share kept growing. But the company scored a coup in 1999 when it won the JetBlue contract—its first in the low-fare sector. Then Britain's easyJet switched from Boeing to Airbus with an order for 120 passenger jets. The vast Asian market lay on the horizon. In 2003, the unthinkable happened. While Boeing announced it would scale back production for the year to 280 planes, Airbus held firm to its projection schedule of 300, giving it a legitimate claim to the title of "world's biggest aircraft manufacturer." In 2004, Airbus reported 366 net airliner orders compared to Boeing's 272. What happened?

As ***Fortune*** reported near the end of 2003, part of Airbus's heady climb to the top could be attributed to its youthful advantage of being nimble and different, unhindered by old ways of doing business. Boeing's outdated production system harkened back to World War II. An even bigger problem was that Boeing couldn't duplicate Airbus's innovations—"such as wider fuselages, cockpits designed for use in more than one aircraft, and electrical rather than mechanical flight controls—without redesigning its aircraft at prohibitive cost." Boeing fell asleep at the controls, lulled by its longtime and overwhelming market dominance.

Even Harry Stonecipher, coming from McDonnell Douglas at a time when Boeing's position was beginning to erode, blamed the company's problems on its "arrogant and insular" culture. Ironically, noted ***Fortune,*** not even Airbus's victory seemed capable of jolting the sluggish behemoth. Boeing had long treated Airbus as an upstart that existed only because of government subsidies, rather than as a threatening competitor. It's true, says the magazine, that Airbus would never have gotten off the ground without government help, but Boeing had its own consistent flow of goodies from Washington. "The larger truth, though, is that Airbus is building more planes that airlines want to buy than Boeing is."

Like denial, arrogance has a way of shielding corporate eyes from such elemental truths, and Airbus continued to steal the march in 2005. With its parent enjoying record profits. Airbus again beat Boeing in total commercial orders and even put itself in contention for the Pentagon's huge order for refueling tankers. But Boeing may be waking up. As of early 2006, orders for its new 787 Dreamliner were outpacing those for Airbus's new A350, and in the long-range market Boeing's more-efficient two-engine 777 was outselling Airbus's four-engine A340. Moreover, Boeing's willingness to accede to a request from Emirates Airlines (for whose business it is competing fiercely with Airbus) to create a special redesign of the 787 may be an even clearer sign of nascent humility.

WHEN DAVID CONQUERS GOLIATH

A second scenario likely to give rise to arrogance is when the new kid in school beats up the playground bully—or when the new entrant in avitation industry knocks the mighty incumbent off the throne. The tech sector is full of these "David and Goliath" stories, and one of the best, of course, is...

MICROSOFT

In its response to an unending stream of antitrust litigation—both in the U.S. and abroad—Microsoft has displayed the arrogance of a monopolist. The company is now the Goliath of the technology world, but let's recall when Microsoft was the puny David.

It's interesting to listen to college dropouts Bill Gates and Paul Mien talk about their early days together. How their friendship began when the "mothers' club" raised the money to put a computer in their high school in 1968. How they then began hanging out at the commercial computer center in town, where they didn't have to pay for computer time as long as they found bugs in the system and reported them. How they designed their first computer to do traffic-volume-count analysis and called their first company Traf-O-Data. How they tweaked the BASIC language they had used for Traf-O-Data and licensed it to MIT for the minicomputer. How the credit line on that first product read "Micro-Soft Basic: Bill Gates wrote a lot of stuff; Paul Mien wrote some other stuff."

They were David. IBM was Goliath. But instead of killing off the young upstart, Goliath came calling. It was 1980, and IBM was looking for programming languages for its secret PC project. Gates and Allen were willing to sell, but as negotiations continued, IBM expressed an interest in acquiring an operating system as well. Microsoft hadn't developed one, but as it happened, Mien was at that same time in the process of buying a system called Q-DOS ("quick and dirty operating system") from a little local company called Seattle Computer. Mien did the deal (for $50,000), and then he and Gates renamed the product MS-DOS and licensed it to IBM.

Even then, David was loading his slingshot. Gates remembers that IBM didn't really pay them that much. "But we knew there were going to be clones of the IBM PC. We structured that original contract to allow them. It was a key point in our negotiations." What's more, IBM was covering all the bases by also offering a version of its PC with the rival GP/M operating system, which had the advantage of being established on other PC brands. Here's where Gates and Allen whetted their appetite for battle. To make MS-DOS the operating system of choice, they promoted their product vigorously and urged other software companies to write applications for DOS first. Within a year, DOS ruled—just as the first of what would become a tidal wave of PC clones began to flood the marketplace.

It didn't take long for Microsoft to begin to wield its monopoly power. I often like to say that Bill Gates is the reincarnation of Tom Watson Sr., a similarly ruthless entrepreneur. (I should note here that throughout this book I want to show how the self-destructive habits afflict institutions and institutional cultures, rather than individuals or individual founders or leaders. But in the case of Microsoft, a still relatively young company with its original founder still in control, it is impossible to separate the company culture from the individual.)

Apple hauled Microsoft into court in 1988 in what was then the most complicated software copyright lawsuit to date, but which was just the beginning of Microsoft's legal entanglements. Had Microsoft's Windows 2.0 stolen the "look and feel" of Apple's Macintosh operating system, as Apple claimed? Was the "look and feel," taken as a whole, protected by copyright? After four years of deliberation, the court answered "no" to both questions. The decision was upheld on appeal in 1994, and a further appeal by Apple to the Supreme Court was denied. Did Microsoft get away with murder? It's not for me to dispute the court's ruling. But it's interesting to note that Apple, once the world's top PC maker, has been relegated to niche status, selling its machines to a devoted cult of desktop publishers and graphic designers. (But stay tuned: the success of Apple's iPod music player has Microsoft mulling an alliance with Sony.)

With the arrival of the Internet, Microsoft's tactics became more brazen. Initially, Gates failed to see the Internet's full potential. He believed that closed dial-up services like CompuServe and Microsoft's MSN would prevail. As journalist Joe Breen puts it, "He was wrong, and, in 1994, an upstart Silicon Valley company called Netscape, with its Navigator browser software, rubbed his nose in it." In response, Microsoft developed its Explorer browser. It was by no means a superior product, but the price was right. It was bundled free with Windows, and thus it appeared on the desktop of every new PC. Netscape, which charged for its software, obviously couldn't compete. The Department of Justice challenged the move, arguing that Microsoft was using the market dominance of one of its products, its operating system, to muscle in on the market for another, Internet browsers. Microsoft argued that it was simply giving added value to the consumer. Thus, the stage was set for the litigation we described in Chapter 1, which Joe Breen calls "the mother of all antitrust suits."

We know how that case turned out, how Judge Jackson ruled that Microsoft should be broken up, and how his ruling was overturned on appeal. But Microsoft wasn't winning any friends. We noted Paul Krugman's comments in ***The New York Times*** that even as the settlement was being worked out, Gates and Ballmer were still up to their old tricks, displaying the same arrogance that got them into trouble in the first place. Even harsher was the judgment of another ***Times*** columnist, Pulitzer Prize winner (and globalism advocate) Thomas Friedman. Viewing Jackson's ruling as an indictment of the high-tech's general arrogance and contempt for government, Friedman wrote that "no one epitomizes this attitude more than Bill Gates." As far as

Friedman was concerned, Microsoft's hiring of an "army of Washington lobbyists" to try to persuade Congress to slash the budget of the Justice Department's Antitrust Division while its case was before the department was more than enough reason for the government to break up the company. "Think about the arrogance behind that strategy." As a comparison, he asked readers to imagine how they would feel if the biggest company in town tried to use its influence to slash the budget of the police department at a time when the police were investigating the company.

Looking back on the case in July 2000, Judge Jackson told Ken Auletta, who was writing a book about the case, that he might now propose a new remedy for Gates. He would require the Microsoft leader to write a review of a recent biography of Napoleon. Why? "Because I think he has a Napoleonic concept of himself and his company. An arrogance which derives from power and unalloyed success, with no leavening hard experience, no reverses."

Another battle looms. At the World Economic Forum in Davos, Switzerland, in January 2004, Gates made a surprising confession; "Google whipped our butts." The last entity to whip Microsoft's butt was Netscape. Now Microsoft is touting Vista (formerly code-named Project Longhorn), the long-awaited replacement for Windows XP that is loaded with new programs and features. It includes integrated search technology for finding and organizing information, whether it is on the Internet or in the user's own e-mails and files. Can Microsoft make its own search technology the default? Will Google be "Netscaped"? Anticipating the battle, Google has launched "Gmail," its own e-mail service that will allow users to store the equivalent of 500,000 pages of e-mail for free.

Google is already huge. This may be a fight between Goliath and Godzilla.

ENRON AND WORLDCOM

There are plenty of other David and Goliath stories out there, stories in which slaying Goliath went straight to David's head, with disastrous consequences. A fine example is Enron, which transformed itself from an obscure gas pipeline operator to the world's largest energy trader—and the nation's seventh-largest corporation, with 21,000 employees and global interests in electricity, water, and telecommunications.

Thousands of news articles, at least a half-dozen books, and a recent documentary have amply exposed Enron's spectacular rise and collapse, along with the greed and arrogance of its top leaders. In books like Kurt Eichenwald's ***Conspiracy of Fools,*** readers are reminded that when reporters or analysts asked too many questions about Enron's soaring profits during the 1990s, they were met with the now-classic rebuke: "It's the new economy, stupid." When securities analysts or auditors persisted, Ken Lay or other Enron executives complained to their bosses and had them removed. Meanwhile, Lay was paying himself ***$40*** million a year while pretending to know nothing when questions began to be raised about Enron's operations and finances. Enron CFO Andrew Fastow, the man responsible for putting together the private partnerships that artificially inflated the company's assets and earnings, was at the same time funneling 30 million into his own pockets.

For a graphic presentation of not just what these guys did, but also the high-handed smugness with which they did it, there is Alex Gibney's documentary ***Enron: The Smartest Guys in the Room,*** which the ***New York Times*** describes as "a tight, fascinating chronicle of arrogance and greed." Gibney managed to get his hands on in-house video from company meetings, so he can show Jeffrey Skilling and Ken Lay as they "strut and brag through the company's boom years." Viewers can hear recorded phone calls of Enron traders gloating over the ***$2*** billion they are milking from the California energy crisis. Then viewers hear them exult over the news that a wildfire was threatening to bring down power lines and shoot up prices further. Perhaps most contemptible is Lay's shocking appropriation of September 11, as he declared to employees in the fall of 2001 that, just like America, Enron was under attack.

As for the smartest guys in the room, Fastow pleaded guilty in January 2004, forfeited ***$23.8*** million in assets, and faces 10 years in jail. Skilling and Lay pleaded not guilty to more than three dozen counts of insider trading, fraud, and lying on Enron financial statements. Their trials got underway in January 2006; the star defendants took the stand in April. Skilling was convicted of 19 of 28 counts of securities fraud and wire fraud. Lay was convicted of six counts of securities and wire fraud. He died of a heart attack on July 5, 2006, before he could be sentenced.

Then there's the story of WorldCom and Bernie Ebbers, the so-called Telecom Cowboy. A better David and Goliath tale could scarcely be written. This one-time milkman and basketball coach, who was said to wrestle bulls for pleasure, began his entrepreneurial career by operating a small motel chain in Mississippi. In 1983, he invested in an obscure long-distance company called Long Distance Discount Services. After becoming CEO two years later, he steered the company through a dizzying series of more than 60 acquisitions. The brash, tough-talking Ebbers planned to make WorldCom—as the company became known in 1995—the world's biggest telecom company, and he neared that goal with the $40 billion acquisition of MCI in 1998. But his $115 billion bid for Sprint, the industry Goliath, was rejected by antitrust regulators the following year, and, as in Greek tragedy, the wheel of fortune turned.

In 2000, as the high-tech boom went bust, Ebbers started facing margin calls on all the personal loans he had collateralized with his WorldCom stock. But that was just the beginning of the end. In June 2002, a couple of months after Ebbers' abrupt departure, WorldCom announced that it had overstated its earnings by 3.5 billion. As investigations into the company's finances began, that figure grew to 11 billion, the biggest corporate fraud in U.S. history. In Mareh 2005, after a six-week trial, Ebbers was found guilty on nine criminal charges—securities fraud, conspiracy, and seven counts of making false filings to the SEC. He faces up to 85 years in jail.

WHEN YOU PIONEER A PRODUCT OR SERVICE NOBODY CAN DUPLICATE

Xerox's patent on xerography and Coca-Cola's "secret formula" spring to mind as obvious examples of this scenario, and arrogance has certainly been a problem at both of those companies. But let's turn instead to the consumer electronics giant from Japan.

SONY

The Sony story starts with transistor radios—when founder Akio Morito wanted to bring radio programming to the parts of the world where there was no electricity. He paid Western Electric ***S25,000*** for transistor technology licenses and in 1955 produced a revolutionary, and affordable, product. It would be the first of many victories for Sony Corp.—a company that came to epitomize Japan's electronics wizardry, and that, according to a Harris poll in the late 1990s, became the world's most recognized brand.

The first home video recorder in 1964, Trinitron color TVs in 1969, the Sony Walkman in 1979, the audio CD in 1983—it wasn't that Sony was creating products that couldn't be duplicated exactly; it's that Sony kept getting to the market first by staying on the crest of the technological wave.

As competition caught up in the 1980s, Sony began to diversify into content, purchasing CBS Records in 1988 for $2 billion and Columbia Pictures (including Tristar) in 1989 for $4.9 billion. Was it an overreach? Another example of now-mighty Japan poking its finger in the eye of over-the-hill America? Had Sony grown arrogant?

Interestingly, at the same time Sony was moving into Hollywood, a book titled ***The Japan That Can Say No*** was selling briskly in Tokyo bookstores. It was coauthored, in alternating chapters, by Morita and Shintaro Ishihara, a politician-turned-author, and its general thesis was that Japan no longer needed to act like the deferential stepchild of the Unites States. Indeed, Japan was superior. "Americans do not manufacture anymore," wrote Morita. "They cannot figure out how to mass-produce goods by applying new technology, or how to market them." Ishihara added, for example, that if Japan were to sell its semiconductor chips to the Soviet Union instead of to the U.S., "that would instantly change the balance of military power." In fact, the book prompted a feud between its authors and then-Ghrysler chairman Lee Iacocca, himself no great paragon of modesty, assailed the book for "America bashing" and said the two authors' "arrogance pours salt into an already open wound."

In 1993, during an early-morning tennis match, Morita suffered a stroke. With his collapse, the company also seemed to stumble. While operating profits had been stagnating since the turn of the decade, the red ink began to flow in 1994. Sony Pictures Entertainment took a $2.5 billion write-off in goodwill and another 500 million to cover losing projects—a huge embarrassment. For the fiscal year ending March 1995, Sony suffered its first-ever loss: ***$2.8*** billion.

From the beginning, Sony Pictures had management problems. The American-based business was put in the hands of Michael Schulhof, a physicist and 20-year Sony veteran who had zero experience in the entertainment industry. His main qualification, apparently, was that he was a protégé of Morita. Schulhof, in turn, hired two producers to run the studio whose principal qualifications were that they knew how to spend tons of money. The occasional success, like ***Sleepless in Seattle,*** was more than offset by stinkers like ***The Last Action Hero.*** Sony Pictures gained a reputation as a dysfunctional family. But problems in management were probably exacerbated by problems in attitude. As a high-ranking cable executive told the ***Wall Street Journal,*** Sony "came into it somewhat naive. They stepped on the accelerator and flooded the engine," trying to grow fast and become a big player.

Meanwhile, Nobuyuki Idei took over at Sony in 1995 (handpicked by Chairman Norio Ohga over several more senior executives). Part of his job was to handle the larger "cultural" issues left simmering during Morita's tenure. "Sony's loner origins and meteoric rise have bred a reputation for arrogance," reported ***Business Week.*** "The ill effects aren't difficult to spot." The article pointed out that Sony supported its own Betamax VCR format long after the rival VHS system had triumphed in the market. More recently, the Sony-Philips digital video disk was also losing the format battle— "because they failed to court the Hollywood film industry. They just assumed the other movie studios would fall in line." Instead, Hollywood chose a setup from Toshiba Corp. and Time Warner.

It appeared Idei might be the man for the cultural overhaul. In the first place, he had jettisoned Schulhof—still a favorite of Chairman Ohga—within nine months. Then he decimated Sony's board, reducing it from 38 members to 10, including three from outside the company. Most important, he fervently embraced the philosophy of "convergence"—bringing together hardware and software, gadgetry and content, digital technology and entertainment, to create a world where satellite communications furnish interactive entertainment to every home. As for the Sony culture, Idei told ***Time*** magazine, "In the 1970s and '80s, this was a founder-driven company. What we need now is a good operating system, a good application system and a good management team."

By 1999, with Sony riding high again—largely on the phenomenal success of its PlayStation video game console—Idei seemed to have turned the company around. London's ***Independent*** rhapsodized that the old days, when Sony's interests were served by the unchecked power of senior management, were gone. "The appointment of Idei immediately wiped away decades of Sony arrogance as the new man instilled a new humility to the company, bringing Sony into the modern world of rational decision making and accountability." As a result, Sony "[has] shone like a beacon on the otherwise dismal economic landscape of Japan during the 1990s."

Then, out of nowhere, came "Sony Shock." For the fiscal year ending March 2003, Sony missed its net profit target by 36% and—even worse—predicted earnings in 2004 of only 50 billion yen, half of 2003's profit and less than a third of what analysts had predicted. In two days after the announcement, Sony shares dropped 27%, wiping out 922 billion yen in market capitalization. Idei's response—a three-year, ***$3*** billion plan to cut costs by eliminating 20,000 jobs—suggested that Sony's problems no longer had anything to do with arrogance.

But what was it? Perhaps Idei's dream of convergence had yet to be realized. Instead of coming together in one magical synergy, it seemed that the huge corporation was coming apart. Suddenly Sony was derided as an "unmanageable giant," a company without focus, a company trying to be in too many businesses and failing as a result. In June 2005, as the company's fortunes continued to decline, Idei stepped down. Howard Stringer, a Welshman who had been in charge of Sony's U.S. business, took over as Sony chairman and chief executive officer. It remains to be seen where he will take the iconic company. Will he continue to pursue Idei's difficult dream, or will he focus narrowly on profitability and ride the success of PlayStation Portable and PlayStation 3?

WHEN YOU'RE SMARTER THAN THE OTHER GUYS

Finally, arrogance is likely to thrive when your scientists have a history of whipping their scientists—that is, when you invent great products first and can therefore reap great profit and renown from patent protection, trademarks, and intellectual property rights in general. Sony might just as easily have fit into this category, but there are plenty of excellent examples. Let's look first at a famous brand from the pharmaceutical industry.

MERCK

Is "arrogant" too harsh a term to apply to venerable Merck & Company? Collins and Porras, in ***Built to Last,*** have nothing but praise for the pharmaceutical giant. They recall George Merck's mantra from the 1920s—"Medicine is for the patient, not for the profits. The profits follow"—and assert that this "core ideology" has shaped the company's vision for more than eight decades. They gush about how Merck elected to develop and give away Mectizan, a drug to cure river blindness, a horrible parasitic worm disease that had blinded more than a million people in the Third World. (At the risk of sounding churlish, I have to note that Collins and Porras don't mention that Merck got out of the flu vaccine business in 1986, despite the thousands of deaths from that disease every year.)

Certainly, the company has much to be proud of. It was founded in 1889, when George Merck came to America and started a firm to import and sell drugs and chemicals from his family's business back in Germany. It began manufacturing operations in 1903, making alkaloids at its new plant in Rahway, New Jersey. After Merck opened its research facility in 1933, a steady stream of brilliant scientists did groundbreaking work there. Merck researchers developed the first steroid, cortisone, in 1944, and five Merck scientists won Nobel Prizes in the 1940s and 1950s. In the 1970s, its unflagging commitment to research and development resulted in the antiarthritic Clinoril, the muscle relaxant Flexeril, and the glaucoma medication Timoptic.

Under legendary biochemist Roy Vagelos, who became the CEO in 1985, the run of major new drugs continued, including Mevacor for high cholesterol and Vasotec for high blood pressure. Merck was the world's leading pharmaceutical company, and its reputation was untarnished.

Then odd things began happening. In December 1992, Merck surprised analysts as well as company insiders when it named fast-rising marketer Richard Markham president, placing him in line to succeed Vagelos. Six months later, industry watchers were even more stunned to learn that Markham had suddenly resigned without explanation. The ***Wall Street Journal*** saw this as a sign that Merck, long considered one of the best-managed companies in the world, was going through a period of remarkable and surprising distress.

Explanations for the departure sounded a central theme: Markham represented too radical a departure from Merck's conservative and stodgy culture. He wanted too much change too fast, and his flamboyant style was marked by a high-profile divorce and remarriage to a Merck employee—a further violation of the company's straight-laced image.

Markham saw the necessity of boosting sales to the fast-growing community of HMOs, rather than selling directly to doctors. But this meant discounts, which the proud Merck culture had always resisted. Even though Vagelos had condoned the move toward HMOs, speculation was that Markham's revolution was moving too far too fast as his "young, brash colleagues from the marketing side" sought to make acquisitions, jettison parts of the company, and cut the workforce.

For example, Markham created a separate business unit to sell generic drugs, a move Merck traditionalists thought cheapened the company's image. As if that weren't bad enough, he also cut the prices of anticholesterol Mevacor and Zocor, a shocking instance of the company's publicly advertising the discounting of drugs.

As one Merck researcher, speaking anonymously, told the journal, "Markham was part of a group of senior Young Turks who seemed to want to do things differently. It was unsettling here."

It was a difficult time for Merck and the industry as a whole. Merck's share price had been dropping for a year, and, industrywide, profits were sagging. All the major companies were holding down prices to blunt the threat of price regulation from the Clinton administration. The profit squeeze was exacerbated by a wave of discounting, as the drug makers hustled for business with HMOs.

Things got even stranger at Merck. The next candidate to succeed Vagelos, Martin Wygod, suddenly dropped out of the running. Wygod had joined Merck a year earlier when it acquired Medco Containment to get into the business of managing prescription benefits for health plans, and he had risen rapidly to become heir apparent. As he neared the top, it sounded like the same song, second verse: The best guess was that the "entrepreneurial" Wygod would be out of place in the "formal" culture at Merck.

Ultimately, Merck brought in an outsider, Raymond Gilmartin, who had been CEO of medical-gear maker Becton Dickinson. There was a lot of talk about changing the corporate atmosphere.

Gilmartin created a 12-member management committee that was intended to decentralize leadership and dismantle a culture characterized by turf battles and defections.

Actually, Gilmartin just happened to arrive at the right time, as he himself liked to joke. Within 18 months after his arrival in 1994, eight new drugs were introduced, all of which had been in development for years. Among them were blockbusters like the AIDS treatment Crixivan, the osteoporosis drug Fosamax, and the antihypertensive Cozaar. Changing Merck's culture didn't seem to be necessary after all.

In fact, Gilmartin reaffirmed Merck's mission and vision. Merck, he said, would remain a research-driven pharmaceutical company, and it would not pursue diversification. He shut down the generic-drug operation and sold off more than 1 billion in assets. He assured Wall Street that he was not looking for acquisitions, despite the fact that mergers among other drug giants had dropped Merck from No. 1 to No. 3 in the industry.

It was a vision in keeping with Merck's proud heritage. Looking back on Gilmartin's tenure in 2003, the ***Wall Street Journal*** observed that as the drug industry was reshaped by a "wave of new hardball tactics," Merck had managed to stay out of the battle. As other companies joined in megamergers, Merck proudly held its independent course. And while other companies spent millions to market new products that differed little from their successors, Merck continued to focus on one-of-a-kind drugs.

Recalling George Merck's guiding philosophy, the journal observed that Merck had always taken pride in its ability to rise above the clamor of "everyday profit-seeking." Although rivals might deride Merck's sanctimonious attitude, the company had established an enviable record of delivering the goods. From penicillin, of which Merck was a leading manufacturer, to cholesterol-lowering statins, of which Merck sold the first one, the company had been a steadfast leader in introducing new medicines to the market. Now Gilmartin was calling the turn of the century the "most productive time ever" for Merck research and promised that Merck would either start selling or seek approval for 11 new medicines by 2006.

Unfortunately, Gilmartin's bet has fallen short. Four of the new medicines have failed, and two others have been delayed. In the six months after May 2003, Merck's stock price was down 30% while other drug stocks were slightly up. Worse, Merck's true Achilles heel was exposed.

As the journal noted, when Gilmartin took over, most people in the drug industry believed that the threat to growth would be the managed-care revolution. Insurers would force drug makers into deep discounts in exchange for getting on approved drug lists. But the managed-care threat was a red herring. The real ***bete noire*** turned out to be utterly different: the challenge of coming up with new mega-sellers as the older blockbusters lose their patent protection and face generic competition. The patents on Vasotec, Mevacor, and Pepcid AG expired in 2001, and the clock is **running** out on others.

Zocor, which recorded more than ***$5*** billion in worldwide sales in 2002, is a prime example of this problem. As a result of loss of patent protection in parts of Europe, sales of Zocor in 2005 were off 16% from the year before. Worse, the expiration of patent protection in the U.S., scheduled for June 2006, was expected to diminish revenues by a whopping ***$2*** billion—a major threat to the company's bottom line. Foreseeing this inevitability in 2003, Merck laid off 3,200 employees, about 5% of the workforce.

As if 2003 weren't bad enough, here came the Vioxx debacle in 2004, when the blockbuster arthritis painkiller was linked to heart problems among users. Merck pulled the drug from the shelves—a huge loss considering the $2.5 billion it had generated in 2003. By the end of 2005, Vioxx users had filed literally thousands of product liability lawsuits against the company. Epidemiologists were speculating that as many as 100,000 heart attacks might be linked to the drug.

Gilmartin had planned to retire in March 2006, when he reached Merck's mandatory retirement age. Suddenly that schedule got moved up. Richard Clark, who had been in charge of Merck's manufacturing operations, became CEO in May 2005. Clark's quicker-than-expected ascension would seem to imply a mandate for change, an acknowledgment that fresh thinking was needed to steer Merck through challenging and perhaps perilous times. The irony is that Clark is the ultimate insider, having spent his entire career at Merck, where he started as a quality control inspector in 1972. Is he the right man to bring Merck down off its high horse?

MOTOROLA

Paul Galvin showed his entrepreneurial bent when he started his first business, selling popcorn, at age 13. Twenty years later, in 1928, he founded Galvin Manufacturing in Chicago to make battery eliminators that allowed early radios to run on household current. From there it was a natural step to car radios (which ultimately would give the company its famous name). In 1940, the company developed the first handheld two-way radio for the U.S. Army.

In 1959, the same year that Paul's son, Robert, became CEO, the company's purchase of a hospital communications systems maker led it to develop its first pagers. By 1977, Motorola was already starting to put together a cell phone system, and in 1990 the company created the 66-satellite Iridium communication system.

In other words, this was a company that enjoyed a well-earned reputation for beating other people to the market with innovative, sometimes revolutionary, products.

A 1992 feature in the ***Wall Street Journal*** called Motorola the "nimble giant" that other companies should look to in order to find "the road back to manufacturing supremacy and market-share dominance." During these halcyon days, under the leadership of George Fisher (who succeeded Robert Galvin), Motorola was the global market leader in cell phones, pagers, two-way radios, and microchips used in devices other than computers. The journal lauded the company for the manufacturing wizardry that allowed it, in the 1980s, to beat back the Japanese advance in both cell phones and pagers. The company's sterling record of achievement was attributed in part to a culture "that kindles rather than stifles conflict and dissent...and generates a constant flow of information and innovation from thousands of small teams held to rigorous, statistically evaluated goals."

George Fisher left Motorola in 1993 to take over at Kodak, and COO Gary Tooker was promoted to CEO. Four years later, on January 1, 1997, the board replaced Tooker with Paul Galvin's grandson, Chris Galvin. Nobody was talking about the "nimble giant" anymore. Instead, Motorola had moved ponderously to digital technology, and now Ericsson and Nokia were stealing the limelight—along with market share—in

Motorola's key segment, cell phones. Rather than receiving universal praise, Motorola was being accused by customers and partners of "arrogance and insularity." It was the smart-guy syndrome; if we build the products, the customers will come.

The new CEO not only heard the charges; he repeated them. "The only time we get off kilter is when we have an initial amount of success," Galvin told ***USA TODAY.*** "People get arrogant or believe that the business model they have is one that will last a long time. They stay with it too long and don't modify." Galvin had also had enough of the "warring tribes" culture that had formerly won so much praise; he vowed that "collaboration," both inside the company and with its partners, would be the new watchword. A year into the job, it looked like Galvin might be the right man to restore Motorola's luster. No less an authority than George Fisher said, "I think in 10 or 20 years the world will look on Chris Galvin as perhaps the greatest leader Motorola has ever had."

It didn't happen that way. In the summer of 2000, SBC Wireless planned to promote a new Motorola cell phone alongside the blockbuster movie ***Mission: Impossible 2.*** It would have been a great marketing coup, but Motorola failed to deliver the phones in time for the movie's release. SBC had to scrap the promotion and almost canceled its order. The story "pretty much sums it up for Motorola these days," wrote the ***Wall Street Journal.*** From mid-2000 to mid-2001, Motorola's shares lost three-fourths of their value, and for the first quarter of 2001 the company reported its first loss in 16 years. Over five years, in the critical cell phone market, the company's global share had fallen from 33% to 14%, while Nokia's share soared from 22% to 35%.

As noted, part of the problem was Motorola's slow shift from analog to digital. But as Verizon Wireless executive John Stratton told the journal, Motorola still exhibited the same old failing: arrogance. It forgot that its most important customers were the carriers, who decide which phones they will stock in their stores and which they will promote with special offers. Motorola's annoying habit had been to tell carriers which phones they should buy and even how to display them in their stores. "Listening, for Motorola, was waiting for you to stop speaking so they could tell you what to buy," Stratton told the journal. "It was endemic to their culture.When you couple arrogance with incompetence—as in Motorola's failure to deliver product on deadline or meet carriers' customized demands—you lose business fast, which is why customers like SBC, Alltel, and Verizon have been turning to competitors like Nokia.

For the third quarter in 2001, Motorola lost $1.4 billion and announced that it would suffer its first annual loss in 46 years. The stock was trading at $17, down from $60 in early 2000. The company was laying off 39,000 workers. Two years later, Galvin was gone. Citing "disagreements with the board," the family scion stepped down, to be replaced by an outsider, Edward Zander, formerly president of Sim Microsystems. Known as a consummate salesman with a working-class Brooklyn background, maybe Zander will prove capable of repairing Motorola's broken relationships, reversing its fortunes, and fundamentally altering its culture of arrogance.

THE WARNING SIGNS OF ARROGANCE

As with the personal habits that insidiously settle upon us, sometimes we're the last to see—or admit to—the behaviors that can prove our undoing. To learn whether your organization might be suffering from arrogance, look for the following signs.

YOU STOP LISTENING

...to customers, employees, investors, consumer advocates, the government. You stop listening to the outside world. You ignore or laugh at others. You believe you've seen it all before.

YOU FLAUNT IT

...in travel, office space, perks, retreats. You like to show off your corporate jets and art collections. Or, like Dennis Kozlowski of Tyco, you throw your wife a ***$2*** million birthday party—complete with scantily clad models in Roman togas—on the Italian island of Sardinia.

YOU BROWBEAT OTHERS

You encourage and even offer incentives to your managers to browbeat employees, customers, and investors. When analysts give your company unfavorable reports, you think you can go to their bosses and have them rebuked or reprimanded. Your company acts like a bully.

YOU'RE HIGH-HANDED

You abuse governance rules and procedures in the belief that they don't pertain to you, that no one can regulate or even question your business. Or, like GM, you abuse or lobby against government regulation because "what's good for you is good for the nation."

YOU CURRY APPROVAL

You bring in consultants and advisors to validate the status quo and inflate your ego. At the same time, you fire those who become critical, including suppliers, customers, and even employees. When ad agencies or research groups suggest strategies you don't like, you hire somebody else.

YOU EXHIBIT THE NIH SYNDROME

Like companies in denial, you believe that if it's "not invented here," it can't be any good.

HOW TO BREAK THE ARROGANCE HABIT

Arrogance breeds in a dark, closed room. To break the habit, open the doors and windows and let some light shine in. The leader must change the culture to one of looking, listening, and learning—especially learning from the experiences of those outside the company. Bring in fresh air, fresh ideas. Here are a few approaches.

ROTATE MANAGEMENT TO NEW CHALLENGES

Give your managers assignments where the odds of success are not guaranteed. Put them to work in unfamiliar and hostile markets, or on projects full of risky innovation, or on major new initiatives (like deregulated businesses for regulated companies). But make it clear that if the manager fails, it is not the end of his career so long as learning has occurred. Jack Welch says he likes managers who have a few failures on their resumes. Failure is a good teacher of modesty.

IMPLEMENT NONTRADITIONAL SUCCESSION PLANNING

Consider selecting someone several levels below the heir apparent—perhaps the COO or vice chair—and testing him or her on a fast track across functions, divisions, and markets. This worked beautifully at Whirlpool when the company elevated David Whitwam. The same thing happened at GE. Jack Welch was three levels down when they fast-tracked him as a way to shake up the culture.

DIVERSIFY THE TALENT POOL BY RECRUITING FROM A VARIETY OF EDUCATIONAL INSTITUTIONS, COUNTRIES, AND DEMOGRAPHICS

Again, insularity breeds arrogance. For years Whirlpool recruited almost exclusively from Purdue University. The benefit was great networking and reciprocity. The downside was insularity. After Whirlpool began hiring highly trained Indian engineers, they quickly drove out much of the Purdue talent.

I like the "Thoroughbred versus mongrel" analogy: the thoroughbred can run a fast mile, but he's fragile. He's not good for the long haul. What you want are the sturdy genes of the mongrel. Make your corporation a mixed-gene mongrel, and you'll prove stronger in the long run.

Another good analogy comes from corn agriculture. To promote uniformity and increase yield, scientists reduced the number of varieties from something like 2,500 to 40. But now the whole crop is susceptible to a single disease. The point is that "genetic diversity" is important to corporate health—and that includes "gender diversity."

Today you can get technical, legal, and accounting talent from across the world. The U.S. no longer dominates. And the best companies know that. P&G is recruiting talent from India and placing it all over the world. Pepsi has also learned this lesson—especially compared to Coke. HSBC (the fast-rising Hong Kong bank) is now at work on the issue of gender diversity. It's no longer a matter of political correctness. It's as urgent as having healthy, oxygenated blood pumping through our systems.

ENCOURAGE OUTSIDE PERSPECTIVES THROUGH LEADERSHIP INSTITUTES

Examples include GE's "Workout," "Action Learning" with Noel Tichy, and Motorola's Participatory Management Process (PMP). Inside the company, encourage an "anybody-can-challenge-anybody" culture. Again, the idea is to break down the walls inside which arrogance festers.

CHANGE YOUR LEADERSHIP

Bringing in an outsider is the most drastic fix, of course. It can work in a crisis, but caution is urged. There are no guarantees. A sensible approach is to bring in an outside board member who has successfully (and humbly) run another company. There have been successes, like Randy Tobias at Eli Lilly and Lou Gerstner at IBM. Perhaps Edward Zander will turn around Motorola. There have also been failures, even when exemplary leaders were brought in. George Fisher, who led Motorola through some of its greatest years, proved unable to ehange the culture at Kodak.

Neither people nor companies are likely to become arrogant overnight. It's a habit formed over the years, and its roots can reach deep into the corporate soul. No one of these five suggestions—not even a change of leadership—can guarantee that the culture of arrogance will be broken. In all likelihood, real change will come only after arrogance has begun to cause visible damage—in lost business, lost customers, lost profits. At that point, the remedies suggested here may help transform the corporate identity—inside and out.

ARROGANCE

Things that lead to arrogance:

- Exceptional achievement in the past warps your perception of present reality.
- David conquers Goliath.
- You pioneer a product or service that nobody can duplicate.
- You're smarter than the other guys.

The warning signs of arrogance:

- **You stop listening:** You believe you've seen it all before, and you no longer listen to customers, employees, investors, consumer advocates, or the government.
- **You flaunt it:** You are extravagantly eager to show off your success.
- **You browbeat others:** Your company acts like a bully—internally and externally.
- **You're high-handed:** You abuse rules and procedures in the belief that no one can regulate or even question your business.
- **You curry approval:** You favor those who validate your views and get rid of those who are critical.

How to break the arrogance habit:

- **Rotate management to new challenges:** Challenge your management, but allow them to fail. Failure is a good teacher of modesty.
- **Implement nontraditional succession planning:** Consider fast-tracking candidates across functions, divisions, and markets.
- **Diversify the talent pool by recruiting from a variety of educational institutions, countries, and demographics:** Make your corporation strong by diversifying your talent genes.
- **Change your leadership:** Consider bringing in an outsider.

CHAPTER 4

COMPLACENCY: SUCCESS BREEDS FAILURE

Complacency is the sense of security and comfort that derives from the belief that the success you've had in the past will continue indefinitely. It breeds in the assumption that the future will be like the present and past, that nothing will change. Complacency likes blindness and inertia; it likes the status quo. It hates urgency and believes in slow, cautious deliberation. It settles easily into large institutions, where size and scale provide a natural armor against the real, fast-moving world outside. Complacency is fostered by the illusion of "sturdy genes"—in other words, bad things can't happen here.

Put another way, complacency rests on three pillars: your success in the past, your belief that the future is predictable, and your assumption that scale will protect you against any setback. A jolt may come, but you won't be shaken.

Obviously, you can't be complacent without having had some success. But where did that success come from? This chapter examines four "success" scenarios that are likely to induce complacency—four scenarios where success ultimately breeds failure. Notice, though, in the following stories how failure likes to hide itself. You'll see that many of these examples are large, vertically integrated companies that depend on cross-subsidies of functions, businesses, products, or customers, so failure in one area or unit of the business can be compensated for by success in another. I find this an interesting hallmark of the complacent culture.

WHEN YOUR PAST SUCCESS CAME VIA A REGULATED MONOPOLY

The only thing better than a monopoly is a government-regulated monopoly. When the government helps you erect the walls of your fortress, protecting your business and holding your competitors at bay, it's pretty easy to become complacent. There's no better example of this scenario than Ma Bell.

AT&T

Alexander Graham Bell invented the telephone in 1876, and the following year he and two partners formed Bell Telephone. In 1885, under Theodore Vail, American Telephone and Telegraph was created to build Bell's long-distance network, and just before the turn of the century it became the parent company. Vail had left to pursue other interests, but he was persuaded to return to AT&T in 1907. Over the next dozen years, until his retirement in 1919, he created the monopoly that would rule the U.S. telephone business until the mid-1980s.

Vail not only reorganized the Bell companies, but, with the financial backing of J. P. Morgan, he set upon a course of acquiring the many independents that had sprung up as the Bell patents expired. Under the famous Kingsbury Commitment of 1913, AT&T agreed to divest itself of Western Union but at the same time was given a governmental green light to fine-tune and strengthen its monopoly strategy. Presumably buying into Vail's philosophy of "one policy, one system, and universal service," the government allowed the company to buy market share from competitors as long as it sold an equal number of phone systems. Between 1921 and 1934 the Interstate Commerce Commission (ICC) approved 271 of AT&T's 274 acquisition requests, through which AT&T strengthened its hold on the lucrative urban markets and consolidated its monopoly on long-distance traffic. In 1934, as part of President Roosevelt's Depression-era New Deal, AT&T was set up as a regulated monopoly (a "natural monopoly") under the jurisdiction of the FCC.

It made sense at the time—when the government saw a need to create jobs by managing huge public businesses. It was also a very sweet deal for AT&T. For 50 years, in effect, AT&T controlled industry regulation. Consider, too, that way back in 1882 Bell Telephone had wrested control of equipment manufacturer Western Electric from Western Union, and that in 1925 it created the renowned research division Bell Labs. Consequently, early in the century AT&T had already established a vertically integrated powerhouse that controlled the research gate at Bell Labs, the manufacturing gate at Western Electric, and the sales and distribution gate by virtue of its monopoly position. This was indeed a fortress nobody could penetrate.

But there's a downside to living in a fortress. It's hard not to get fat and lazy. Looking back at AT&T's long history, the ***Wall Street Journal*** noted that in the 1950s and 1960s, the company's "secure and growing" revenue and protected markets caused its "combative muscle" to atrophy. Federal and state regulators had put a cap on its profits, "so the company placed little value on entrepreneurial ventures ... Its managers were homegrown and so inculcated with the company dogma that they were called 'Bellheads'. . . ." For the rest of AT&T's life, its monopoly status would be a double-edged word.

The winds began to shift in 1949 when the government tried to force AT&T to sell Western Electric. A consent decree in 1956 allowed the company to continue manufacturing phones but otherwise forced the spin-off of AT&T's global manufacturing arm. (Today, that arm exists as Nortel in Canada, ITT in Europe, and NEC in Japan.) So a part of the vertical hierarchy had been eliminated, but AT&T held on to its service monopoly.

At the same time, AT&T was trying to deal with the threat posed by Jack Goeken, a story worth telling in some detail.

Goeken's MCI had started as a store selling two-way radios, mostly to truckers, in Joliet, Illinois. The truckers liked them, but the problem was that they had a range of only about 15 miles. Goeken figured that if he could set up some towers along the heavy-traffic route from St. Louis to Chicago, he would be able to sell a lot more radios, so in 1963 he set off to Washington, D.C. to get FGG approval. (I should point out that Goeken's strategy represents the typical competitive attack against cross-subsidized monopolies. He took aim, naturally, at the customer-heavy St. Louis-to-Chicago market, the kind of market AT&T would depend on to subsidize less lucrative segments. In other words, he "cream-skimmed.")

At the hearing, AT&T argued that MCI could not build its system at a cost that would allow it to charge competitive prices, that the public interest would not be served, and therefore the license should be denied. Since AT&T still had the regulators pretty much in its pocket, the FGG took the company's word for it.

But Goeken had heard at the FGG about a confidential report on microwave communications systems that AT&T had prepared for internal use only. He wanted to see a copy, so he flew to AT&T headquarters in New York to try to get his hands on it. As it happened, it was cold and snowing in New York when he landed, and he had left his overcoat at the Hartford airport. When he walked into AT&T without an overcoat on, the receptionist he encountered assumed he had to be an employee and told him the report he was looking for was in the library. As historian John Steele Gordon tells it, Goeken "asked where—meaning 'Where is the library?'—and she apparently thought he meant where in the library. She wrote out an official interoffice request form with the document name and number. Goeken realized what was happening, had enough sense to shut up, and found the library on his own." He got his hands on the report, and in it he discovered that AT&T itself had estimated far lower costs than it had reported to the FGG.

"It would take another six years for the FGG to grant MCI a license to operate," wrote Steele, "but when it did, the camel's nose was under AT&T's tent."

What Goeken started, the Department of Justice finished. The FGG might have tried to protect AT&T's monopoly forever, but the courts were less amenable. This was the fortress gate AT&T had left unguarded. Entrepreneur William McGowan took over MCI in 1968 and initiated the court challenge that would eventually topple the monopoly. He liked to say, when asked how he could take on such a giant, "My R&D department is my legal department." When AT&T tried to shut down MCI by tripling its interconnection fees, MCI filed suit and was awarded damages in 1980—the beginning of the end for Ma Bell.

Thanks to its monopoly-bred complacency, AT&T had difficulty competing after it was forced to break up in 1984. Unbelievably, the company didn't even have a marketing department until 1979. As a result, when it was broken up, AT&T was by no means a well-known consumer brand. Customers were familiar with the Bell logo, of course, but in fact less than 10% of the public knew AT&T by name, and 50% confused it with ITT. The company immediately went to work on branding, planning to call itself ABI—American Bell International. But Judge Harold Greene, who oversaw the breakup, ruled against the name. He gave to the Baby Bells exclusive rights to the Yellow Pages and the Bell name. AT&T could use the name, only in reference to Bell Labs, a national treasure. (I still have a tie that Randall Tobias, who was in charge of the marketing effort, gave me at the time—with the ABI name and newly designed logo on it. He told me to hold onto it; it would be a collector's item one day.) The upshot was that the company kept the AT&T name—but in initial form only. The words meant nothing; there was no telephone/telegraph business, and "American" was an anachronism in the global business environment. The company spent 1 billion a year on the brand and made it a household word.

But AT&T needed more than a brand. It needed competitive muscle. It needed to see the future. It needed vital management. None of these things had been important before, and now they were in short supply. Arch McGill was brought in to be the change agent. He succeeded in being an irritant, like the sand in an oyster, but he didn't survive. He was succeeded by Charlie Brown, who oversaw the final stages of the breakup and then turned the company over to Jim Olsen. Olsen's task was to find the company's direction in the rapidly changing telecom environment. Unfortunately, he died suddenly on the job in 1988. Here's when the company should have elevated Randall Tobias, who was being groomed for the job by Olsen, but in the absence of a formal succession plan the position instead was filled by Robert Allen. His nine-year tenure was marked by turmoil in the upper ranks and the widely publicized departures of a number of high-level executives, including Alex Mandl, Jerre Stead, Joe Nacchio, and John Walter.

Not surprisingly, strategic confusion ensued, most dramatically with AT&T's purchase of NCR—a last-minute attempt to get into the computer business—in 1991. The deal was widely regarded as a disaster, and NCR returned to being a separate company in 1997. In 1993, AT&T moved into the cellular phone business with the purchase of 33% of McCaw Cellular Communications, the biggest firm in the wireless market with a network covering 40% of the U.S. population and almost all major cities. The price—$11.4 billion—was seen as the cost of correcting the strategic error AT&T had made in the early days of cellular, when it opted to be only an equipment supplier. Then, in 1996, the company spun off the remainder of its equipment manufacturing business as Lucent Technologies.

In 1997, it was Michael Armstrong's turn. He was recruited from Hughes Electronics to come in and set AT&T on a "bold new course." His idea was that AT&T would use its powerful brand identity, technology know-how, and vast scale to become the first company to offer consumers a bundle of services, including local, long distance, and cellular, along with Internet access, basic television, and even video.

The first thing Armstrong had to do was get into cable, so he spent 100 billion to buy Tele-Communications Inc. (TCI) and MediaOne Group, which in one stroke made AT&T the biggest cable operator in the United States. At the same time he sought regulatory approval to connect into the copper-wire networks of the regional Bells.

It was a good strategy, but Armstrong, as would become clear, had paid way too much for the cable companies, which needed additional billions of dollars worth of upgrades. At the same time, the Baby Bells fought back to keep AT&T and anybody else from hooking into their networks and challenging their monopoly on local service. As if that weren't bad enough, the telecom boom turned to bust, and prices for long distance and cellular began to plummet, robbing AT&T of the profits it needed to pay the interest on the huge debt it had assumed to buy the cable companies. Needless to say, AT&T's stock price tanked as a result.

In October 2001, AT&T and British Telecom dissolved their joint venture, Concert. It was supposed to have created a global telecom powerhouse by combining the two companies' corporate clients and selected network assets into one entity. It had been one of Armstrong's big initiatives but had bled money from the outset. AT&T announced a $5.3 billion charge against earnings to scrap the enterprise. At the same time, AT&T's high-speed ISP, Excite@Home, filed for bankruptcy—another major snag in Armstrong's tapestry. He had paid ***$6*** billion for 38% of the company's stock and control of its board. Now the company's market value was about ***$19*** million.

Armstrong was forced to beat a hasty retreat. Rejecting the grand plan, he announced that the company would be broken up. The cellular division was spun off to raise cash and pay down debt, and then a badly battered AT&T had to accept Comcast's unsolicited offer of $46 billion for its cable division. It was about half what Armstrong had paid, and, perhaps wisely, when the cable enterprise went to Comcast, Armstrong went with it. "It's been a lousy couple of decades [for Ma Bell]," wrote the ***Washington Post*** after Armstrong had made his exit, "going from having a monopoly on the telecommunications business to being an industry also-ran in one of the fastest-growing sectors. Its strategic blunders are now the stuff of business school legend.

Armstrong still gets credit for seeing what others failed to—that long distance was doomed. He just ran out of money before he could make his dream a reality, and the failure no doubt left a bad taste in his mouth. In fact, he blames industry fraud for AT&T's demise. If competitors like WorldCom hadn't lied about their numbers, says Armstrong, Wall Street might have looked more favorably on AT&T—and given his strategy more time to work.

Still, his acquisition binge left AT&T with 65 billion in debt just as revenues were falling, and analysts agreed that all the bleeding ultimately proved fatal. To add insult to injury, Armstrong had originally stipulated that the merged company was to be named AT&T Comcast, but the AT&T half was dropped at the last moment.

In 2002, Armstrong was succeeded by David Dorman, whom he had named president two years earlier. But Dorman inherited little except problems. A year into his tenure, revenues were falling fast as the company's core long-distance business continued to erode. He scrambled to reassemble at least a part of Armstrong's dream, counteracting the shrinking long-distance business by offering broadband services, Internet-based phone services, and mobile calling plans. He also cut thousands of jobs. But he was swimming upstream. Add to its other problems the ***$11*** billion in "access fees" AT&T was required to pay to the Baby Bells to hook into their networks, and the problems became insurmountable.

The end came fast. In 2004, efforts to slash jobs and cut debt were no longer part of a turnaround strategy. AT&T was trying to pretty itself up for suitors. The next year, in a fine irony, one of the children ate the parent. SBC announced the purchase of AT&T for ***$16*** billion, pending approval of federal regulators. Ten years earlier, the company's market value had been ***$78*** billion.

And so the fortress walls came crashing down at last. Nobody doubted that AT&T's monopoly position had fostered a culture of complacency—and, when crunch time came, an inability to survive the rough-and-tumble, super-competitive high-tech battlefield. "AT&T grew fat and complacent in the 1970s and 1980s while the telecommunications market was getting lean and hungry," wrote the ***Wall Street*** Journal. More generally, as John Steele Gordon put it in the ***American Heritage*** piece cited earlier, "All monopolies, whether owned by 'the people' or shareholders, tend to become fat, lazy, and uninnovative."

"In reality, just six years after the 1996 Telecom Act [which was intended to remove the last vestiges of telephone monopoly by allowing the Baby Bells into the long-distance market], AT&T was left without any clear strategy for its future." So wrote Philip Weiser, a professor of law and telecommunications and a former antitrust lawyer at the Department of Justice. Interestingly, Weiser goes on to wonder whether it makes any sense for SBC to buy AT&T. "Even though the merger symbolizes the technological advances that have changed the industry, the new Goliath could also become a victim of the next wave of innovation."

One thing is certain, though: SBC won't be using government regulation to build its fortress walls.

AIRLINES IN FREEFALL

Our "legacy" airlines provide another great example of companies that were organized and protected by regulation—and that grew complacent as a result.

The numbers today are pretty incredible. Based on stock market value, the best performers now are American and Continental. Both of them even turned a profit in the second quarter of 2005 (the traditionally busy summer season), and their shares are trading at just above 10. Below this layer of cream, the milk appears to have curdled. By the end of 2005, Delta and Northwest, plagued by high fuel prices, pension burdens, and other costs, had both filed for bankruptcy protection. Virtually no shareholder value is left. United, which finally emerged from three years in bankruptcy in early 2006, still faces a host of problems, including $100 million in attorneys' fees.

What happened? Same story: regulation erected the fortress walls, and when those walls came down in 1978, the legacy carriers, which had never had to compete, were at a loss. The deal was struck in the 1930s. The government divided up the country among the airlines, telling each one which cities it could serve and how much to charge for tickets. Those government-mandated ticket prices were high enough to guarantee that the airlines made money. It was a great deal for the airlines, which were virtually assured profitability, and for their union workers, who easily won labor concessions since the airlines could depend on the government to raise ticket prices as needed. It just wasn't a good deal for consumers, since lack of competition kept ticket prices high.

When Garter administration economist Alfred Kahn, as head of the Civil Aeronautics Board, pushed through deregulation in 1978, airlines were suddenly free to fly wherever they wanted and to compete on fares. At the same time, of course, new airlines were permitted to enter the market, and many took the opportunity.

With the opening up of the industry, that fundamental problem with "fortress" industries appears again: cross-subsidization. The legacy carriers had leaned heavily on this strategy. Business travelers subsidized coach travelers. Lucrative routes subsidized unprofitable ones. In fact, we see the problem in the earliest days of the industry, when revenue from carrying mail kept planes in the air that might have only a handful of passengers on board, or when Pan Am's successful Panagra line subsidized its first transoceanic flights.

Again, cross-subsidization works as long as the walls stand, but when they fall, the barbarians are poised to invade. Needless to say, the new competitors are not interested in your unprofitable business; you can bet they will cream-skim your high-profit area. This is exactly what has happened in the airline industry with the low-cost carriers. Unfettered by the hub-and-spoke model, carriers like Southwest fly point-to-point, and in choosing which airports to serve, they focus on the top 100 cities.

According to Duane E. Woerth, president of the Air Line Pilots Association, "The United States has 429 airports with scheduled air service—and Southwest serves only 60 of them. They'll never serve Waxahachie, Texas. Their business model doesn't work in Waxahachie."

As Robert Sobel points out in ***When Giants Stumble,*** airline regulation made sense in the early days of the industry, when nobody saw the real future of air travel. If the new industry were to grow, it would need government help in the form of subsidies and generous airmail contracts. Consequently, the airlines grew fat and complacent feeding at the trough of a generous Civil Aeronautics Administration (CAA) and the Civil Aeronautics Board (CAB). "By the 1950s the airlines no longer had to rely upon airmail to break even and make money," writes Sobel. "That was the time to recognize the time for deregulation had arrived, and had this taken place then, rather than 20 years later, the old dogs of the airlines might have learned new tricks in a more favorable business environment, and Pam Am, as well as Eastern, a strong TWA, and some other companies of the period might be with us today.

Not surprisingly, many people blame deregulation for the sorry plight of the airline industry today. But Alfred Kahn, the "father of deregulation," has no regrets. At a conference at the University of Colorado School of Law in 2005, Kahn reminded the audience that "Consumers have benefited to the effect of 20 billion a year." The arch-defender of free enterprise added, "Where competition is feasible, the government should get the hell out of the way."

Despite the current woes of the legacy carriers, Kahn remains pleased that they are being challenged by the availability of lower-priced competition from airlines that fly to smaller airports near major cities. "The incursion of the low-cost carriers satisfied me, vindicated me," he said. He's not opposed to the government's trying to help the airlines get over the effects of 9/11, but enough is enough. "I think we've gotten to a point in which we can't have the government decide who survives."

WHEN YOUR PAST SUCCESS WAS BASED ON A DISTRIBUTION MONOPOLY

The classic example of a distribution monopoly is the United States Post Office. When other earners are prohibited by law from leaving anything in your mailbox, that's a distribution monopoly—in spades. It's clear, also, that the complacency bred by this monopoly left the postal service vulnerable to competitive attacks from UPS on the ground and FedEx in the air. In fact, the postal service's blase attitude became the brunt of FedEx's derisive ad campaign: "Would you trust this package to the Post-Office?" More recently, its core profit center, first-class mail, has suffered a withering attack from the e-mail revolution. It's an interesting story, but let's take a more in-depth look at a company that created its own distribution monopoly.

Controlling distribution can be a compelling business strategy. Even if other companies can produce a product to compete with yours, they still can't get their product into the marketplace. You've created a "limited-access" highway, and you control the traffic. One of the best examples of this scenario is De Beers, whose century-long hegemony in mining and marketing diamonds is the stuff of business legend.

DE BEERS: THE ICE KING

Talk about a de facto monopoly. For most of the 20th century, De Beers sold 85% to 90% of the diamonds mined worldwide and controlled prices by matching supply to world demand. Here's how the company put together the world's most exclusive ***supply chain.***

Cecil Rhodes began the operation before the turn of the century, when he consolidated South Africa's diamond mines into the company that would become De Beers and then formed a cartel with 10 of the largest London-based diamond merchants. Each merchant was guaranteed a percentage of the diamonds coming out of the De Beers mines, and in exchange De Beers got the market data it needed to ensure that supply met demand. Over the years that group of 10 members expanded to approximately 125, but the purpose of the cartel remained the same: virtual control of the diamond pipeline.

As the 20th century was coming to a close, the operation looked like this: the company's selling arm, until recently known as the Central Selling Organization (CSO), purchased all the diamonds produced by the 13 mines in Africa owned or co-owned by De Beers—amounting to about 44% of world output. In addition, diamonds the CSO bought from mines in Russia and Canada pumped another 25% into the De Beers pipeline, bringing the total to close to 70%.

At CSO offices in London, all these diamonds are combined, categorized, and divided into lots called "boxes." Every five weeks De Beers distributes the boxes among the 125 partners, now known as "sightholders." The price, quantity, and quality of the diamonds in each box are set by De Beers—and are nonnegotiable. The sightholders take the rough diamonds back to their factories in Antwerp, Tel Aviv, New York, Bombay, Johannesburg, and Smolensk, Russia, where they are cut, polished, and finally sold to the sightholders' wholesale and retail customers throughout the world.

In the 1990s, however, a series of discrete events began to erode the De Beers monopoly. The first of these was the collapse of the Soviet Union in 1991.

The discovery of huge diamond deposits in Siberia 30 years earlier had made the Soviets the world's second-largest producer, and De Beers had moved quickly to negotiate with the Soviet regime to have all those Siberian diamonds sold to the GSO. But the collapse jeopardized that arrangement, and since that time an increasing percentage of Russian diamonds have been sold outside the De Beers network.

On the micro level, an example of De Beers' problems in Russia can be seen in the story of Lev Leviev, a Russian-born Jew who was once a De Beers sightholder. Leviev opened his first diamondcutting factory in Israel in 1977, when the industry was starting to soar in that country. Soon he had expanded to 12 factories, and in 1987 De Beers invited him to join the cartel. He agreed to, but by then he had become one of Israel's largest manufacturers of polished stones, and he grew tired of De Beers' high-handed treatment of cartel members. In 1989, when Russia's state-run diamond mining industry asked Leviev for help in establishing its own cutting factories, Leviev was happy to get in on the business—and effectively cut De Beers out of the loop. De Beers kicked Leviev out of the cartel in 1995, but that didn't stop him. As of 2003, he was the world's largest diamond cutter and polisher and, in direct competition with De Beers, a major seller of rough stones.

A second blow to De Beers' hegemony came in 1996 when Australia's Argyle diamond mine had the temerity to terminate its contract with De Beers. Instead of selling to the GSO, Argyle opted to sell directly to De Beers sightholders as well as to other merchants, thus threatening De Beers' stranglehold on price. Argyle is known for quantity—the mine produces more volume than any other in the world—rather than quality, and the new arrangement directly competes with De Beers at the fast-growing low end of the market.

Third, in the same decade Canada began to emerge as a new power in diamond production. Although De Beers has been angling for control of the three major deposits discovered in the Northwest Territories, it has not been able to secure the kind of dominant position that would have seemed its birthright in the past.

And a final challenge to De Beers has come from the burgeoning diamond industry in India. Known for "cutting the uncuttable," India has long been a force in diamond cutting, and today 80% of the world's diamonds are cut and finished there. At the same time, Indians have been moving rapidly not only up the diamond value chain, cutting larger and more costly stones, but also into diamond trading. In Antwerp, still the diamond-trading capital of the world, Indians are crowding Hasidic Jews out of the business. By working seven days a week (which most Orthodox Jews refuse to do) and by sending their diamonds back home to be finished (where labor is much cheaper), Indian traders have taken over about 65% of Antwerp's ***$26*** billion-a-year diamond business.

None of this directly threatens De Beers, of course, as long as Indian traders are buying their rough stones from the cartel. But the latest initiatives in the home country do indeed pose a threat. The Indian government and the domestic industry are working on deals to buy stones directly from African mines. The plans call for Indian companies to set up manufacturing plants in African mining nations, boost employment among the native population, and send rough diamonds directly to India to be cut and polished. The role of De Beers' Diamond Trading Corporation (the current name of the old Central Selling Organization) would be eliminated. Eventually, the Indian industry will complete its integration by developing its own retail outlets.

But give De Beers credit. If its unquestioned monopoly in distribution bred complacency, the erosion of that monopoly has spurred action. De Beers has devised a new game plan: if it can't sell all the world's diamonds, it will get a better return on the ones it does sell. In the increasingly competitive diamond marketplace, De Beers will no longer be "supplier by force"; it will be, as its new marketing campaign puts it, "Supplier of Choice."

In other words, De Beers is getting in on the branding game—with two new initiatives. The first is something called "Forevermark," a sort of signature inside the diamond that assures its quality. The second is the De Beers name itself, to be marketed as part of the eompany's reach into retail. A stand-alone De Beers store has already appeared on London's Bond Street and in Tokyo's shopping district. Others are in the works.

It seems "a brilliant response to the changing conditions of the diamond business," according to ***Fortune*** magazine. Finding it increasingly difficult to control every facet of diamond production and distribution, De Beers has introduced a method by which the diamonds it does control are more valuable simply because they have the company's seal of approval. But, the magazine notes, a century of history is difficult to change. "Transforming its corporate culture from that of a ponderous colonial-era monopoly may in fact be De Beers' greatest challenge as it implements Supplier of Choice."

WHEN YOU HAVE BEEN "CHOSEN" FOR SUCCESS BY THE GOVERNMENT

In the United States, with rare exceptions like the utilities and airlines, our free-market economy enjoys operating with a minimum of government intervention. In other parts of the world, however, even up until the most recent decades, government has continued its presence in what Lenin referred to as "the commanding heights" of the economy. Often, as in Japan, Korea, and some Western European nations, this arrangement has not amounted to government ownership of business. Instead, it has created a tight alliance between government and business in which the government favors certain companies or groups of companies for success. Needless to say, being "blessed" by the government is an easy road to complacency—and often, ultimately, to a jarring return to reality. Let's look at a few examples.

JAPAN, INC.

The rapid industrialization of Japan before World War II was marked by the rising power of the zaibatsu, those huge industrial conglomerates organized around a single family and chosen by the government to spearhead economic growth. The most dominant zaibatsu—Mitsui, Mitsubishi, Sumitomo, and Yasuda—were likely to have interests in all important areas of industry, and they all had their own banks as a means of mobilizing capital.

At the end of World War II, the Allied occupation authorities ordered that the zaibatsu be dissolved, but the system did not exactly go away. The zaibatsu were replaced by the so-called keiretsu, less-tight-knit groupings of banks and industrial companies, with much of the old management still in place. More important, very close government–corporate collaboration also remained in place to oversee the nation's postwar rebuilding. At the center of the collaboration was the Ministry of International Trade and Industry (MITI), run by a cadre of government bureaucrats who steered the course of the national economy. MITI regulated virtually every aspect of Japanese business during the postwar boom. It set prices and quotas, issued licenses and quality standards, managed domestic competition and controlled incursions from foreigners, organized mergers, and strongly supported growth through exports.

The system worked spectacularly through the 1960s, the 1970s, and into the 1980s, and there were few dissenters. One of these was Masahisa Naitoh, a MITI director who saw the inherent weakness in such an overregulated economy and who began to speak out in favor of deregulation. He was fired for his trouble in 1993, but by then it was already too late to avoid an impending economic meltdown.

A colossal speculative bubble in real estate had begun to burst in 1990, and as real estate values plunged over the next couple of years, they took Japan's banks, overloaded with real estate loans, down with them. The crisis threw a spotlight on the weakness of a protected, complacent banking industry—one in which government favoritism had replaced rigorous accountability. For years, MITI's "administrative guidance" had made sure that banks made cheap money available to the growing industrial sector, with too little regard for companies' prospects for repayment. When the real estate market crashed, banks were suddenly revealing huge portfolios of bad loans, and yet the banks were regarded as too big and important to be allowed to fail. This banking collapse—and Japan's unwillingness to impose any radical fix—dragged Japan's economy backward for the rest of the decade.

Indeed, as recently as October 2002, with the banking sector still straining under the weight of ***$423*** billion in bad loans. Prime Minister Junichiro Koizumi elevated cabinet minister Heizo Takenaka to the position of "economy czar" with the express mission of bringing an end to the long-running crisis. Takenaka favored using taxpayer money to refloat some of the country's banks, as well as forcing some of the weaker banks to close. Three years earlier, the government had invested ***$75*** billion in propping up the ailing system—without demanding substantial reform. That hadn't worked, reaffirming the 15-year-old message: government fat is a poor diet for an industry already weakened by a lack of vigorous competition.

For an interesting comparison, consider Honda. Back in the 1960s, in a characteristic effort to position Japan's auto industry for international competition, MITI wanted to hold down the number of entrants to ensure economies of scale. Part of its strategy was to convince Honda to stay out of the auto market and stick with motorcycles. Honda rebelled and struck out on its own, jumping into the competitive waters without MITI's guiding hand and help. Honda, currently Japan's No. 3

automaker (behind Toyota and Nissan) and the world leader in the manufacture of internal combustion engines, has clearly succeeded by going it alone. And, apparently, the company likes it that way. When merger fever gripped the industry a few years back, Honda stated publicly that it would remain on its own.

FIAT—THE EUROPEAN VERSION

In Europe, too, venerable family-run companies were favored by government to facilitate postwar rebuilding. As in Japan, these "champions" were encouraged to diversify into a number of key industries and, eventually, to go global. The model worked in Europe as it did in Asia, and, similarly, once the "economic miracle" had transpired, the system's weakness, from a market point of view, lay exposed. A perfect example is Fiat.

Founded by Giovanni Agnelli in 1899, Fiat was already Italy's dominant auto company before World War II. After the war, with the government's blessing, the company diversified into jets, railway cars, tractors, insurance, construction, and newspapers, among other enterprises. Today, the $50 billion conglomerate remains Italy's largest private employer. But it is in deep trouble.

Fiat amply demonstrates how the government–business partnership, even though it might begin out of necessity, devolves into an unhealthy symbiosis. It becomes too easy (like so many self-destructive habits) for the government to protect the corporation and for the corporation to pay for that protection. True, open competition is thwarted by cronyism and corruption, a culture in which complacency is at home.

In Italy, long-festering problems came spectacularly to the surface in 1992 when magistrates in Milan began investigating kickbacks at a home for the elderly. Within a year, "Operation Clean Hand" had implicated most of the nation's political parties, and corruption cases were under way in 21 cities. Ministers were resigning in droves, and some of the nation's top corporate officers were under arrest, including two at Fiat.

For Fiat, shocking times were at hand. Its share of the domestic car market was in sharp decline—from more than 60% in the early 1980s to 45% in the early 1990s. A 27% decline in sales from 1991 to 1992 required an emergency ***$2.5*** billion recapitalization by the company's bankers. Fiat was facing the new reality: there really wasn't such a thing as "foreign" cars anymore. No longer could the company complacently depend on the subservient domestic market to buy its cars just because they were "homegrown."

By 1997, "Operation Clean Hand" had finally finished sweeping up at Fiat. Cesare Romiti, who had succeeded Giovanni Agnelli as chairman a year earlier, was convicted of falsifying company accounts, committing tax fraud, and making illegal payments to political parties. The company's chief financial officer was convicted also. The crux of the allegation against the two men was that from 1980 to 1992 they had approved slush funds for illegal political contributions and had falsified accounts to conceal the payments. (Corruption ran deep throughout the nation. Among the convicted were former Olivetti chairman Carlo de Beneditti and fashion magnate

Giorgio Armani. Once and future prime minister—and business tycoon—Silvio Berlusconi also came under investigation.)

Fiat's protected market was its crutch. It has never learned how to live without it. In 2002, crisis loomed again. Fiat Auto had lost 1.3 billion in 2001, and a new restructuring was in the works—closing 18 plants and cutting 6,000 jobs outside Italy. Market share in Italy had lost another 12 percentage points over the past decade and was down to 32%. Jack Welch, brought in to consult on human-resources issues, told the company it suffered from too many layers of management and a "consensus culture" that protected underperformers. He was right. It was also an old, deeply entrenched culture, formed over the decades during which Agnelli had been able to persuade politicians to shelter Fiat's domestic market from real competition.

Fiat Auto's CEO, Paolo Gantarella, had to resign, and the losses were still mounting. ***Business Week*** reflected on the predicament of Prime Minister Berlusconi. A free-market advocate, Berlusconi was in no position to offer "a big old-style government bailout," but neither could he afford to bear witness to the collapse of the nation's most revered industrial icon. Noting that the carmaker's fundamental problem was overcapacity, the magazine's sensible recommendation was that the prime minister should encourage a radical downsizing—one that would bring capacity in line with market-based output. "Fiat is an object lesson on the perils of old-style Italian protectionism. By helping Fiat shrink to a size commensurate with its capacity to sell cars, Berlusconi would be writing a fresh chapter in the carmaker's troubled history, rather than its epilogue."

In the fall of 2002, the crisis had deepened. Fiat announced that it would lay off 8,000 workers; sales were plummeting, and losses for the year were projected at close to ***$2*** billion. Berlusconi was sequestered at his private estate with top Fiat officials, still considering the possibility of an emergency bailout. Then, in January 2003, Giovanni Agnelli died. The passing of the company's longtime patriarch and the grandson of its founder diverted attention, momentarily, from Fiat Auto's difficulties, but it did not resolve them. As a lengthy obituary in London's ***Independent*** noted, Fiat's problems were in large part a result of the company's inability "to produce a new generation of cars that can meet the demands of the highly competitive European market.... Once fiercely loyal to their unreliable Fiats..., in recent years the Italians have started to demand quality."

With the sudden death in 2004 of Giovanni's brother Umberto, who had been serving as Fiat Chairman, the company made some uncharacteristically decisive moves. It brought in turnaround specialist Sergio Marchionne as the new group CEO, and he in turn quickly began firing managers who had resisted change and hiring top international industry talent. Marchionne was given added responsibility the following year when he became Fiat Auto CEO as well, marking the first time in a century that the same person was in charge of both the holding company and the car unit. Can he save Fiat Auto? Maybe so. At the end of 2005, the company announced that its auto unit had posted a profit for the first time in 17 quarters. In any case, there's nothing like the threat of imminent demise to jolt a company out of complacency.

WHEN THE GOVERNMENT OWNS OR CONTROLS THE BUSINESS

The slide into complacency is hastened when, rather than merely bestowing its blessings upon an enterprise, the government actually controls or owns it. We might discuss the U.S. Post Office under this heading or Britain's public sector industries like its railways, airlines, airports, and seaports—infrastructure industries typically funded by taxpayer monies. But let's look instead at India, where, because of its postwar infatuation with the Communist model, state ownership was much more pervasive and ruinous.

While much of the rest of the world was abandoning the "mixed" economy in favor of free markets, India was headed in the opposite direction. Between 1960 and 1990, the public sector expanded from 8% of the gross domestic product (GDP) to 26%. The central government owned approximately 240 enterprises, excluding traditional state industries such as utilities, railways, and airlines. Like the favored companies we examined in the preceding section, these state-owned businesses luxuriated in sheltered markets, oblivious to the competitive world outside. Consequently, they set a new standard for inefficiency, unresponsiveness, and, of course, complacency.

Daniel Yergin cites the "truly brilliant" example of the Hindustan Fertilizer Corporation, which had been in existence for 12 years when India's economy reached its crisis point in 1991. The company's 1,200 employees had been faithfully clocking in every day during those years, but the plant had not yet produced its first bag of fertilizer. It seems the plant had been built, at considerable public expense, using machinery from Germany, Czechoslovakia, Poland, and several other countries—purchases driven by the fact that they could be financed with export credits. "Alas," writes Yergin, "the machinery did not fit together and the plant could not operate. Everyone just pretended that it was operating.

Since the ascension of P. V. Narasimha Rao to prime minister in 1991, India has been on the road to reform. But reform is never easy, especially when you are trying to push noncompetitive, government-owned businesses into the unforgiving arena of the free market. The story of Air India aptly illustrates India's ambitious, but problematic, transformation.

AIR INDIA

What came to be known as the airline of the Maharajah was founded in 1932 by J. R. D. Tata, of the illustrious Indian commercial family. From the beginning, Tata conceived of his airline as among the world's best, and he spared no expense in fulfilling his vision. He insisted on the latest and finest aircraft, and in 1962 Air India achieved the distinction of being the world's first all-jet carrier with a fleet of six 707s. Tata's intent was to combine Western efficiency with Eastern hospitality, and the result was excellent service and a broad range of unique amenities. The planes featured elegant decor, fine cuisine (including vegetarian meals), and hostesses clad in saris. The eye-catching mascot with the oversized moustache and striped turban made his first appearance in 1946 and soon came to symbolize all that was gracious and sophisticated about the airline.

Air India came under state ownership in 1953, but Tata remained its chairman for another 25 years. His status and prestige were such that, for much of that time, he was able to insulate the airline from too much government interference. But all good things must come to an end. Eventually the airline, which had been granted a monopoly on international travel, succumbed to inefficiency and bloat. By the turn of the century, when it was put up for sale by the government as another step in the privatization program, it had been operating in the red for five years.

How bad was it? In 2000, the company employed 17,700 people, or 770 per aircraft, compared with a global average of 250 employees per plane. Moreover, the average age of the 23 aircraft in its fleet was 14 years, compared to less than five years for highly competitive Singapore Airlines and only three for the 30 planes in India's privately owned Jet Airways. A foreign correspondent for the ***Wall Street Journal*** awarded Air India the title of "worst airline in Asia," with "notoriously bad service," planes that "sometimes look like they're held together with duct tape," and "employees who seem to regard their positions as sinecures for life." With its small fleet of aging planes, the once-venerable airline was flying to only 19 of the 90 destinations it was licensed to serve.

As part of the disinvestment program, the government floated a plan to sell off 40% of the airline, keep 40%, and divide the remaining 20% between employees and financial institutions. It looked like a partnership between the Tata Group (owned by the same family that founded the airline) and Singapore Airlines was about to make an offer, but then SIA pulled out, explaining that there was just too much social and political opposition to the deal in India. Tata shopped around for another airline partner, but then September 11, 2001 shook the industry, and none of the major carriers was in the mood for expansion. Consequently, Tata also backed away from the table.

Since that time, India's expanding economy, along with the worldwide recuperation of air travel, may have restored some hope to the still-government-owned Air India. In April 2005, it announced the purchase of 50 new jets from Boeing, at a price of 6.9 billion—its first fleet expansion in 15 years. The airline also said it would increase the number of flights to the United States, adding San Francisco and Houston to its itinerary.

In a more promising move, Air India is now planning to merge with the government-owned domestic carrier, Indian Airlines. In this case, the whole will be greater than the two halves because the combined airline will have the ability to connect international flights from any airport within the country, something that the separate airlines could not do.

Will these moves enable the crippled airline to fly again? Possibly, but there are major obstacles to overcome. The combined Air India-Indian Airlines will have to merge two entrenched government organizations. It must also develop a company-wide customer service orientation. And this fact remains: in 1990, Air India had 40% of the traffic flying into and out of the country. In 2005, that share was down to 18%. A sizable portion has gone to European and other Asian airlines. And on the domestic side. Jet Airways, which only came into existence in 1992, is now the No. 1 carrier. It began by taking business away from Indian Airlines, the government's domestic carrier, and now has expanded into international routes. Like the upstarts in America and Europe, Jet Airways is unburdened by government regulation, is free to cream-skim the lucrative routes, and wins over customers with great service and amenities. Just like Air India 50 years ago.

THE WARNING SIGNS OF COMPLACENCY

It's like what they say about quality. You know complacency when you see it. Here are several recognizable symptoms.

YOU ARE IN NO HURRY TO MAKE DECISIONS

Your cycle times are long and leisurely. The Baby Bells are a great example. It took them years to decide to get into the broadband business and the Internet business. Your whole culture is geared to moving slowly. Speeding up goes against the grain. Every action or idea is subjected to double checks and triple checks. GM suffered from this syndrome in the extreme. It took 60 months to move from concept to market. Honda shook up the industry with 36-month cycle times, and Toyota followed Honda's lead.

YOUR PROCESSES ARE OVERLY BUREAUCRATIC

Your decision-making is thwarted by a tyranny of committees, as we typically see in nongovernmental organizations (NGOs) and large volunteer organizations. Each committee member has veto power, and the cultural differences between them are irreconcilable. For example, your committee has representatives from finance, marketing, sales, engineering, procurement, and so on, and each member brings his group's culture to the table. I will return to this point of cultural differences in Chapter 8, "The Territorial Impulse: Culture Conflicts and Turf Wars." For now I'll just suggest that the cultural differences among a German, a Frenchman, and an Englishman are less divisive than those among an engineer, a salesperson, and an accountant.

This is a bureaucratic problem, and it is the leader's responsibility to break down the bureaucracy's walls. While he's at it, he should get rid of the other obstacles—not just culture, but processes, structures, systems, regulations—that are hallmarks of the "no-hurry," complacent organization.

YOU HAVE A BOTTOM-UP, DECENTRALIZED, CONSENSUS-BASED CULTURE

You need to get everybody on board, as in the famous Japanese style of "consensus management." This style was in vogue in years past, but in today's fast-changing environment, it's counterproductive. It makes change too difficult in our global arena. We still see it in nonprofits and universities, where, for example, every "search" takes a full year. Why not three months? Then, once the new president or VP takes office, he or she spends another year "consensus building." That's fine—as long as the world remains predictable.

I like to say that there are three things you should never do from the bottom up:

- Visioning. People will always have different visions. You will never get a consensus; you will debate forever. If you are the leader, it's your job to decide where the company is going. If people aren't on board, let them go, as the new leader Marchionne is trying to do at Fiat.
- Designing information technology (IT) infrastructure. Don't even try it. There are too many different solutions, too many different systems of hardware and software. In mergers and acquisitions, the biggest nightmare is that your IT system is incompatible with mine.
- Branding. Try branding by consensus and you'll end up all over the map. As the leader, you decide what your brand is.

YOUR COST STRUCTURE IS HIGH

You have a very expensive way of doing things. Excess baggage—in the form of gold-plating without accountability—drags down the company's core competency. You live in a protected environment, so you do everything lavishly. Pan Am was the classic example. Its lounges seemed to have been appointed with kings and emperors in mind. Your driving ideal is "best in class." Your overhead is outrageous, but inside your fortress, cross-subsidizing helps you cover the problem. At the time of the breakup of the Bell system, its total training and education budget was five times bigger than MIT's: ***$1*** billion versus ***$200*** million, in 1980 figures. Such lavish volume obsession is a hallmark of the complacent culture. (Note: It's not just complacent companies that have trouble controlling their costs. In fact, the self-destructive habit of "volume obsession" is the subject of Chapter 7.)

YOUR COMPANY STRUCTURE IS COMPLETE VERTICAL INTEGRATION

You do everything internally. A friend who was an executive in AT&T's consumer products' division took me to a Western Electric factory in Indianapolis. It was a huge, beautiful facility, absolutely top of the line. He showed me the furnace and explained that it was used to make the company's special charcoal, from coal that came from the company's very own mine. Not only that, the company had its own truck line dedicated to picking up the coal from the mine and bringing it to the factory. All this went into supplying charcoal for the company's telephone sets. That's what you call doing everything in house. Of course, I can buy that charcoal in the marketplace four or five times more cheaply, but, again, vertical integration provides ample opportunity for cross-subsidization, which allows you to use internal pricing mechanisms. Evidence suggests that the more vertically integrated you are, the more you are likely to be a legacy company—and a complacent company. Think of GM. Or think of Lucent in telephone manufacturing, and how Cisco blew competition out of the water with what it called "virtual integration"—a system not of controlling every function but merely coordinating every function. (See the section of Chapter 7 titled "Move from Vertical Integration to 'Virtual Integration'.")

YOU HAVE ENORMOUS CROSS-SUBSIDIES BY FUNCTIONS, BY PRODUCTS, BY MARKETS, AND BY CUSTOMERS

Average costing and average pricing prevail in your company. You try to look good by aggregating costs, but the numbers are deceptive. You end up cream-skimming from the lucrative segments of your own business. At the same time, you render yourself vulnerable to competitive attack. Recall how the Baby Bells put telephones next to the restrooms in restaurants across the nation. These never made any money. The Bells did much better with banks of phones at airports, in prisons, and in shopping centers. That's where the attack came. The competition wasn't interested in the phone booth at the gas station; alternate phone companies looked for high-profit areas. Then, of course, cell phones practically wiped out the pay-phone industry. The message that complacent companies never quite get is that the world of tomorrow is not the world of yesterday.

HOW TO BREAK THE COMPLACENCY HABIT

As noted, complacency is most likely to flourish in old, legacy companies. It's also likely to be a chronic condition, not easily rooted out by the quick fix. Here are a few suggestions.

REENGINEER

This is Mike Hammer's advice in ***Reengineering the Corporation.*** You've come to realize that thanks to years of complacency, your processes are poorly designed, inefficiencies have been built into the system, your cycle times are too slow, and your product quality has slipped. It's time to reengineer.

For all its other problems, Motorola gets credit for developing the Six Sigma program, a process of reengineering to achieve high quality, eliminate waste, and curb inefficiency. When the company realized how costly product defects could be, CEO Bob Galvin and engineer Bill Smith instituted the now-famous **program** designed to reduce defects to 3.4 per million parts manufactured. The program, with its DMAIC methodology (Define, Measure, Analyze, Improve, Control), has since been embraced by other big companies, most notably GE. This hyper-emphasis on quality control, however, actually comes from the Japanese, who have long been masters of efficiency, just-in-time manufacturing, and zero tolerance for defects.

REORGANIZE

Typically, the path is toward centralization in the name of tighter control, efficiency, and economy. Consider Hewlett-Packard, whose decentralized organization consisted of subsidiaries around the globe, each with its own managerial structure to sell all HP products in that particular market. Until fairly recently, this model made sense for political reasons. But, as Carly Fiorina realized, it doesn't make sense in the global economy, so she reorganized into worldwide product management responsibilities. If you are in charge of printers, you have the worldwide market, not just one country. Reorganizing this way also shines a glaring light on cross-subsidies and makes it more difficult to sweep them under the rug.

DIVEST NON-CORE BUSINESSES

General Electric has led the way here. As mentioned in Chapter 7, when Reginald Jones began his paring initiative, GE had hundreds of businesses. Continuing the process, Jack Welch has brought the number down to about 14. His mantra has become famous: "If you are not No. 1 or No. 2, you must fix, sell, or close" the business. He even got rid of his consumer electronics business, which was No. 1, because he realized it would not ***stay*** No. 1.

Of course, diversification was all the rage a couple of decades ago. Energy companies got the bug, diversified into a range of nonenergy concerns, and then later were forced to divest. You saw in earlier chapters how Xerox moved away from its core business and later retrenched. Until recently, Beatrice Foods owned an absolutely baffling array of companies. It made no sense. In Europe, too, the old model of the family-based diversified conglomerate is no longer sustainable, as big holding companies like the Philips Group, the Shell Group, and ThyssenKrupp are finding out.

A better idea for the current environment is to get back to your core business and take it global. This will force you to become truly competitive, rather than complacent and will also prohibit you from using one profitable business to conceal the weakness of another.

OUTSOURCE NON-CORE FUNCTIONS

The reason outsourcing is so controversial today is because so many companies are engaging in it. The reason so many companies are engaging in it is because it makes so much sense. If it's not a core activity, contract it out, whether to India, to Ireland, or to another company close to home. Warehousing, distribution, even manufacturing—contract manufacturing—is becoming the industry standard.

It's a wonderful solution to the bloat, sloth, and inefficiency that characterize complacent companies. The fact that I make computers doesn't mean that I have to hire thousands of people to staff help lines. The fact that I fly planes doesn't mean that I have to take reservations. Business process outsourcing (BPO) is here to stay, and competitive companies will be taking advantage of it. As you'll see in Chapter 7, outsourcing is also a great way to bring costs back into line.

REENERGIZE THE COMPANY

A strong new leader with a positive, opportunity-oriented vision might be what you need to transform your company's culture. It can work. Gordon Bethune shook up Continental Airlines (and wrote a book about it called ***From Worst to First).*** IBM was a huge, bloated monster before Lou Gerstner arrived from R.J. Reynolds. At 3M, a long history of success seemed to be inducing complacency until Jim McInerney was brought in from GE. At Home Depot, the culture created by founders Bernie Marcus and Arthur Blank was too slow to respond to the competitive challenge from Lowe's. Bob Nardelli has proven to be the solution to that problem.

On the other hand, why wait until your self-destructive habits threaten to become terminal? Why wait until you have lung cancer to quit smoking, or until you've had a heart attack to change your diet? The best hedge against complacency is to look at the future instead of the past, to hold firmly to the truth that the future is not predictable, and to focus your thoughts on what you can do, not what you have done.

COMPLACENCY

Things that lead to complacency:

- Your past success came via a regulated monopoly.
- Your past success was based on a distribution monopoly.
- You have been "chosen" for success by the government.
- The government owns or controls the business.

The warning signs of complacency:

- **You are in no hurry to make decisions:** Your whole culture is geared to moving slowly, and speeding up goes against the grain.
- **Your processes are overly bureaucratic:** Your decision-making is thwarted by a tyranny of committees.
- **You have a bottom-up, decentralized, consensus-based culture:** You have to get everybody on board before making a decision.
- **Your company structure is complete vertical integration:** You do everything internally.

You have enormous cross-subsidies by functions, by products, by markets, and by customers: Average costing and average pricing prevail in your company.

How to break the complacency habit:

- **Reengineer:** Reengineer to achieve high quality, eliminate waste, and curb inefficiency.
- **Reorganize:** Decentralize profit and loss by creating business units around products or geographies.
- **Outsource non-core functions:** If it's not a core activity, contract it out.
- **Reenergize the company:** A strong new leader with a positive, opportunity-oriented vision might be what you need to transform your company's culture.

CHAPTER

5

COMPETENCY DEPENDENCE: THE CURSE OF INCUMBENCY

Most companies depend on a core competency for success, but your "competency dependence" becomes a self-destructive habit when it limits your vision and blinds you to other opportunities. The competency-dependent company is like Mao Zedong's frog at the bottom of the well. He thinks the sky is only as big as the top of the well. If he surfaced, he would have an entirely different view.

What do you do when your core competency has become obsolete or noncompetitive? What do you do when somebody else (like an offshore company) is doing a better job, and all your customers are deserting you? If you can't figure out what to do, if you feel trapped, you have become competency-dependent.

When you are the incumbent, you need to be particularly wary of this self-destructive habit. It's hard to change when you're No. 1. Your competency is deeply rooted in your culture; it's what you are, what you stand for, what your logo signifies. GM is Chevy. Coca-Cola is Coke. That's hard to change, even when the market for your iconic product is in decline. Digital Equipment ***was*** the minicomputer—until the company's incumbency became its curse and it collapsed.

When you're competency-dependent, your strength becomes your weakness—like Aladdin's lamp or Samson's hair. Suddenly it seems you're out of options. Let's look at a couple of examples.

SINGER SEWING MACHINES

If you are a baby boomer, chances are good that your mother owned a sewing machine, and there's an equal chance that you, or your spouse, do not. If you are a generation or more younger than the boomers, you may never have laid eyes on a sewing machine.

It was a great idea 150 years ago, when I. M. Singer started selling his machines in Boston. Such a good idea, in fact, that by 1913 he had sold three million of them. Singer even invented the installment plan so that the rural poor, who needed them most, could afford to buy his machines. But by 1970, who knew how to sew? And more to the point, with discount retailers available everywhere, why bother to learn? In America, at least, the market for the sewing machine had vanished.

Actually, Singer tried to reinvent itself. When Joseph Flavin arrived from Xerox in 1975, he saw the company's future in defense technology. A decade later, the sewing machine unit was spun off as Singer Sewing Machine Company (SSMC), leaving the original Singer as a manufacturer of aerospace electronics.

In 1989, SSMC—which at the time employed 24,000 people at its sewing machine factories in Italy, Taiwan, and Brazil—was bought by Shanghai-born entrepreneur James Ting's Semi-Tech Microelectronics. Leveraging the famous name, he called the company Singer N.V. and moved it to the Netherlands Antilles, where he began trying to assemble a home appliance conglomerate. The Asian collapse in the late 1990s caught Ting overextended. The company lost $238 million in 1997 and another ***$208*** million in 1998. It filed for bankruptcy in 1999. At the time of the filing, it had ***$25*** million in cash and liabilities of 1.25 billion. The great American sewing machine company was dead at last.

So what happened to the original Singer after the 1986 spin-off of the sewing machine division? It hasn't fared any better. A few months after Joseph Flavin's unexpected death in 1987, Singer was acquired in a hostile takeover by a Florida-based corporate raider named Paul Bilzerian. Flavin may have seen the future; Bilzerian, apparently, saw only the money. He renamed the company Bicoastal and quickly sold off eight of its 12 divisions, inciting a storm of employee lawsuits and other litigation. In June 1988, he was convicted of nine counts of securities fraud, among other crimes, sentenced to four years in jail, and fined 1.5 million. In 1989, Bicoastal petitioned for bankruptcy.

ENCYCLOPAEDIA BRITANNICA

If you think selling a Singer sewing machine to today's consumer would be difficult, how about a 32-volume, 150-pound encyclopedia?

The world's premier encyclopedia was first published in Scotland in three volumes between 1768 and 1771. Benjamin Franklin and John Locke were among its early contributors. By the time the ninth edition appeared a century later, Thomas Huxley and James Clerk Maxwell had added their expertise. Yet another century later, Britannica's content remained superb, but the format was facing a serious challenge.

A funny thing happened on the way to the digital age. In the mid-1970s, Britannica bought out rival Compton's Encyclopedia. In 1989, the Compton's division released Compton's Multimedia Encyclopedia on CD-ROM, the first in the industry. But the CD-ROM market was still in its infancy, and Britannica, in a failure of prescience, sold Compton's NewMedia division to Chicago's Tribune Company in 1993. Worse, in a noncompete arrangement, Britannica also agreed not to publish its own encyclopedia in multimedia format for another two years. The company was still betting on bound volumes—a bet it lost.

Talk about a vanishing market! In 1991, Britannica sold 4,00,000 units worldwide; by the end of the decade, that number was down to 25,000. In 1998, an era came to an end with the dismissal of Britannica's last 70 door-to-door salesmen.

The next year, in a furious game of catch-up, Britannica.com was created to offer the complete encyclopedia online, free, hoping for substantial revenue from advertising on its site. That plan was aborted in 2001 when ad revenues failed to materialize and costs continued to rise. The new plan would be to charge customers for access to the site. At the same time, the cash-strapped company was soliciting offers for Miriam-Webster, which it had owned for 40 years.

The company signaled its retreat when wounded Britannica.com was folded back into Encyclopaedia Britannica. In 2002, in a remarkable illustration of competency dependence, the company published the 2,000-page hardback Britannica Concise Encyclopaedia.

Typically, a company's competency grows out of its core functional area, out of the function that drives the company. In high-tech companies, it's likely to be engineering. In the hotel industry, operations. In Avon, it's sales; in Nike, it's marketing. As noted in the preceding chapter, the cultural differences between functional areas can be vast and virtually unbridgeable, so it's not surprising that one function becomes dominant.

The point is, with this dominance comes the potential for competency dependence. If a company's functional areas were better integrated and more cooperative, its vision would naturally be more expansive and its options more open. The sales force would be able to communicate to research and development (R&D) that the new product line was shriveling on the vine. Alternatives could be discussed and new strategies plotted. But when functional cultures are at war, the winning function forms the company's bias. That dominant function drives the company regardless—even if it's into a brick wall.

Let's look at several different scenarios (R&D, design, sales, and service) and consider how functional bias can precipitate competency dependence.

R&D DEPENDENCE

Pharmaceuticals provide a dramatic example of an industry whose core competency is research and development, and, in the United States, an industry that is courting peril because of competency dependence. The reason is the high cost of American R&D, which is being seriously undercut by emerging pharmaceutical industries in India and China. Studies coming out of India are showing that, while in America the costs associated with developing a blockbuster drug approach $900 million, the Indian pharmaceutical industry can produce the same drug for about ***$20*** million. India is already one of the largest producers of generic drugs in the world. When your HMO tells you to fill your prescription with generics, you're almost certain to find an Indian manufacturer on the label.

Moreover, if R&D is what you do, and if you do it at the expense of other basic functions such as marketing or sales, you run the risk of developing products for which there's no market. Sticking to pharmaceuticals for a moment, in ***The Innovator's Dilemma,*** Clayton Christensen tells the story of Eli Lilly and its development of a "100% pure" insulin. Thanks largely to Lilly's persistent efforts over the decades, insulin purity had improved from 50,000 impure parts per million (ppm) in 1925 to 10 ppm in 1980. Still, despite the dramatic improvement, the fact that insulin extracted from animals is slightly different from human insulin meant that a fraction of a percent of patients built up resistance in their immune systems. Lilly attacked this problem with a $1 billion R&D effort (in partnership with biotech firm Genentech) to create genetically altered bacteria that could produce insulin proteins that were the structural equivalent of human insulin proteins and therefore 100% pure.

The project was technically successful, and Lilly introduced its Humulin brand insulin with a 25% price premium over animal-extracted insulin. The problem was, because of its significantly higher price, the product had no takers. As a Lilly researcher told Christensen, "In retrospect, the market was not terribly dissatisfied with pork insulin. In fact, it was pretty happy with it." Development of the pure insulin was an R&D triumph, but to no avail. As Christensen puts it, "Lilly had spent enormous capital and organizational energy overshooting the market's demand for product purity."

Those who live by R&D die by R&D. What happens when the other guy's R&D effort produces a product that knocks yours out of the marketplace? One response is to develop another self-destructive habit—denial—and pretend it isn't happening. Or if you have good researchers and deep pockets, your response might be to go back to the lab and develop the next-generation product. Most difficult of all, if you live and breathe an R&D culture, is to break your habit of competency dependence. Let's look at how this has played out in the artificial sweetener industry.

TEMPEST IN A SUGAR BOWL

Benjamin Eisenstadt and his son Marvin invented Sweet 'N Low in 1957 and have distributed it ever since through their family-owned Cumberland Packing Corp. Nobody confused the saccharin-based sweetener's taste with that of real sugar, but it was the only low-cal sugar substitute out there. Two decades later, a supposed link between saccharin and bladder cancer in laboratory rats almost got the sweetener banned by the government. The FDA settled for slapping a warning label on the little pink packets. Still, without a competitor in view, the business prospered.

All that changed with the appearance of aspartame in 1981. To back up briefly, aspartame was actually discovered by a researcher at G. D. Searle in 1965, but it too ran into regulatory roadblocks. It took a new FDA commissioner appointed by President Reagan to get the product approved as a tabletop sweetener and food additive. That same year, 1981, Searle sold the aspartame formula to Monsanto, which brought the NutraSweet brand to market. When the FDA approved aspartame in soft drinks a couple years later, saccharin's clout as a low-cal sweetener was on the wane.

At first, both Coke and Pepsi started sweetening their diet drinks with a mixture of saccharin and aspartame. But in 1984, Pepsi led the way to an all-aspartame concoction. Aspartame was more expensive, but consumers preferred it overwhelmingly, according to Pepsi's research. Plus, Diet Pepsi could get rid of the warning label and promote itself as "saccharin-free." Coke soon followed suit. At the same time, NutraSweet's Equal bumped Sweet 'N Low from the No. 1 spot on the tabletop.

By 1992, in terms of dollar sales. Equal had 54% of a market that a decade earlier had belonged entirely to Sweet 'N Low. That's when the NutraSweet patents expired. All of a sudden, NutraSweet's price—two to three times more per serving than Sweet 'N Low—became a problem. To reduce costs, the company cut its workforce by 15%. At the same time, to hold on to its key customers, it signed new contracts with Pepsi and Coke that reduced the product's price.

More interestingly, in a clear case of competency dependence, both NutraSweet and Sweet 'N Low immediately began to eat their own tails. Sweet 'N Low went after Equal with aspartame-based NatraTaste, at about half the price of Equal. Not to be outdone, NutraSweet rolled out a lower-priced aspartame sweetener called SweetMate, hoping to lure Sweet 'N Low's price-conscious loyalists. As a NutraSweet executive told the ***Wall Street Journal,*** SweetMate "has a different taste profile that's very much like Sweet 'N Low, but we've taken out the saccharin and the warning label." The question was, why wouldn't Sweet 'N Low users defect to NatraTaste, and Equal users to SweetMate? The answer, said industry analysts, is that they probably would. "What they'll end up doing is cannibalizing their original product," as one market consultant told the journal.

Still, the two brands dominated the market throughout the 1990s. Deep-pocketed NutraSweet (still a division of Monsanto) continued to take swipes at low-end Sweet 'N Low by featuring a succession of celebrity spokespeople—Cher, Lauren Hutton, Tony Bennett, Jamie Lee Curtis— who often could be seen choosing the blue packet over the pink one. Not even fraud charges against company president Marvin Eisenstadt, accused of trying to influence Congress to continue its stand against banning saccharin, could quite sound the death knell for stubborn Sweet 'N Low. Then, 20 years after aspartame's entry, the landscape took another dramatic shift.

In September 2000, a new sweetener hit the market: Splenda, a no-calorie sugar substitute developed by London-based Tate & Lyle and distributed by McNeil Nutritionals, a division of Johnson & Johnson. Two-and-a-half years later, it had soared to No. 1 in the product category, with a 33% share of the market. Within another year, Splenda had captured 48% of the table top market, sending erstwhile leader Equal into a nosedive. In fact. Equal's plunge was so dramatic that Merisant Worldwide, which had acquired Equal from Monsanto in 2000, brought in an outsider from Sara Lee, Paul Block, to try to stage a comeback.

Splenda, made from sucralose, looks to have its way in the meantime. The R&D team at Tate & Lyle came up with a product that has twice the shelf life of aspartame and that, unlike aspartame, does not react to heat and so can be conveniently used in baking. Whether or not they have been misled by advertising that touts the product as "made from sugar so it tastes like sugar," consumers have embraced Splenda at the very time that the nation seems to have become obsessed with the obesity epidemic. It hasn't hurt that Splenda has been endorsed by Dr. Arthur Agatson, whose South Beach Diet cookbooks have sold millions of copies. Not only are the yellow packets substantially outselling the blue packets and the pink packets, but the number of new products entering the market that include sucralose is skyrocketing, from roughly 600 in 2003 to twice that many in 2004. In fact, Splenda's only problem at the end of 2004 was that its one manufacturing plant could no longer meet rising demand.

How badly have the historic players been hit? While Splenda's share was surging from 37% to 48% between 2003 and 2004, Equal's was falling from 24% to 19%, and Sweet 'N Low's from 18% to 15%. The trend has continued. In 2005, retail sales of Splenda far outstripped those of Equal and Sweet 'N Low combined.

Of the responses to R&D dependency mentioned earlier, NutraSweet (which sells aspartame to Merisant and others) opted for the second: developing the next-generation product. The company returned to the lab and is now pushing a new product called Neotame, said to be far sweeter than any of its competitors and roughly half as expensive as sucralose. Sweet 'N Low, apparently, opted for the first: denial. Ignoring its declining share in a changing marketplace, the company has counted up the little pink packets on tabletops around the world, declared that it is still No. 1, and spent a lot of money on an ad campaign to send that message to an audience that's not likely to care.

DESIGN DEPENDENCE

Another core function that can come to define a company's culture is design. Clothing springs immediately to mind. After all, especially at the high end, clothing is all about design. The manufacturing component is negligible. Sales are driven by word of mouth and "prestige" pressure. And what a perfect example of competency dependence. What do these people do when their styles are no longer hot and their names have grown cold? Where was Tommy Hilfiger yesterday? Where will he be tomorrow? Not that I'm worried about him. He'll probably be on a yacht in the Mediterranean. But when your competence must accommodate the whims of fashion, competency dependence is a self-destructive habit indeed.

In lots of other industries, too, consumer choice is driven not by which product is better made (manufacturing) or more advanced (technology), but rather by which has the combination of form and function that we call "good design." Obviously, the automobile industry is an example, and Detroit's "competency" in this area—its confidence that boxy sedans would remain the ideal automotive design forever—has played a significant role in U.S. carmakers' loss of market share.

Yet another interesting example is the toy industry, which brings us to a story from northern Europe.

LEGO

The famous "construction toy" company began in 1932 in Billund, Denmark, when carpenter Ole Kirk Christiansen started carving wooden toys. Two years later, Christiansen held a contest among his employees to come up with a company name, and Lego (a combination of the Danish words "leg" and "godt," meaning "play well") emerged as the winner. Plastic began to replace wood after World War II, just as Lego's "Automatic Binding Blocks" made their way into the market. But it wasn't until the late 1950s, when the company introduced its first play sets with the revolutionary "stud and tube" snap-together building blocks, that sales soared and Lego became one of the most popular toys in Europe. Through an exclusive license arrangement with Samsonite Luggage, Lego made it to the U.S. in 1961. Twelve years later, when Samsonite declined to renew the license. Lego set up a sales and production facility in Connecticut, and the U.S. business took off. Lego seemed indeed to have discovered the building blocks to profit. It was one of the highest-margin businesses in the world, and it offered a unique product that no one could copy. In 1999, ***Fortune*** magazine cited Lego as "toy of the century."

In the 1990s, things began to go awry. In 1994, for example, sales dropped for the first time in 20 years. The company blamed the decline on the glut of imitators flooding the market during the height of the Christmas selling season. (The patent on the Lego brick had expired in the early 1980s, but Lego's exacting design specifications continued to discourage knockoffs.) The business press noted at the time, though, that Lego's workforce of extremely loyal employees was unaffected by the decline and that the company had cut hours rather than cutting jobs and preserved full benefits.

In 1996, with the business having returned to normal, Lego opened its second LEGOLAND Theme Park outside London and announced an ambitious plan to open 14 more around the world at three-year intervals. But in 1998, the company reported its first loss since the worldwide depression of the 1930s. The "loyal" workforce was cut by 10% (from 10,000 to 9,000), with plans to revamp operations worldwide. The loss was blamed in part on the wholesale shift in the industry away from construction toys toward computer and video games, but a spokesman told the ***Wall Street Journal*** that the company was also to blame: "We haven't been too good at managing costs. We let things grow without thinking, and we have too much double work." The restructuring was expected to save 150 million and put Lego back in the black for 1999.

Of note, the poor 1998 performance also prompted Kjeld Kirk Kristiansen, grandson of the company founder, to step aside in favor of turnaround specialist Poul Plougmann, the first non-family member ever to lead the company. Plougmann promised a 10% rise in sales, annually, and he did boost sales by pushing the company into more electronics-related products and expensive licensing deals. But profits stagnated, and in 2000 the company reported a loss of $105 million. Analysts were wondering whether, under the new leader, the company had lost its way.

In 2002, Lego suffered its worst loss ever, and Plougmann was fired before the year was over. His initiatives, like the merchandising spin-offs with Harry Potter and ***Star Wars,*** had proved a failure, and Kristiansen stepped back in to take control. As he told a group at MIT's Lego Learning Institute: "We went into too many categories, [and made] too many different products without really being aware of what they are about, or what our brand stands for. It was time to return to the basics and to restore the luster of the Lego brand."

It hasn't happened yet. Losses continued in 2003, to the tune of $170 million. Predicting even higher losses in 2004, Kristiansen stepped down at the end of the year and appointed an insider, senior VP Jorgen Vig Knudstorp, to take over the company. The LEGOLAND Theme Parks (which now numbered four—in Denmark, Germany, England, and San Diego) were put up for sale to pay off debt. With ever-increasing pressure from electronic toymakers, 2006 brought the shutting down of a plant in Switzerland and, most tellingly, significant job cuts at the original production facility in Billund.

To me, it's a sad story about a great product—and a classic case of competency dependence. The company's culture was formed around the care and skill with which the founder designed those early building blocks, and the design of that one product remained the company's single forte. In the 1980s and 1990s everything else changed—including a sea change in kids' leisure-time pursuits—but Lego did not.

SALES DEPENDENCE

Of course, every company depends on sales, but not every company develops a sales approach or technique that becomes its core competency. Some products, borne along on the crest of a fad, "sell themselves." Many others, like automobiles, are simple necessities. Although one company's sales efforts may be more aggressive than another's, the sales function is not likely to become the defining element in the company's culture.

Then there are the uniquely sales-oriented companies, the so-called direct sellers—companies whose sales force is their chief asset. These companies—purveyors of vacuum cleaners, encyclopedias, and life insurance, among other products—made the "salesman" an archetypal figure in American business, and that gave life to the expression, "Nothing happens until somebody sells somebody something." Direct selling thrived during America's postwar prosperity, when our middle class was expanding and consumers were buying lots of things they had never bought before. But it was also a more innocent and hopeful time in America—a time of open neighborhoods rather than gated communities, a time when people were willing to open their front doors and take a moment to listen to an eager drummer's sales pitch.

Can such companies survive today? We've already seen what happened to Encyclopaedia Britannica, but let's look at another company where the sales approach is clearly the core competency.

AVON

Avon's first "direct seller" was its founder, David McConnell, who started out by selling books door to door. He ingratiated himself to the New York housewives willing to listen to his pitch by giving them a small bottle of perfume, and he eventually realized that the perfume was more popular than the books. In 1886, he created the California Perfume Company and began hiring a sales force based on an additional insight: women would be more likely to buy perfume from other women. In 1939, returning from a trip to England during which he had been taken with the beauty of Stratford-on-Avon, McConnell renamed the company after the famous river.

After World War II, many of the housewives who had joined the workforce in place of their soldier husbands were no longer content to fix supper and do laundry. They wanted to keep working, to make a little extra income. For thousands, Avon offered a way to realize this desire, and these women, selling Avon products door to door, made Avon the world's largest cosmetics company.

But if the emancipation of the homemaker enabled Avon's rise to the top, the same phenomenon appeared to be the company's undoing. By the mid-1970s, being an "Avon lady" was losing its appeal. Younger women were going to college and pursuing "real" careers, and in increasing numbers housewives, too, were returning to school. Moreover, as the middle-aged woman was changing her image, the target market for Avon's products began to shrink. Consequently, over the next 10 years Avon's core business—selling cosmetics door to door—declined steadily and took the stock price with it. From a high of $140 in the early 1970s, the stock had plummeted to ***$20*** by 1985.

If you bought Avon at ***$20*** a share in 1985, however, you were smart. What Avon realized, even then, was that its selling platform would never recover—in America— but that women in other countries would be demographically similar to American women of the 1950s and 1960s. In other words, Avon could keep right on "calling"—overseas. Not that the company's struggles were over. It lost $400 million in 1988, despite trimming almost 200 employees from its corporate staff. Through the early 1990s, U.S. sales continued to decline, but steady growth in the international business had returned the company to profitability by 1993.

Let's take a closer look at Avon in Latin America, where the company's "homey door-to-door sales tactic is a perfect fit," according to Fernando Lezama, who heads up the Mexican and Central American divisions. In the first place, Lezama points out that the average Mexican household size is 5.2, twice that in America, so there's always someone at home to open the door. Also because there's virtually no other retail presence in Mexico's remote towns and villages, Avon's is often the only sales pitch people hear—which explains why the company also does well with apparel and home products, not just cosmetics. Then, too, just like in America 40 years ago, Avon represents one of the few employment opportunities for women, especially in more rural regions.

In 1995, when the Mexican peso was devalued by 50%, Avon stood to be hurt by a sharp decline in sales. Instead, because the devaluation meant layoffs in the male labor force, more women signed up to be Avon reps, and unit sales increased 10%. "There is one way to compensate for the loss of purchasing power," explains Lezama. "Demand slows down, so we increase the sales force and go to more customers." Ten years ago, Avon's sales in Latin America already totaled ***$1.2*** billion, out of ***$4*** billion worldwide.

Five years later, Avon's worldwide revenue had climbed to ***$6*** billion, thanks at least in part to the ascension of Andrea Jung to CEO (and subsequently chairman), a promotion that brought a woman to the company's top post for the first time in its 115-year history. Despite the continuing success of Avon's traditional direct sales approach in its overseas markets, Jung clearly saw the potential danger of competency dependence. Her strategy was to put muscle into the company's other functions. In marketing, she ditched the company's ancient "Ding-dong. Avon calling!" jingle and replaced it with the contemporary-sounding "Let's Talk" campaign. In design, she called for an overhaul of the products' packaging to give it the look of the more upscale Lancôme and Estée Lauder brands. In R&D, she demanded a "breakthrough" new product under a two-year deadline, and the lab responded with "Retroactive," an anti-aging skin cream that's been a huge hit. Analysts credit her initiatives with improving sales growth from 1.5% a year to 6%.

Still, the overseas markets remained the growth engines for Avon, as Jung fully realized. By 2005, the company was selling in 143 countries, including Kazakhstan and Vietnam. It's the market leader in Hungary, Poland, Russia, and Slovakia. Sales in foreign markets have been climbing 15% annually and now account for roughly two-thirds of Avon's ***$7*** billion in worldwide revenue. Best of all, China still beckons.

Fearing pyramid schemes and other forms of corruption, Beijing banned door-to-door selling in 1998, and Avon's efforts in China have been limited to retail beauty boutiques and sales counters in department stores. Sales have been impressive nonetheless, rising from $157 million in 2003 to $220 million in 2004. But for Avon, retail is not as profitable or conducive to building market share as the model that has proven so effective in other developing economies, wherein its army of Avon Ladies scour the rural countryside, pushing Avon where other brands have no presence.

In April 2005, the company got word: the ban was being lifted "on a trial basis," and Avon could begin its direct sales effort in Beijing, Tianjin, and Guangdong province. "We are fully prepared," Jung told investors.

SERVICE DEPENDENCE

When was the last time someone came out to fill up your tank and check your oil at the gas station? It was probably right before the last independently owned station in your neighborhood closed its doors. A funny thing is happening in what we used to think of as our service industries. Nobody's there anymore. In fact, it's hard to find the word itself without the contemporary modifier in front of it: "self." Let's look at an example.

TRAVEL AGENTS

Until recently, travel agencies constituted the classic service industry. Booking a trip was something anybody could do themselves ("I want to go to Nassau. I'm sure if I write the chamber of commerce I can get a list of hotels to pick from..."). But why bother? That's what the travel agent was for. And the travel agent was not only helpful and service-oriented, because he or she was paid on commission, his or her service to the customer was free.

Now the travel agent's services are, if not obsolete, at least not quite as alluring as they used to be. Of course, there's the Internet. With online providers such as Expedia and Travelocity, people who are already accustomed to shopping and paying bills online are very likely to make their own travel arrangements as well. The sector is growing fast. Online-travel revenues topped $54 billion in 2004—a quarter of all industry bookings. $24 billion of that went to Internet agencies as opposed to airline and hotel websites. Online agent revenues are expected to grow another 50% by 2009.

What's more, the services of the traditional travel agent—the one you used to call on the phone—aren't free anymore. Since airlines no longer pay commissions to travel agents, agents now collect on the front end, in the form of a service fee usually in the ***$25*** range.

"There is a sea change going on," William Maloney, executive vice president of the Society of Travel Agents, told the ***New York Times.*** "Travel agents for a long time had a monopoly on two things. One was information. They had the airlines' computers. The second thing was documents. If you wanted a ticket, you went to a travel agency." Those monopolies no longer exist. Not **surprisingly** added Maloney, membership in the society is declining steadily, down 25% over three years.

It seems independent travel agents have two choices. One, they can give up and shut the door. Many have done so. Industry analysts predict a drop in the number of agencies from a high of 32,000 in the mid-1990s to a low of 15,000 when the shakeout is finally over.

The other option, paradoxically, is to offer more and more specialized services. The first step might very well be a vocabulary upgrade, from "travel agent" to "vacation planning consultant." The point is to let the customer know you are offering something that can't be duplicated on the Internet.

An increasing number of agents are pushing the service envelope by moving their business in home so that they can accommodate the client's schedule. Many, in fact, are now offering house-call service. One of these, David Thrower, told the ***Boston Globe*** that he's ready to serve his customers "at all hours" and that it's to their benefit that he's not confined to a nine-to-five business. He's happy to meet clients at their homes or, if necessary, will even meet them at the airport with their travel documents. "I'll go almost anywhere to help a client," says Thrower. More generally, the metamorphosis in the industry, another agent told the ***Globe,*** is "from order takers to travel professionals selling personal service."

It's a perplexing case of competency dependence. It seems for the old-line travel agent, whose service is in decreasing demand, the route to survival is to offer ***more*** service. I suspect that the point of diminishing returns looms on the horizon.

THE WARNING SIGNS OF COMPETENCY DEPENDENCE

What are the symptoms of competency dependence? It's not hard to tell when your strength has become your weakness and your incumbency has become a curse. Here are a few things to look for.

YOUR EFFORTS TO TRANSFORM THE COMPANY HAVE BEEN FUTILE

You have tried reengineering and reorganization, but your problem remains. You have brought in the advisors who have told you to retool processes and functions, and still nothing has happened. You have driven out the costs, but you are still trapped. You can't find the rainbow that tells you the storm is over.

THE THRILL IS GONE

Inside the company, there is a feeling of malaise, helplessness, and inevitability. The company seems to suffer from a terminal illness—like the smoker who's already developed lung cancer and says, "Why quit now?" Your people are disheartened and disillusioned, but they don't know how to get out of their funk. (Of course, it's the leader's job to pull them out.)

STAKEHOLDERS ARE JUMPING SHIP

Loyalty to the enterprise is gone. First to leave are the investors, who realize it's time to bet on somebody else. Second to leave are the suppliers, who realize they need to do business elsewhere. Last to go are the customers; they have been faithful to the brand, but finally they too see the light.

The textile industry in the Southeast provides a great example. To illustrate more specifically, consider the venerable Georgia-based company WestPoint Stevens. Over the last couple of decades, the nation's second-largest manufacturer of bedding and towels has seen its core competency (textile manufacturing) increasingly threatened by goods from overseas. Emerging from bankruptcy in 1992, WestPoint came under the control of investor Holcombe

Between 1997 and 2001, according to ***the Atlanta Journal-Constitution,*** Green spent almost $600 million in an effort to bring the company's mills up to speed (reengineering). He also closed plants and fired hundreds of workers to stay competitive (restructuring, driving down costs).

All to no avail. In June 2003, buried under ***$2*** billion in debt, the company was back in bankruptcy. Investors had fled in such a hurry that the stock's price had dropped to three pennies a share. Green was out; president and COO "Chip" Fontenot was in, but the company's problems remained. As one analyst told the Atlanta paper, WestPoint needed more than debt relief. It didn't help that Kmart, its biggest customer, was also in bankruptcy, but the central problem continued to be competition from imports. It's a problem that wasn't about to go away. The company's strength had become its weakness.

By June 2005, WestPoint had shed 2,500 employees, just over a fifth of its workforce. That's when investor Carl Icahn stepped in to buy the company for $700 million—a deal that would allocate more than $500 million to pay off creditors and leave the company debt-free. Odds are that Icahn, who no doubt saw value in still-popular WestPoint brands like Martex, will shift the remaining manufacturing operations overseas, ignore the company's historic obligations to the community, restore it to profitability, and then sell it.

It may work—for Icahn—but for WestPoint, as well as for the textile industry in the Southeast more generally, the end has come.

HOW TO BREAK THE HABIT OF COMPETENCY DEPENDENCE

In some of the cases we've looked at, competency dependence has morphed from a self-destructive habit to a fatal illness. But it doesn't have to be that way. To break the habit, try one of the following five remedies.

FIND NEW APPLICATIONS

Escape the competency trap by finding new applications where the same competency yields new value.

For a perfect illustration, consider what Church & Dwight Co. has done with its Arm & Hammer brand baking soda: Dr. Austin Church founded the company in 1846 to make bicarbonate of soda for bread baking, and making bread rise remained a worthy mission for a hundred years. But over the last half-century home bread-baking has yielded to commercial bakeries, leaving the high-margin customer—the housewife—with no further need for the product.

No further need as a baking ingredient, that is. Actually, the company had begun investigating other uses for its product as early as the 1920s, but this effort was intensified after World War II. Baking soda's cleansing and foaming properties made it ideal for brushing teeth, so the company marketed it as a toothpaste. When more contemporary products like Crest and Colgate pushed it out of that market, baking soda saw a new future as a laundry detergent. It could even be touted as a "natural" (nonphosphate) product, good for the environment and beneficial for people who were allergic to traditional detergents. In fact, Arm & Hammer's effectiveness as a cleanser was put on spectacular display in 1986 when it was used to clean the inner walls of the Statue of Liberty in preparation for the landmark's 100th anniversary.

Next to be exploited was the product's effectiveness as an odor killer. Of course, knowledgeable consumers had long been keeping an open box of baking soda in the refrigerator; the company simply commercialized this use. Not only is the market for the product as a deodorizer huge (refrigerators, cat litter boxes, carpets), but the larger-sized (and more expensive) box has now become the standard.

Most recently, health benefits are coming to light. The company manufactures a medical-grade sodium bicarbonate for use in kidney dialysis, and sports medicine research reports that you can get an energy boost from drinking a spoonful of baking soda dissolved in water or juice. And, by the way, the 160-year-old company continues to thrive.

Nylon is another product whose versatility has provided an escape from competency dependence. When the supply of silk from China was disrupted by the communist revolution there, DuPont scientists quickly went to work on a synthetic. The company sold its first pair of nylon stockings in 1940. A few years later, when the manufacturing sector turned its efforts to producing war materiel, factories that had been making stockings began making nylon parachutes. During the postwar years other materials, especially polyester, took over the hosiery market, and nylon found a new use as an upholstery fabric. Next it found a huge new market in wall-to-wall carpeting; and then in artificial turf; and then, most unlikely of all, in artificial ski slopes. Now nylon is replacing metal in the human-parts industry—heart valves and hip prosthetics.

Both baking soda and nylon exemplify "new applications" of the same product. Sometimes, however, survival, demands refocusing the company's competency on an entirely different product or product category. Consider forward-looking Monsanto.

Foreseeing a growing market for the artificial sweetener, John Queeny founded Monsanto Chemical Works in 1901 to manufacture saccharin. Long before the use of saccharin was linked to cancer in laboratory rats, the company had already moved into textile chemicals and synthetic fibers. And even before the textile industry went to Asia, Monsanto was making its move into agricultural chemicals, most notably with the herbicides Lasso (in 1969) and Roundup (in 1973). Incidentally, the company stopped making saccharin in 1972.

Its interest in developing seeds that tolerate Roundup while resisting insects led the company to refocus once again—this time on bioengineering crops such as soybeans, corn, cotton, and canola. Despite public resistance to biotech crops, Monsanto is betting its future on the need to alleviate world hunger. Its core competency—chemistry—finds its latest application in increasing crop yields through biotechnology and genomics.

FIND NEW MARKETS

A second way to break this habit is to find new markets where the same competency remains an asset. Such markets are likely to be overseas, especially in emerging economies such as India, China, the Association of Southeast Asian Nations (ASEAN) bloc, Russia, and Eastern Europe. This is the strategy Avon has pursued so successfully—capitalizing on the idea that many of these emerging economies have demographics much like America's used to be.

Direct seller Amway has followed Avon's example, pushing its Artistry cosmetic and Nutralite vitamin lines in markets around the world. The company established a beachhead in Asia when it set up its first distributorships in Hong Kong in 1974, and it has never looked back. Today, most of the company's sales come from outside North America, and two-thirds of those foreign sales are in Asia. The company is doing great business in Japan, Korea, and Thailand, but China is where the real action is. Unlike Avon, Amway wasn't stymied when China banned direct selling in 1998 because the company was allowed to have its distributors enter China as sales reps. As a result, China is now Am-way's biggest single market. In 2004 alone, sales there topped $2 billion, and in 2005 the company opened flagship stores in Taipei and Kaohsiung.

Similarly, as Chinese, Indian, and other Asian economies surge, international staffing companies are finding new life by matching their competence to this explosive market. Paris-based Ecco, for example, moved into Asia in the mid-1980s, opening offices in Tokyo, Singapore, and Hong Kong. It has found a huge Asian demand for temp services, but it's also doing well in executive placement as established businesses expand and new ones appear. Another big player, Toronto-based Drake International, arrived in the Pacific Rim in 1988 and has since grown a lucrative business in executive recruitment. Kom/Ferry, the world leader in executive search, reported tremendous growth in its Asian operations 10 years ago when it opened a second office in India. After a slowdown during the "Asian crisis" of 1999, its business is surging again.

In fact, the staffing business in Asia is so hot that it's attracting companies that are too young to have developed competency dependence. For instance, there's DSS Software, the high-tech staffing firm that opened in Oakland in 1996. Its founder, Atul Parikh, saw a growing need for high-tech professionals and also saw a very deep talent pool in India, where he quickly opened a branch office. The company's growth was so explosive (350% in 2000) that it was snatched up by Diversinet in 2002.

There's also the story of India-born entrepreneur Ranjan Marwah, who arrived in Hong Kong to visit his father in'1969 and never returned home. After dabbling in a variety of businesses, he found his calling as a headhunter. He founded Executive Access in 1988, which is one of Asia's biggest executive search firms.

MOVE UPSTREAM, MOVE DOWNSTREAM

A third escape from the competency trap is expanding the range of your competencies by moving up or down the value chain.

Perhaps the best example is IBM, which has successfully moved in both directions. When its big-box business maxed out, the company realized that most of its big-box expertise could be put to other uses. The strategy has propelled it to the forefront as a merchant supplier, selling servers, chips, and software to other computer makers like Dell and HP. The move upstream has been powered by acquisitions (Lotus in 1995 and Tivoli in 1997, among others), and today IBM sells more software than anyone else except Microsoft. At the "streamhead," IBM remains at the forefront of high-tech areas like nanotechnology and cell processing, developing technologies that it leases to Hitachi, Sony, and other global manufacturers.

Meanwhile, the company has also moved downstream by developing its services business, which now accounts for almost half of its sales. The push in this direction is generally credited to Louis Gerstner, the outsider who arrived in 1993, and who understood that the stream didn't have to dry up after the sale was made. Products could also be profitably managed and maintained. To expand the services arm into high-end management consulting, IBM bought PriceWaterhouseCoopers in a huge $3.5 billion deal, and on the low end it bought Daksh eServices, one of India's biggest call center businesses. Heavy advertising has supported the downstream move—witness the high-visibility TV campaigns for IBM Global Services and "E-Business Solutions."

In most cases, moving downstream is the viable option for large-scale manufacturers like GE, ABB, Westinghouse, Siemens, Lucent, Alcatel, Nortel, and others. GE is a case in point. The company no longer makes power generators, for example, but it does a huge business in maintaining existing power plants—including nuclear facilities. Along the same lines, the famous maker of jet engines now creates as much revenue from maintaining and repairing engines as it does from manufacturing them.

While it was at it, GE created GE Capital to finance the sale of all its major manufacturing undertakings. Historically, the financing for a power plant or for aircraft engines would be handled by import/export banks, but GE eventually decided to dip into this revenue stream. Out of this effort has come the surprising fact that GE is now the world's largest airline leasing company. The big manufacturers such as Boeing and Airbus sell their aircraft to GE, and GE leases them to the airlines. This arrangement is easier on the budget-constrained customer than an outright purchase. For example, with the military's budget so closely scrutinized, the Pentagon might prefer to pay $5 billion for years than $100 billion today. Interestingly, GE Capital itself grew into such a behemoth that in 2002 Jeff Immelt, Jack Welch's successor, split it into four units—GE Commercial Finance, GE Consumer Finance, GE Equipment Management, and GE Insurance. GE Commercial Finance alone now brings in 15% of the company's total revenues.

DEVELOP A NEW COMPETENCY

A more drastic fix for the habit of competency dependence is to develop a new competency and grow your business there. This strategy is likely to require an uncomfortable transition period during which you cannibalize your old business to invest in the new one. But breaking self-destructive habits—especially long-entrenched ones—is never easy.

Consider Kodak's current difficulties, for example. Its core competency, of course, has long been the manufacture of photographic film, and it remains the world's No. 1 film producer. But the folks in Rochester didn't have to be geniuses to see that dependence on that competency would become a terminal illness. Now the company is in the middle of a wrenching transformation into a digital photography leader. It's been expensive. The company announced a $3 billion investment in the new technology, much of which would be generated by continuing to sell traditional film and cameras in emerging markets like China, India, Eastern Europe, and Latin America—by milking its old competency. The company has also been forced to raise cash by cutting its stock dividend by 70%.

The new strategy has also been tough on the workforce. In July 2005, Kodak announced another 10,000 layoffs, in addition to the 12,000 to 15,000 it had announced a year earlier. Originally, the company's restructuring plan had called for the elimination of 25,000 jobs by 2007, but now it looks as though that estimate was too low.

Still, the company has little choice. It must develop this new competency, and it is moving aggressively to do so. It has made deals with Intel and Adobe Systems that allow its consumers to edit, print, and send photos from their PCs. A joint venture with HP will produce photofinishing equipment for digital pictures. Deals with U.S. and European cell phone companies have also gotten Kodak into the camera-phone market. Another series of deals and acquisitions have made the company a player in health imaging, where it sees a robust future. There's a lot of pain now, but not many companies have been so cursed by incumbency as Kodak.

A contrasting example is provided by India-based Wipro Limited, which has avoided Kodak-style turmoil by developing new competencies before dependence set in. The company's founder, Hasham Premji, had been in the rice mill business in Burma. He returned to India in 1946 to start a vegetable shortening distribution company (Western Indian Vegetable Products or Wipro). Since animal fat, or lard, is not used in India, there's an enormous market for vegetable shortening, and Premji tapped that market by cutting out the middleman. He bought in bulk, repackaged the product into small units, branded it, and sold it directly to street vendors. In other words, his core competency became distribution.

Before he died of a heart attack in 1966, Premji had already moved upstream by making the shortening. Since he was now manufacturing, he also found other uses for it, diversifying into bath soap and hydraulic fluid. When Premji died, his son, Azim, cut short his engineering studies at Stanford to return home and run the business. Having become familiar with computers as an engineer, and having inherited a distribution business, he added Epson printers to the Wipro pipeline. When IBM was asked to depart from India in 1977 over investment and intellectual property disputes, Azim saw the opportunity to begin distributing computers. However, since India was still a closed economy at that time, with very high import duties, manufacturers preferred to have Wipro assemble the computers in India. They would simply sell Azim the components and thus avoid the onerous taxes. Soon Wipro computers were a leading national brand.

A move into software in the early 1980s was followed at the end of that decade by the development of the competency that constitutes Wipro's growth business today: software services. An alliance with GE in 1989 to form Wipro GE Medical Systems attracted a steady stream of global clients, including AT&T, Lucent, Cisco, Hitachi, and Alcatel. Now, more than 75% of Wipro's revenue comes from software services, an arena in which it competes successfully with IBM. Recent acquisitions have expanded Wipro's services offerings by making it a global leader in business process outsourcing (BPO) as well.

Wipro has done well, but as Kodak's experience shows, developing a new competency can be a difficult strategy. Nor should it be confused with simple diversification. The diversification mania that seized American business in the 1970s and 1980s has played itself out and has left many maimed bodies in its wake. Beatrice, Coca-Cola, Xerox, Alcoa, Sears, and all three major American television networks are but a few of the iconic American companies that have been hurt, not helped, by diversification.

The idea is not to wildly diversify, but to identify and develop a single new core competency. Ideally, the choice should grow naturally out of your company's previous success, culture, and values.

REFOCUS YOUR RESOURCES

On the other hand, you may not need a new competency. You may simply need to redirect your efforts and resources into areas with more growth and profit potential.

Here, BellSouth offers an instructive example. The company rode the cellular revolution to virtually every corner of the globe—Argentina, New Zealand, Germany, Israel, China—before deciding to focus its foreign efforts in South America. Pursuing that strategy, it bought major stakes in telecoms in Nicaragua, Ecuador, Peru, and Venezuela, while pulling out of Europe and Israel. Eventually, BellSouth held stakes in 10 Latin American countries, but then it shifted focus again and sold its Latin American Group to the Spanish giant Telefonica.

Fittingly, the new strategy has the company refocused on its original nine-state home territory. It was the first Baby Bell to be allowed to offer long distance in its local service area, and that hasn't hurt. But as demand for land lines decreases, BellSouth plans to offer its customers the entire spectrum of communication services. Its combination with SBC to form Gingular Wireless and its subsequent acquisition of AT&T Wireless has made it the nation's No. 1 mobile phone operator. In its effort to bundle services and give customers the convenience of seeing just one bill, it has even hooked up with DIRECTV. At the same time, BellSouth is working with Dell to offer DSL-equipped PCs and is starting to bring Voice over Internet Protocol (VoIP) technology to its business customers. (There is an interesting backstory here. In its initial regulation of the cell phone industry, the government allowed the so-called A-carriers—companies other than the Baby Bells—into the market on the basis of a lottery. However, that system allowed too many players who weren't competent, so the government narrowed the field by charging these A-carriers enormous license fees. By contrast, all the Baby Bells got a free license to operate their cell companies, along with their given territories. BellSouth and the other Baby Bells were slow to recognize this advantage—until they saw the tremendous boom in cell phone demand, at which point BellSouth and SBC quickly joined forces. In effect, BellSouth took all the revenue from its land lines (including 6.5 million long-distance customers) and, since that business was destined to shrink, invested the money in wireless. Again, it's not so much a change in competency as a realignment of resources. Indeed, BellSouth did such a fine job of reshaping and expanding its competencies in the fast-changing telecom world that it became an irresistible marriage partner. The suitor? None other than AT&T, which must have seemed confusing to many outside the industry. Of course, as noted in Chapter 4, there is no Ma Bell these days. AT&T is really SBC, the child that ate the parent (but kept the parent's famous name).

Competency dependence is an easy habit to fall into. After all, being competent—doing something well—makes you feel good. This is especially true when you're the incumbent, when you're not just good—you're the best. You like the feeling. You get hooked onto it. You're like the drug user who can neither see nor think of anything beyond his next fix. Or like anyone whose vision is limited by his or her own narrow conception of the possible.

Remember that there is a wide world out there. Your company may have great potential in underutilized functional areas. Who knows what might happen if your engineers accepted a little feedback from the marketing department or if your manufacturing arm moved downstream toward services? As you've seen, there may be new uses for the product your company makes or new markets for it in the global economy.

A clear, wide-ranging vision that opens up possibilities is the first step to breaking the habit of competency dependence. The time to embrace change will come sooner or later.

COMPETENCY DEPENDENCE

Things that lead to competency dependence:

- R&D dependence
- Design dependence
- Sales dependence
- Service dependence

The warning signs of competency dependence:

- **Your efforts to transform the company have been futile:** You have tried reengineering, reorganization, retooling—and still nothing has happened.
- **The thrill is gone:** Your company seems to be in a funk.
- **Stakeholders are jumping ship:** Investor, supplier, and customer loyalty has disappeared.

How to break the habit of competency dependence:

- **New applications:** Find new applications where the same competency yields new value.
- **New markets:** Find new markets where the same competency remains an asset.
- **Move upstream, move downstream:** Expand the range of your competencies by moving up or down the value chain.
- **Refocus your resources:** Redirect your efforts and resources into areas with more growth and profit potential.

CHAPTER 6

COMPETITIVE MYOPIA: A NEARSIGHTED VIEW OF COMPETITION

You suffer from "competitive myopia" when you make the mistake of defining your competition too narrowly, when you acknowledge only the competitors that are in your face, whose challenge is direct and immediate. You lack the peripheral vision that would discern less obvious challengers—those whose threat is, for whatever reason, not on today's radar screen but is nonetheless very real and dangerous.

It's surprisingly easy to think of examples of iconic global companies that have fallen into this self-destructive habit: Coke worries about Pepsi; Caterpillar watches KOMATSU. Boeing frets about Airbus, while Bombardier and Embrace plan their flanking maneuvers. Most famously, while GM, Ford, and Chrysler competed with each other, Japan invaded and conquered the market. In fact, we see the problem even in competition among nations. For four decades the United States was locked in military and economic conflict with the Soviet Union. Only after the Great Bear collapsed did we discern in the looming threat of instability and upheaval in the Middle East a danger that had been quietly growing for years.

At one point or another, virtually every company succumbs to competitive myopia. Why is this habit so widespread? Here are four reasons.

THE NATURAL EVOLUTION OF THE INDUSTRY

In the early days of the typical industry, competitors spring up like mushrooms. We saw this graphically in the infancy of the automobile industry, when 500 companies jumped into the game. A century later, the dot-com boom offered another illustration. Competitors swarm like flies, and, like flies, most have limited mortality. A better analogy might be a road race, where, at the starting gun, thousands of runners are basically in the same place. At that point, you have no idea who your real competitors will be. Eventually, though, as the pack thins out, you see who you are running against, and that's who you pace yourself against. You focus on the guy running stride for stride beside you or maybe the one who's one stride ahead. What you probably don't see is the outsider, the guy who wasn't even mentioned by the oddsmakers, sneaking stealthily up from behind.

Once the evolving industry has completed the shakeout phase, only a handful of serious competitors will have survived. It's my theory (as outlined in ***The Rule of Three***) that industries typically support three dominant players, but whether the number is three, two, or four, the premise remains: It is among themselves that these alpha companies find their competition. They ignore the niche players; they ignore the newcomers. They even tend to ignore the industry consolidators, as Ford foolishly ignored General Motors—until it is too late. In other words, they develop competitive myopia.

This pattern is beautifully illustrated in the story of Firestone, one of the Big Three in the U.S. tire industry.

FIRESTONE: WHEN THE RUBBER LEFT THE ROAD

After the shakeout of the domestic tire industry, the three big survivors were Goodyear, Firestone, and BF Goodrich. All enjoyed complete vertical integration, with control over raw materials, manufacturing, and distribution. Goodyear was No. 1, and Firestone was the cocky challenger, the No. 2 player determined to take over the top spot. Firestone focused solely on Goodyear, barely acknowledging No. 3 BF Goodrich. More important—and quite typical—all three companies failed to notice the winds of change blowing across the Atlantic. They paid no attention to Michelin, which, with its new radial tire, was rising to become the European leader and was looking for a gateway into America.

Well, why should they pay attention? They had distribution locked up, just like the U.S. auto industry did. They wouldn't let Michelin in. End of problem. But they overlooked one fact: With its platform of tires, batteries, and accessories (TBA), Sears had actually become America's largest tire retailer, controlling about 25% of the market. The Big Three had managed to ignore this fact because they had all said no to Sears. They didn't want their tires sold by the giant retailer because Sears would have put its private label on them, and thus they would have been competing against themselves. Sears had its own dedicated suppliers, and it was selling plenty of tires.

Sears didn't have any radial tires, though, and it was happy to talk with French manufacturer Michelin. The talks were productive. Because the Michelin brand had no presence in America and Sears had no presence in Europe, Michelin saw no problem whatever with Sears' private label. In fact, it was a perfect marriage, and Sears became the "market maker" for Michelin in America. Soon, Sears was selling radials both under its private label and under the Michelin brand. With the two-brand strategy. Sears began to destroy the long-standing U.S. manufacturing platform—bias belted and bias ply. Suddenly the radial tire was ascendant, and American manufacturers were behind the curve.

Firestone ran into special difficulties. The historic company, which was founded in 1900 and produced a warm friendship between its founder, Harvey Firestone, and Henry Ford, seriously fumbled at the transition to radial technology. Radials were problematic for the U.S. industry anyway since the new process entailed enormous retooling costs and then hurt manufacturers again by eroding the market for replacement tires. But Firestone compounded its problems by rushing into the market with a faulty product, the radial Firestone 500, a mistake with devastating consequences. In 1980, the National Highway Traffic Safety Administration fined Firestone a then-record $500,000 for failing to recall 400,000 tires it made in 1973 and 1974—tires that, according to the NHTSA, Firestone knew were faulty. Meanwhile, as the result of a subsequent NHTSA investigation in 1978, the company agreed to recall another 14 million tires, the largest tire recall in history. Firestone had to set aside ***$234*** million to cover that disaster.

In 1979, the company hired turnaround specialist John Nevin, who had become experienced with the hatchet while at Zenith. Within a year he had closed seven U.S. factories and eliminated close to 8,000 jobs. But it was too late to restore Firestone's luster as a tire maker, and Nevin knew it. He pushed the company toward auto repair and retail sales rather than manufacturing, and he also cast about for a suitor. Pirelli came calling in March 1988, offering $58 a share for a company whose stock had been trading in the mid-30s. That was all Bridgestone, the Japanese tire leader, needed to hear. Bridgestone, which had badly coveted a piece of the U.S. market but which had been bashfully standing on the sidelines, swooped in and carried the bride away for $80 a share. Nevin's work was done.

At the time of the Firestone sale, the competitive myopia that had plagued all three major U.S. tire companies was put into perspective by a Goodyear executive. "We no longer have U.S. competition," Dennis Rich told ***the Los Angeles Times.*** "They're all foreign names now. They're rapidly growing and they're very capable."

As it turns out. Firestone has not been the ideal spouse. First, within weeks of the announcement of the deal, GM cut off Firestone as a supplier, immediately costing the company 10% of its business. Two years later, with Bridgestone/Firestone $3 billion in debt, it was becoming apparent that Bridgestone had paid too much. A decade later came the Ford Explorer catastrophe, which began with media reports of crashes caused by tire tread separation. By late 2000, Bridgestone/Firestone had recalled 6.5 million tires, most of them on Fords. The next year. Ford preemptively recalled another 13 million Bridgestone/Firestone tires, causing Bridgestone/Firestone to dump Ford as a customer and effectively bringing to an unhappy end the old alliance between the two companies. At the end of 2001, Bridgestone/Firestone agreed to pay $500,000 to each of the 50 states to avert lawsuits stemming from hundreds of accidents that might have been caused by faulty tires.

Bridgestone Corp. president Yoichiro Kaizaki suggested that the company would henceforth "move to rely more heavily on sales of Bridgestone-brand tires in the U.S." Thus was the death knell quietly rung for another venerable American brand.

By the way, the tire story has a great irony. The inventor of radial technology was BF Goodrich. Typical of the German-American R&D model, Goodrich wanted to cream-skim some profit from its new invention, so it went first to its highest-margin customer—the aerospace industry. Passenger car tires constituted a commodity business, with lots of price pressure and thin margins, so there was little motivation to apply the technology there. At the same time, rather than retool its factories to accommodate radial manufacturing, Goodrich licensed the technology, and Michelin bought the license. The French maker was fortunate enough to be holding it when

Europe went completely radial, by law, because radial tires are demonstrably safer. This plot line came full circle in 1989, when Michelin bought Uniroyal Goodrich Tire Co for $1.5 billion.

FROM ZENITH TO NADIR

What the French did to the American tire industry, the Japanese did to the American television industry. The parallels are striking. Just as BF Goodrich licensed radial technology to Michelin, RCA— thinking its competition was Zenith, Magnavox, and GE—licensed TV technology to the Japanese. In fact, while on a trip to visit Japanese industry and government leaders in 1960, RCA's legendary leader, David Sarnoff, was awarded the Order of the Rising Sun for the aid he had given Japan's electronics industry.

After Sarnoff handed the reins to his son. Bob, RCA's plunge was spectacular. By 1974, its share of the color TV market, a category it had largely developed and utterly dominated, had fallen to 20%. Japanese companies, led by Matsushita, had an equal stake. Zenith, with 24%, had become the U.S. leader. Soon RCA had departed the market, selling sets manufactured by others under the RCA brand. "As a graphic sign of its humiliation," writes Robert Sobel in ***When Giants Stumble,*** "RCA had become a licensee—to Matsushita."

RCA's board dumped Bob Sarnoff in 1975, but by then the highly diversified and unfocused company's problems had become intractable. In the early 1980s, CEO Thornton Bradshaw divested a number of enterprises and got the company out of debt. Then in 1986 he sold it to GE for $6.3 billion. The RCA-manufactured television set passed from the American scene, but that's not the end of our story. GE's Jack Welch promptly turned around and sold the RCA and GE television brands to Thomson SA of France in 1987. Philips Electronics NV of the Netherlands had previously bought Magnavox and Sylvania. That left Zenith as the last remaining U.S. TV manufacturer.

Zenith led the market in sales of color TVs from 1972 to 1978. While enjoying this nice run, in 1974, the company's controller had this to say: "We are basically a U.S. company and are likely to stay that way." No problem, except that Zenith failed to foresee the beating it was about to take from Asian, not American, competitors. By 1984, forced into price cuts by less expensive imports, Zenith had ceased making money once and for all. Over the next 10 years, under the leadership of Jerry Pearlman, the company fought a rear-guard action by cutting its payroll and moving production increasingly to Mexico. In 1995, it sold 58% of itself for a cash infusion of $351 million. The buyer? Korea's LG Group (formerly Lucky-Goldstar, one of the old-line chaebols).

It didn't help. Zenith lost a record $300 million in 1997, the same year it cut its workforce by 25%. In 1998, it closed its last U.S. manufacturing facility, the famous color picture-tube plant in Melrose Park, Illinois. The next year it entered into bankruptcy protection. As part of the proceedings, LG Group canceled $200 million of the company's debt in exchange for 100% ownership. Completing its transformation into a marketing and distribution entity, the company sold what was left of its manufacturing operations, including its TV plant in Reynosa, Mexico. So it's not just that Zenith was no longer a U.S. company; it was no longer even a TV maker.

In the case of this industry, and in consumer electronics more broadly, the consequences of competitive myopia have been truly staggering. As Robert Sobel puts it, "Today one can't buy a TV manufactured by an American-owned and -based company. The Japanese victory in consumer electronics was more complete and startling than that in automobiles."

THE CLUSTERING PHENOMENON

The clustering in one location of companies in a given industry is a natural phenomenon. In earlier times, it was simply a matter of the availability of natural resources. Pittsburgh became the steel capital because of rich deposits of coal and iron ore in the area. Cotton mills proliferated in the South where cotton was cultivated. Paper mills, too, located in the South because kaolin, the whitener, was plentiful there. Transporting such raw materials to distant factories would in many cases be more expensive than the extraction, so economics dictated that industries locate where the materials were abundant.

Clustering offers other advantages beyond the efficient use of natural resources. It makes sense for competitors to locate near each other. Supply lines have already been established into the area, and a qualified and motivated labor pool is likely to be available. There is a synergistic sharing of ideas and information, and advances by one player spur further innovation from another. Competition pushes the industry forward, and it's healthy—up to a point.

In a number of great American industries, that point has been reached. The automotive industry, clustered in Detroit, is now in decline. Same with the tire industry in Akron and the steel industry in Pittsburgh. The defense industry (Hughes, Boeing) in Los Angeles might also be cited. Whether the high-tech industry in Silicon Valley thrives or collapses remains to be seen.

The point is that, whatever its advantages, clustering contributes to competitive myopia. Clustering makes it too easy to focus on the competition in your backyard. How can it be otherwise, when competing executives are members of the same clubs and their children attend the same schools? Nobody wants to lose market share to his next-door neighbor. That would be worse than being cuckolded. Clustering makes for a closed society, and a much too narrow view of the competition.

Of course, problems create opportunities. The company located in the midst of its competitors can continue to slug it out with its neighbors. But if it manages to tune out the local noise and raise its eyes above the walls of the compound, it might find itself with a huge global advantage.

WHEN NO. 1 IS ALSO THE PIONEER

If you're at the top of an industry you also pioneered, be careful. As you focus on the one or two players coming up from behind, stealing your market share and trying to take your crown, you're prone to fall prey to competitive myopia. Let's take McDonald's as an example.

BURGER WARS

The national appetite for what McDonald's created—fast food—turned out to be so voracious that there was no way a single company could supply the demand. Competitors proliferated—some local, some regional, some national. Many died off. After the shakeout, McDonald's was focused on Burger King and to a lesser extent on Wendy's. First let's concede that McDonald's has done many things right. It has made vertical integration an art, and, as a result, its operations are beautiful. Rigid adherence to its core philosophy of "Quality, Service, Cleanliness, and Value" continues to lure millions of customers and to maintain the company's position as No. 1 in the industry. As Peters and Waterman put it, in exalting McDonald's as one of their "exemplar" companies, "McDonald's is above all, better at the basics."

It's true, also, that McDonald's had good reason to watch Burger King. Burger King noticed how McDonald's kept tight control over its franchisees, limiting each one to a very small number of stores so that none could get too powerful. When it began its own franchising effort in 1959, Burger King took the opposite tack, giving franchisees large territories, sometimes whole states, which promoted rapid expansion. Burger King also took aim at McDonald's with its "Have It Your Way" campaign, which kicked off in 1974. By claiming that "Special orders don't upset us," Burger King scored points against the regimented preparation of McDonald's burgers. By 1982, Burger King had clearly established itself as the No. 2 player, and it had McDonald's attention.

While focusing on its direct challenger, though, McDonald's was overlooking the peripheral, nontraditional competition. More specifically, it was forgetting that the hamburger is not the only possible fast food. Suddenly the fast-food landscape was cluttered with fried-chicken outlets. Taco Bells, pizza joints, and Chick-fil-A's. This last enterprise, with its appealing "Eat more chicken" ad campaign, epitomizes the nontraditional challenger. It comes out of left field into the formerly all-beef category; it offers a more contemporary, healthier alternative while beef is plateauing; and it doesn't mind jabbing the big players in the eye. It also maneuvers nimbly into places others haven't penetrated, like university food courts, shopping malls, and office buildings.

I should note that the McDonald's platform has always been to own its own real estate and lease it to its franchisees. It often acquired land at rock-bottom prices as a concession from local governments since it would likely draw additional commercial development to the same area. Until recently, McDonald's was the largest owner of commercial real estate. Niche players like Chick-fil-A couldn't afford to go that route; by necessity they leased other people's real estate—in airports, malls, and the like. Where consumer foot traffic is high, that can be an advantage. For McDonald's, wedded to the automobile culture, owning its own property became a double-edged sword.

Admittedly, with about 1,200 outlets, Chick-fil-A may not by itself constitute a direct threat to McDonald's, which has 31,000 stores in 100 countries. But when you add up the other serious "nonburger" competition—the KFCs, the Taco Bells, and the Pizza Huts—you do have a threat. And adding together these three big brands is exactly what Pepsi did when it spun off its fast-food acquisitions as TRICON ("three brand icons") in 1997.

Five years later, in 2002, TRICON added Long John Silver's and A&W Restaurants to its stable and changed its name to Yum! Brands. At this point, we can assume that McDonald's has noticed because Yum!, with 33,000 restaurants worldwide, is now No. 1 in total fast-food store locations. What's more, while McDonald's must feel pinched by what we might call the "share-of-stomach phenomenon," Yum! is actively capitalizing on giving consumers a choice. Its new strategy is "multibranded units," single locations where several Yum! Brands restaurants are available. Close to 3,000 such locations have been opened, and customer reaction has been highly favorable. In what is now a veritable smorgasbord of fast food, McDonald's single-minded focus on the threat from Burger King constitutes a serious case of competitive myopia.

Another area in which McDonald's is getting beaten up by its peripheral challengers is in the thinness of the margin on hamburgers. McDonald's only really high-margin offering is its Coke products. The total cost per serving for a soft drink is about a nickel, but the company charges close to a dollar (and includes lots of ice). Although they don't compare with the beverages, the French fries are also relatively high-margin. This explains the emphasis on "Value Meals," which include both. It's the same as the disposable camera scheme, in which the very inexpensive camera preloaded with film is the main attraction for the customer, but the profits are in the processing.

Meanwhile, the niche players are minding the margins on their main food, and nobody is doing it better than the pizza purveyors. The total cost of one pizza (including ingredients and preparation) is about a buck and a half. And think of the other ways the pizza business is driving out costs. Some are all-delivery, without the expense of leasing square feet for tables and chairs, and the delivery is jobbed out to kids driving their own cars who rely on tips more than salary. (It's for these reasons, certainly, that single-store independents—especially in college towns—continue to persist in the pizza business.)

Finally, while McDonald's focused on its burger-centric rivals, consumer tastes began to change. Greasy burgers on high-carb, white-bread buns fell from favor as a more health-conscious generation began to demand fresh salads and broiled chicken. Like giants we've seen in other industries, McDonald's was slow to respond to this trend, which offered an opening to niche players like Subway and the ever-innovative Wendy's.

McDonald's narrow view of the competition no doubt contributed to the company's downturn in 2000. After three straight quarters of declining profits, the company announced a major restructuring in 2001, slashing 700 corporate jobs and reorganizing its service regions. Those moves didn't seem to help. After cutting another 600 jobs and closing 175 underperforming stores, McDonald's reported its first quarterly loss ever at the end of 2002. Interestingly, though, in the midst of all this turmoil, McDonald's was engaged in a furious price war with traditional rival Burger King. Early in 2002, Burger King introduced a special menu of 11 items priced at 99 cents. McDonald's fired back with its own one-dollar menu. The irony was not lost on the business press. "Burger wars have broken out in the U.S.," the ***Knight Ridder Tribune*** reported, "but the first casualties seem to be the fast food chains themselves. In spite of fierce price competition, consumers seem to have lost their appetite for junk food stalwarts such as Burger King and McDonald's. Both experienced a downturn in trading this year."

McDonald's seems finally to be looking beyond the burger and bun, however. The chain is trying to win back its customers with healthier fare, including a line of premium salads and a promise to remove the trans fats from its cooking oil. Perhaps stung by the satirical film ***Supersize Me,*** the super-size French fries have been shelved. The company is also test-marketing espresso drinks, is planning to reintroduce the McCafe concept, and is working on a national rollout of premium coffees. This broad-based attempt to respond to the changing market and to evolve beyond the all-beef mentality appears to be producing results. Business began to turn around in 2003, and same-store sales surged 14% in 2004. The upward trend continued, and when the company posted first-quarter results for 2005, it noted that same-store sales had increased for 24 straight months, something the chain hadn't accomplished in 25 years. The company's profit for the last quarter in 2005 was up an impressive 53%, and revenue for the year was up 8%.

Given the intensity—and variety—of the fast-food competition, that's quite an achievement. Maybe McDonald's is myopic no more.

THE OPPOSITE SCENARIO: WHEN NO. 2 CHASES NO. 1

Perhaps this is the easiest route to competitive myopia: when you are No. 2 and gaining. If you have No. 1 in your crosshairs, if you are seen as the only viable challenger, it's only natural for you to focus all your competitive energies on the market leader, to the exclusion of everybody else.

TRYING HARDER

Hertz was the undisputed car rental pioneer and long remained the industry leader. Founded in 1918, it had already introduced a car rental charge card by 1926 and had established itself at Chicago's Midway Airport by 1932. It initiated the first "rent it here/leave it there" plan the following year. When Avis came along three decades later, what could it do but "try harder"?

The campaign built around "trying harder because we have to," a slogan that somehow found virtue in being No. 2, is now 40 years old. Robert Salerno, currently CEO of Cendant Car Rental Group, Avis's parent, came to Avis 20 years after the campaign's debut. He says he is "still in awe of a campaign that broke every rule in the book and is credited with the company's overnight profit improvement in 1963." The campaign worked, says Salerno, because "we were No. 2 [and] we said it, and our honesty resonated with every customer and business owner who had ever felt like the underdog."

While Avis was trying harder to catch industry leader Hertz, and while both companies were competing for the business of the air-traveling executive, neither paid much attention to the emergence of Budget. Budget didn't try harder; it tried something different. It saw a new market for car rentals: the vacationing family, or tourists who want to drive to a variety of destinations. To tap this market, it created a new concept: unlimited mileage. Mileage hadn't mattered to the traveling executive, who picks up his car at the airport, drives it to the conference downtown, and returns it to the airport. But Budget saw that the "pleasure market," especially among vacationers in hotspots like Florida and California, could be bigger than the business market, and it went after it.

Now under the Cendant umbrella, Budget is in a virtual tie with Avis in terms of total U.S. locations and annual revenue. But here's the odd thing: They are not tied for No. 2. More surprising. Hertz is no longer No. 1. Budget succeeded in making the other big players aware of the leisure market, but there was still another market—the biggest one yet—that all had failed to see. As ***Fortune*** explained it, while Hertz, Avis, and Budget "were cutting one another's throats to win a point or two of the 'suits and shorts' market from business and vacation travelers at airports. Enterprise invaded the hinterlands with a completely different strategy." A strategy so brilliant, in fact, that in a little over 40 years, Enterprise has blown past everybody else in the industry. What is this strategy? To provide a spare car for the family. If your car has broken down, or if you've been in an accident and your car has to sit in the body shop for a few days, or if it is at the dealership for routine maintenance, you're in Enterprise's hands. A few decades ago, your spouse might have ferried you about. But now your spouse works, too and can't serve as your chauffeur. This is the point of the "We pick you up" campaign. Focused on each other and on the traditional markets, Hertz and Avis and Budget missed this yawning ocean of opportunity.

Of late, Enterprise has been eyeing a share of the airport market too, but its great innovation was to be everywhere else. Instead of massing its fleet at the major airports, it opened cheap storefronts in strip malls across the land. Andy Taylor, current CEO and son of the company's founder, likes to boast that "90% of the American population lives within 15 minutes of an Enterprise office." When Enterprise staffers aren't behind the desk, they are out making friends with local body shop owners, tow truck operators, and car dealers. As a result, word-of-mouth business is a mainstay. Taylor can't see the business slowing down because, increasingly, people are renting from Enterprise even when their own car is running fine. This includes the small-businessman who needs a car better than his own to pick up clients, or people who don't trust, or who simply prefer not to use, the family car. In such cases, he says, Enterprise supplies the "virtual car."

It's astounding. As of 2005, Enterprise's total fleet numbered more than 600,000 vehicles, nearly twice as many as Hertz, and it has also taken a sizable lead in total revenues. As long as it keeps opening more than 400 new locations a year, as it has done every year since 2000, its market share growth is not likely to slow.

As for Avis, it may have tried harder, but it clearly suffered from the competitive myopia that seems to afflict the big players in so many industries. Once again the industry leaders were put to flight by an outsider that, instead of focusing narrowly on the competition, was focused on an innovative strategy.

THE WARNING SIGNS OF COMPETITIVE MYOPIA

How do you know you have become myopic? Not surprisingly, with a habit so easy to fall into, there are several symptoms to watch out for.

YOU ALLOW SMALL NICHE PLAYERS TO COEXIST WITH YOU

Because you're focused on the big guys, you don't see the niche companies as a threat. This isn't a matter of arrogance or denial; you simply don't believe these guys are a viable challenge. They're too small, they don't have the capabilities or resources, and they're not even really in your category. Besides, you believe coexistence is working for you, as we see in the example of Sears and The Limited.

Sears looked into the future and saw automobiles and highways. It helped shape that future by building shopping centers along those highways—shopping centers it would anchor. It was a beautiful vision, but maintaining a shopping center's infrastructure is an expensive proposition. Therefore, Sears invited the specialty retailers to come in to help defray those fixed costs—people like The Limited. Sears' competition was other big department stores; it didn't see The Limited as a threat.

Now, it was The Limited's turn to see the future. When Leslie Wexner opened the first Limited store in Columbus, Ohio, in 1963, his ambition—from which the store took its name—was limited. He wanted to do one product line well: moderately priced fashionable clothing for young women. By 1976, The Limited had 100 outlets (most in suburban malls), and it was becoming clear that demographics were on Wexner's side. He had tapped into a customer base—young professional women—that was expanding fast. Meanwhile, the target market for Sears' female clothing—the traditional middle-class housewife—was shrinking as more and more women headed into the workplace. Sears was slow to recognize this trend.

The "limited" concept worked. The chain went after women from 18 to 30—women who had been or were going to college, women who needed stylish clothes to wear to work, women whose view of life was broader than the "husband/breadwinner, wife/homemaker" model. The Limited took the concept a step further by hiring saleswomen who looked like the clientele—young, stylish, professional-looking. They even sold a limited range of sizes.

Next, The Limited expanded the boundaries of its market by buying or creating additional brands. To cater to young teens, it created Express in 1980. For larger women, it acquired Lane Bryant in 1982. For more budget-minded young women, it bought The Lerner Stores in 1985, and Limited Too, for girls, opened in 1988. To cover the lingerie segment, it bought the catalog company Victoria's Secret and took it retail. By this point, its clout was such that it could dictate that its various stores be grouped close to one another in the mall. There was no longer any reason for women to buy clothing in the department store. As a mall executive in Chicago told ***Crain's Chicago Business,*** "One by one, store by store, Les Wexner is redefining what used to be the department store business."

By the mid-1990s. The Limited's great run had slowed, and its strategy shifted from expansion to contraction. It spun off some brands (Victoria's Secret, Limited Too), sold some others (Abercrombie & Fitch, Lane Bryant, Lerner), and closed some stores. But the specialty retailing revolution was complete. With respect to Sears, The Limited had killed the women's clothing category.

Moreover, letting the niche players into its malls hurt Sears in some other product categories, too. A particularly good example is shoes because the story has an ironic twist. As Sears thrived on the suburban mall phenomenon, its one-time competitor, Woolworth, collapsed. Sears must have snickered to see the demise of the old five-and-dime, shackled to its decaying downtown location near the abandoned train station. But Woolworth wasn't quite done yet. It took the advice offered in the preceding chapter and shifted its competency to a related business—specialty retailing. It milked the Woolworth brand and invested the returns in the shoe business, first by buying Kinney and then, spectacularly, by introducing Foot Locker. It helped create the now-huge athletic shoe category.

So picture Sears, locked into its department store model. Within it is the family shoe center—a generalist enterprise selling shoes for men and women, dress and casual, sandals and sneakers. Athletic shoes are a small part of the business, so Sears isn't worried about Foot Locker. But then Foot Locker branched out with Lady Foot Locker and Kids Foot Locker, and at the same time everybody in the world started buying sports-type shoes to walk around in. Nobody would buy these shoes at Sears. Another category had been killed by the specialty guys.

The same thing happened with toys when Toys R Us arrived—not inside the mall but on the mall property. The department store lost another category. (Now Walmart's strategy—standing alone in its great big box—makes penetrating sense. If you're in any category that Walmart's in, you won't get on the property.)

YOUR SUPPLIER'S LOYALTY IS WON BY A NONTRADITIONAL COMPETITOR

Failing to realize that your supplier can become your competitor is another sign of competitive nearsightedness. Let's say that you're so focused on your immediate competition that you seek an edge by squeezing your supplier on price. You think you can get away with it because you're a big customer. But you've been taking your supplier's loyalty for granted, and now that supplier says, "Wait a minute. I don't like what you're doing to me. I'll sell my capacity to somebody else." Suddenly your supplier has become your competitor. (In his valuable book ***Competitive Strategy,*** Michael Porter makes the important point that the direct competition among the major players is but one of the five "competitive forces" driving any industry. The others are the bargaining power of suppliers, the bargaining power of buyers, the threat of new entrants, and the threat of substitute products or services.)

Again, the lesson is that we must have a broad, peripheral view of the competition. If we're in the retail business, our suppliers aren't looking to compete there. They don't want to start retailing. But what they do with their capacity is a "competitive force" that we need to be aware of. As an example, let's look at what happened to the relationship between Procter & Gamble, the supplier, and the supermarkets that had traditionally been the company's biggest customers.

What happened to that relationship is, in a word, Walmart. The supermarkets never saw it coming. They conceived of Walmart as a dry-goods store—textiles, clothing, home furnishings—and failed to foresee Walmart's expansion of its product lines. They also failed to note the growing alliance between their favorite supplier and the world's No. 1 retailer. Supermarkets didn't understand that "general merchandizers" could become their competition, but it has happened—big time. In 1990, Walmart did $500 million worth of business with P&G; 15 years later that business was worth more than $10 billion a year, and an amazing 18% of P&G's product was going to the behemoth from Bentonville, Arkansas.

As early as 1992, the supermarkets should have been feeling this "competitive force." P&G's ability to divert a growing share of its capacity to Walmart allowed it to force "everyday low pricing" on its supermarket customers, at the same time slashing the discounts it had used to persuade the grocery chains to stock up on its brands. The supermarkets weren't happy. The lower prices for P&G products cut into sales of their more profitable private labels, and the loss of P&G's discounts was a huge blow. But what could they do? With Walmart standing by, the stores' threat to stop carrying P&G lines was empty, and they couldn't afford to do that anyway. According to industry figures at the time, P&G supplied grocery stores with products in 44 different categories, and its brands were No. 1 or No. 2 in a remarkable 32 of those categories. The irony, of course, is that P&G learned "everyday low pricing" from Walmart, which had no private labels to protect and which didn't demand the big supplier discounts. Instead, Walmart had volume.

In 1997, P&G curtailed its long-standing policy of taking back damaged or discontinued items from its supermarket customers. Instead, it mandated "no more returns" and began issuing lump quarterly payments to cover the cost of damaged shipments. The move seemed designed to bring a Walmart-like efficiency to the order-and-distribution process. The payments figured to benefit retailers with the smoothest operations and to hurt those with sloppy ordering and handling systems. Regardless, the point is that P&G, the supplier, was in a position to dictate terms to the supermarkets.

We might add that although supermarkets are getting pinched from above by "the bargaining power of suppliers" like P&G, they are also getting sucker punched by the nontraditional competitors entering the arena. In early 2003, Walmart announced plans to open its first grocery supercenter in California and to build 39 more in the state within five years. Ralphs, Vons, and Albertsons, the largest grocery chains in California, were not thrilled with the news. After all, Walmart was already credited with helping shove a dozen national supermarket chains into bankruptcy within the previous decade. In the very few years since it expanded into the grocery business, the Walmart juggernaut had already surged to become No. 1 in the category, with 19% of the nation's grocery sales. If it adhered to its five-year plan to open 1,000 new supercenters nationwide, industry projections saw that 19% share growing to 35% of the domestic food market.

In retrospect, could the supermarkets have done anything to hold onto P&G's loyalty? They might have done more to support P&G's brands, but their huge investment in their own store brands would have made that difficult. They might have reduced the fees they charged for shelf space, but Walmart, the hungry new entrant, no doubt would have been willing to go lower. The lesson is that by the time they recognized the full dimensions of the competitive arena, not many good options were left.

A similar phenomenon took place when appliance manufacturers started to shift their capacity away from department stores like Sears and JCPenney to Home Depot and Lowe's. From the narrow competitive perspective of the department stores, stores such as Home Depot and Lowe's were "plywood guys," just overgrown building supply stores. So their entry went unnoticed—until the threat became all too real.

This syndrome is most prevalent in retailing, but we can find examples in manufacturing, too. IBM, for example, created two key suppliers, Microsoft and Intel, and assumed that all that capacity would keep flowing in its direction while it focused on direct competitors like HP and Compaq. Then out of nowhere came young entrepreneur Michael Dell. Dell created a new paradigm in the computer business, and both Microsoft and Intel, which had about as much loyalty as arms merchants, diverted their capacity his way. Dell became No. 1 as a result. Again, the real competitive threat for IBM was the possibility that its suppliers would take their capacity elsewhere.

YOUR CUSTOMER'S (OR CHANNEL PARTNER'S) STRATEGY SHIFTS FROM BUY TO MAKE

Here, competition comes from the customer rather than the supplier, but it's not just that your customer's loyalty is shifting. As I see this scenario, the real danger is when your customer moves upstream and starts to make the product.

The classic example is American Express, with its formerly prestigious credit card and traveler's checks. (By the way, American Express's traveler's check business was great while it lasted. Think of it: You give me your money up front. I give you a promissory note, which you may or may not redeem. Meanwhile, I take your money and loan it out. To you! On your credit card! This is what you call a highly synergistic business.)

American Express did an admirable job of destroying the old Diner's Club and Carte Blanche card businesses. In the first place, it invested massively in mainframe technology and compiled a tremendous database. In that one move, it basically left the old players behind. Then, too, the company figured out that the executive market (the target for all the early card companies) spends money not only on dining, but also on air travel and hotels, so it pushed this aspect of the business. And as if that weren't enough, the company also created a number of memorable, and highly effective, advertising campaigns (like "Do you know me?" and "Don't leave home without it").

The point to keep in mind, however, is that American Express's real customers were banks. Traveler's checks were sold through banks, and all the card processing—from the merchants that accepted the card—went through banks. In fact, these merchants—with their small and medium-sized enterprises (SMEs) like car dealerships, restaurants, and shops—constitute a huge bloc of bank customers.

Perhaps inevitably, banks finally decided to get in on the credit card business. First, on the West Coast, came Visa from Bank of America, which recruited other banks to cooperate. On the East Coast, Citibank brought out MasterCard, also with the participation of other banks. Soon the participating networks grew so wide that both cards became virtually universal. Today, even the executive customer, who formerly would have embodied the prestige and clout of the American Express cardholder, has lots of other attractive choices. And he doesn't want to pay American Express's high fees.

In this way American Express's customers moved upstream and directly into the competitive arena. American Express fought back, with some success, by coming out with the corporate card. Of course, this strategy was designed to get the card in the hands of all of a company's employees, and Ameriean Express sweetened the deal by offering to monitor and classify all the charges. This was a real value-added service, and American Express had the computer system to do it. Next the company offered treasury management—in other words, it would take care of all of the client's cash on hand. Here, obviously, American Express was striking back by offering not just card services but banking services. If the banks could compete in the credit card business, American Express could respond in kind.

Visa and MasterCard went for the jugular by offering lower fees to merchants that accepted their cards. This explains the proliferation of establishments—especially SMEs—where American Express is not accepted. The proprietors don't want to pay American Express's higher percentage (a situation that Visa has been eager to capitalize on in its aggressive advertising). Also while Visa and MasterCard charged merchants lower fees, they allowed card users to pay a "monthly minimum" instead of paying off their entire balance—which had been American Express's practice. This seeming convenience for consumers expanded the cards' popularity among the credit-loving middle class, even while interest charges became a huge profit center for the card companies. To stay in the game, American Express introduced Optima, its first revolving-credit card, in 1987.

As cut-throat competition has brought thinning margins to the credit card business, American Express has survived through adaptation and diversification. It has become more like a full-service financial institution (even offering online mortgage and brokerage services), and its card services are now less distinguishable from those of its rivals. Ironically, even Citigroup now distributes American Express cards.

Ultimately, while its erstwhile customers morphed into competitors, American Express itself mutated to fully answer the challenge.

YOU UNDERESTIMATE NEW ENTRANTS, ESPECIALLY FROM EMERGING ECONOMIES

New entrants threaten to force their way into virtually every industry, but your myopia is apparent when you fail to acknowledge this threat. You have a natural tendency to focus on the existing competition, and if you're one of the big players, you may also have a touch of arrogance. In any case, the last thing you're worried about is a new player from an emerging nation.

Sony, for example, had plenty of direct competition to worry about. Coming from outside the old keiretsu organization of "blessed" companies, it had to first take on its big Japanese rivals like Matsushita, Hitachi, and Sharp. Expanding into Europe, it faced established rivals like Thomson and Philips. In America, Zenith and GE awaited. As it stormed into the global marketplace and became one of the best-known brands in the world, perhaps Sony could be forgiven for failing to look back over its shoulder at humble Korea.

Even if it had looked over its shoulder, it might have had trouble discerning Samsung, which had its origins in milling rice and trading dried fish. Its entry into the electronics industry in 1969 was similarly unassuming. It simply disassembled Western-designed TVs, VCRs, and microwave ovens and figured out how to manufacture them cheaply. It didn't even bother to assert its own brand, but rather sold to Western manufacturers like GE and retailers like Sears. But in the mid-1990s, chairman Lee Kun Hee, the founder's son, decided to transform Samsung from a low-end manufacturer to a high-end brand, and suddenly the game was on.

"We want to beat Sony," declared Eric Kim, Samsung's global marketing head, in 2001. "Sony has the strongest brand awareness; we want to be stronger than Sony by 2005." Company leaders figured that the digital revolution would give it the opportunity. Already the world leader in the production of DRAM memory chips (ironically, including those used in Sony's PlayStation 2), Samsung rolled out a huge effort to establish itself as the "digit-all" company—the maker of innovative, appealing, and affordable chip-based electronic gadgetry. Still a technology borrower, it would emphasize design. By 2001 its MP3 players, digital cameras, and flat-screen monitors were already winning awards.

Eric Kim's dream was realized a year early. Although perhaps it still wasn't a more recognized brand, by the end of 2004 Samsung had become the world's most profitable consumer electronics company, leading the global market in color TVs, VCRs, liquid- crystal displays, and digital memory devices. It was second only to Nokia in cell phones and was closing fast on Sony in DVDs. In addition to cutting-edge design, it added another element to its digital-age strategy: speed. The company's ***modus operandi*** is to pounce on new technology, immediately improve upon it, and then pour out more products faster than anyone else. "Even expensive fish becomes cheap in a day or two," CEO Yun Jong Yong explain to ***Newsweek.*** "For both sashimi shops and the digital industry, inventory is detrimental. Speed is everything." For example, although Samsung didn't invent the cell phone, it introduces 100 new models a year, compared to Nokia's two dozen.

Sony's business model was geared to an earlier age, when it could introduce a big-splash item like the Walkman every few years and gradually bring down the price as the market widened. Samsung, as ***Newsweek*** points out, is the master of the new age, wherein "companies need to bring out a constant stream of new products that sell immediately at high volume for a relatively low price, [then] are quickly displaced by the next new thing."

With Samsung earning a record 12 billion in 2004 and eclipsing its archrival in total stock market value, Sony would have to concede that "made in Korea" had a whole new meaning.

Another global giant that runs the risk of being blindsided by competition from an emerging economy is France's Lafarge S.A., the world's biggest cement maker. Not that the 170-year-old company is doddering about in its old age. On the contrary, since 1970 it has been expanding steadily. It raised a formidable profile in North America with the acquisitions of Canada Cement and General Portland, and in the last 15 years it has seen its operations expand from 12 countries to 70. It bought India-based Tisco's cement plants in 1999 and moved into China by purchasing a stake in Chongqing Cement in 2003.

But when its huge plant in Indonesia was destroyed by the 2004 tsunami, what company hustled to ship product and gain market share? Not Lafarge's traditional European rivals like Heidelberg Cement and Holcim from Switzerland, but rather CEMEX from Mexico. By 1976, CEMEX had become Mexico's largest cement maker, but its international visibility remained low until Lorenzo Zambrano, the founder's grandson, took over in 1985. Zambrano grew the company through a steady stream of acquisitions in South and Central America, and by 1996 it had become No. 3 in the world. It acquired big U.S. producer Southdown for ***$2.8*** billion in 2000, but its boldest move was yet to come. In 2005, CEMEX made a stunning move into Europe with the purchase of U.K. giant RMC group for ***$5.8*** billion. The deal not only made CEMEX the No. 2 cement maker in the world; it threw the gauntlet at Lafarge's feet by making Europe CEMEX's largest market.

WHEN YOU HAVE BECOME HELPLESS AGAINST A SUBSTITUTE TECHNOLOGY

It's a threat that's always there. Perhaps we discern it in time to adapt, change strategy, or roll out the next-generation technology. But if we suffer from competitive myopia, we might throw up our hands and surrender.

The preceding chapter discussed Kodak's struggle to catch up to an industry that changed beneath its feet. Did it wait too long before committing itself to the digital revolution? Its massive infusion of capital and technical know-how may have come just in time. In any case, what a perfect example of an industry being roiled by the emergence of a new or "substitute" technology!

Perhaps an even better one is the revolution taking place in the telecom industry. The Baby Bells must have thought halcyon days had arrived when regulators permitted them to move into Ma Bell's long-distance franchise. But then came the cell phone, which, depending on your calling plan, makes no distinction between local and long distance. Take recent figures from Qwest as one example. For the second quarter of 2005, the company reported a net loss of $164 million. The only good news there is that it was much less than the $776 million it lost a year earlier. The losses are not a mystery. People are giving up their land lines—a trend abetted by two recent FGG rulings. The first allowed consumers to switch wireless providers without having to change phone numbers. The second, a keener blow to the traditional industry, allows land-line customers to switch to wireless and still keep their same number. Now the Baby Bells are scrambling like crazy to get into the cell phone business—often by acquiring or merging with an established provider.

But once their cell phone business is up and running, the phone companies' problems won't be over. Now there's VoIP. It's the cheapest communication platform yet, and start-ups are offering the service at 30% less than standard land-line rates. It also drastically reduces the size of the provider's employee roster. Vonage, out of New Jersey, offers VoIP to 70,000 customers for $24.99 a month, and it does so with only 220 employees.

Now all the Baby Bells are scrambling again. Qwest, Verizon, SBC, and BellSouth all have announced plans to roll out VoIP service. "The large phone companies would be stupid not to," as one telecom analyst told the ***Wall Street Journal.***

It's "the latest example of how quickly a new technology can help reshape an industry," says the journal. Indeed, the change seems to have come in the blink of an eye. All of a sudden, if you're in the land-line business, you're out of business.

HOW TO BREAK THE COMPETITIVE MYOPIA HABIT

The signs are there. You've been focused on your direct competitors, so you've ignored peripheral challengers and, more important, the whole industry. You've been nearsighted, and now you're losing market share. You've failed to acknowledge and adapt to the full range of competitive forces shaping your industry's landscape. How do you open your eyes and see the whole picture? Here are some suggestions.

REDEFINE THE COMPETITIVE LANDSCAPE

You have finally understood, perhaps after the sudden erosion of your position, that you need to broaden your definition of competition. You need to check the entire perimeter and see where you are vulnerable. IBM offers a case in point.

As you've seen, Big Blue made the smart move downstream and reinvented itself as a services company. But that move created a new problem: it changed the competitive landscape. Because it was a "big box" company, IBM's competitors had been the other domestic manufacturers. Because of the huge capital investment necessary to become a player, IBM hadn't had to worry about any threat from emerging nations. But in the services business, things were very different. A huge challenge from India appeared on the horizon, and IBM had to refocus. The tech consulting firm

Infosys, for example, now has operations in 15 countries, including North America, which accounts for 65% of its sales. TCS (Tata Consultancy Services, part of the Tata Group) is another fast-grower, now operating in 30 countries and continuing to expand through acquisition. Then there's Wipro Technologies, the consulting division of Wipro Limited, with offices in 35 nations. It is doing a vigorous business with U.S. companies looking to reduce costs through outsourcing. These and others have moved to the front line in the industry, challenging IBM for key customers on its own turf.

To its credit, IBM has not simply acknowledged the threat; it has decided to counterattack by establishing a massive presence in India. Part of its strategy is to decimate the leadership of the Indian firms by luring away their senior executives. Big Blue has also started recruiting in India, offering higher wages to new college graduates and entry-level technicians and engineers. IBM keeps these new recruits at its offices in India, where wages are lower than for comparable positions in the U.S. but are higher than those typically paid by Indian firms. In this way, IBM is squeezing the margins of the Indian competitors since they'll be pressured to raise wages too. Finally, IBM is going after India-based customers. In India as elsewhere, the government is usually the biggest client, and IBM is now aggressively bidding on Indian government contracts. As IBM redefines the competitive landscape, the other big American players in the industry—EDS, Accenture, Oracle, and others—are following suit.

Of course, not all nontraditional challengers come from emerging economies. Home Depot's growing awareness of Walmart, Hertz's recognition of Enterprise, Cadillac's acknowledgment of the threat from German and Japanese luxury carmakers—all these illustrate the necessity of redefining the competitive landscape.

BROADEN THE SCOPE OF YOUR PRODUCT OR MARKET

When you maintain your existing products in your existing markets, your basic strategy is entrenchment. But beating the competition will probably require a more aggressive strategy. You can expand the market for your existing products, or, conversely, you can expand your product lines in your existing markets. The ultimate option is to diversify—to offer new products you haven't sold before in markets you haven't been in before.

HSBC (Hong Kong & Shanghai Banking Corporation) shows how to enlarge your competitive vision by broadening the scope of your products and markets. Founded in 1865 to finance the growing trade, in opium, silk, and tea between Great Britain and Asia, the bank remained focused on the import-export business until fairly recently. But the changes that shook up the banking industry over the past couple of decades—deregulation, globalization, megamergers—convinced HSBC that it would have to evolve and expand to survive. Rather than being a bank for international trade, it would have to become a "universal" bank.

Its first big move was to purchase Midland, Britain's third-largest bank, in 1992. The acquisition broadened HSBC product lines to include corporate and consumer banking. The next step was into consumer finance, with the huge $14.8 billion takeover of Household International (formerly Household Finance) in 2003. The move pushed HSBC into the thick of the consimier credit card business while greatly expanding its U.S. operations. A year later it bought a 20% stake in China's state-owned Bank of Communications, the largest-ever foreign investment in a Chinese bank. That same year, 2004, it set its sights on Iraq's commercial and investment bank Dar Es Salaam, hoping to become the first foreign bank in Iraq since Saddam Hussein expelled all foreign financial institutions 35 years earlier. Of the full range of banking services, it remains weakest in investment banking, but it is moving to shore up that division. As of 2004, it had hired 700 investment specialists, and rumors were circulating that HSBC was lusting to acquire a big U.S. player like Morgan Stanley.

By whatever measure, the bank's progress has been remarkable as it transformed itself from a staid trade bank into a bold global player. It now has 9,800 offices in 80 countries throughout the world, offering consumer and commercial banking, credit card services, asset management, private banking, securities trading, and insurance, along with its growing investment banking business. No wonder that in 2004, ***The Banker*** named HSBC "Global Bank of the Year" for the third year in a row, and ***Euromoney*** cited it as "World's Best Bank."

CONSOLIDATE TO SQUEEZE OUT EXCESS CAPACITY

This has been a key strategy in the airline industry, especially among the European carriers. A perfect example is Air France's acquisition of Dutch airline KLM in 2004. The move benefited Air France in two ways. First, it vaulted the French carrier past British Airways and into the No. 1 position in Europe. Perhaps more important, it squeezed excess capacity out of the industry. Too much capacity, by increasing buyers' bargaining power, itself becomes a force of competition. Having too many flights between the same destinations, too many available seats, drives down prices and heats up competition. Consolidation reduces capacity. Between them, Air France and KLM might have had 20 flights a day between Paris and Amsterdam. The merged company, obviously, can cut the number of flights and increase the number of ticket holders on each one. Air France has also moved to consolidate the domestic market by buying regional carriers like Proteus Airlines and Flandre Air.

This story was repeated with Lufthansa's acquisition of Swissair in early 2005. The German company strengthened its hold on the No. 3 position in Europe while, again, reducing capacity in the highly competitive industry. As an indication of how fierce the rivalry is, as soon as the merger is completed (in 2007, according to predictions), Lufthansa will carry about 60 million passengers a year, compared to Air France's 65 million. In the meantime, British Airways is said to be looking for a European partner and has been seen holding hands with Spanish carrier Iberia.

COUNTERATTACK THE NONTRADITIONAL COMPETITORS

You've seen how IBM pursued this strategy in India, but the appliance industry offers another example. Confirming the "rule of three," the U.S. appliance industry had come to be dominated by No. 1 Whirlpool, No. 2 GE, and No. 3 White Consolidated.

White Consolidated was cobbled together in the 1960s and 1970s from appliance makers that had fallen out of the race when Whirlpool and GE battled for market share. Edward Reddig, the CEO of the old White Sewing Machine Co., bought up Gibson, Kelvinator, the appliance division of Westinghouse, and Frigidaire, among others. and "consolidated" these "white goods" brands into the third-largest U.S. appliance maker.

That was how the U.S. industry stood when, in 1986, Electrolux, the world-famous vacuum cleaner company, swept across the Atlantic from Sweden. Thanks to a string of acquisitions starting in the 1970s, Electrolux had already expanded from vacuum cleaners to a full line of appliances and had assumed the mantle of No. 1 in the European industry. Now it wanted to go global; more specifically, it wanted to move aggressively into the U.S. market with a major acquisition. This Viking-like raid culminated with the successful purchase of White Consolidated. Suddenly Electrolux was not just the European leader but the world's No. 1 producer of household appliances. White Consolidated had remained a relatively weak challenger to Whirlpool and GE, but Electrolux's clear ambition was to gain U.S. market share.

Given the unlooked-for attack from Europe, Whirlpool had no choice but to counterattack. Responding in kind, it fired back across the Atlantic and formed Whirlpool Europe, a joint venture with Philips Electronics, in 1989. By 1991, the joint venture had become a buyout, and Whirlpool was suddenly Europe's No. 2 appliance maker (stronger than Electrolux's No. 3 position in America). It now shared with Electrolux the position of world leader, and, more important, it effectively met the challenge of Electrolux's global aggression.

REFOCUS ON THE CORE BUSINESS

This "entrenchment" strategy may sound counterintuitive, but it can be very effective. When companies diversify, they often lose management bandwidth, and instead of redefining the competitive arena, they sometimes fragment it. Beatrice Foods is a classic example, as was GE under Reginald Jones.

Some of the huge Indian conglomerates, after decades of diversification, are now also moving toward retrenchment. Aditya Birla Group (ABG) is now returning to the basics of textile fibers, carbon black, and cement. Its Indian Rayon division, for example, reported increased profits and improved operations once it dumped its stake in Indo Gulf Fertilizers. Mahindra & Mahindra is refocusing on its core business, big time, with the announcement of its plans to become the world's largest tractor. But perhaps the best example is India's largest industrial conglomerate, the Tata Group. Pursuing an overall strategy of divesting non-core businesses, Tata has shed its businesses in the toiletries and cosmetics, cement, oil, pharmaceuticals, and paint industries, and it sold its stake in Tata Honeywell to Honeywell International. Much as Jack Welch did at GE, is working on refocusing the company on its areas of strength—like tea, steel, autos, telecom, energy, and information technology.

In conclusion, if your problem is myopia, your solution is better vision. As so many of these stories illustrate, to focus on your one or two strongest and most direct competitors is—like many self-destructive habits—a strong temptation. Similarly, performing well against your industry's big benchmarks is gratifying, reassuring; it makes you feel good. But if you don't constantly check the periphery as well, danger lurks.

It's imperative to be aware—not just of your immediate competitors, but all the other forces of competition as well—your suppliers' capacity, the possibility that your customers might move upstream, the threat posed by new or nontraditional players, and the ever-present danger that new technologies might leave you behind the curve.

A thorough familiarity with every feature of the competitive landscape is the surest cure for your myopia. Walk the full perimeter of your industry every day.

COMPETITIVE MYOPIA

Things that lead to competitive myopia:

- The natural evolution of the industry
- The clustering phenomenon
- When No. 1 is also the pioneer
- The opposite scenario: when No. 2 chases No. 1

The warning signs of competitive myopia:

- **You allow small niche players to coexist with you:** You're focused on the big guys, so you don't see the niche companies as a threat.
- **Your supplier's loyalty is won by a nontraditional competitor:** You fail to realize that your supplier can become your competitor.
- **You underestimate new entrants, especially from emerging economies:** You fail to acknowledge the threat of new entrants.
- **You have become helpless against a substitute technology:** The threat has always been there, but you have not reacted in time and must surrender.

How to break the competitive myopia habit:

- **Redefine the competitive landscape:** You need to check the entire competitive perimeter to see where you are vulnerable.
- **Broaden the scope of your product or market:** Diversify by expanding the market for your existing products or by expanding your product lines in your existing markets.
- **Consolidate to squeeze out excess capacity:** Decrease buyers' bargaining power by removing excess capacity from the industry.
- **Counterattack the nontraditional competitors:** Return fire on a unique competitor by attacking its home turf.
- **Refocus on the core business:** This "entrenchment" strategy may seem counterintuitive, but it allows you to concentrate limited resources in your most successful area.

CHAPTER

7

VOLUME OBSESSION: RISING COSTS AND FALLING MARGINS

Perhaps a more businesslike term for this self-destructive habit would be "cost inefficiency." But it comes to the same thing: Your costs are too high for the revenue you're generating, or, in the simplest formulation, you're spending too much money to make money. In a non-monopoly situation, this occurs when prices have crashed due to intense competition or excess industry capacity, but your costs remain the same.

Like most of our self-destructive habits, this one usually seems to be a by-product of growth. The human analog would go like this: After I am past my "growth spurt," I stop burning my calories productively, and I end up storing unused fat in my body. I'm using my energy less efficiently. Athletes offer an even better illustration. During their active careers, they are paragons of health. They consume huge numbers of calories but, in a model of efficiency, burn them off to achieve peak performance. However, when they retire, they often continue to take in excess calories but no longer burn them. What had been a necessary component in an efficient cycle has become a self-destmctive habit—and sometimes a dangerous one, given how quickly some athletes deteriorate. In any case, the syndrome is the same for the mature corporation and the over-the-hill human body: consuming too much and producing too little.

The myriad "restructurings" that provide constant fodder for the business press make it clear that this unhealthy imbalance between costs and revenue is a widespread problem—one confronted sooner or later by businesses big and small. But why is this? Why does a company's cost structure get out of whack? Let's examine a few typical scenarios in which the cost/revenue ratio moves implacably into the danger zone.

THE HIGH-MARGIN PIONEER

As we've noted, business and industry here in the United States are influenced by the Germanic predisposition in favor of science and invention. Our giants, our icons, have been those who have made the discoveries that sparked new industries, like Alexander Graham Bell. Or those who have implemented new processes (Henry Ford and the assembly line) or invented products (John Pemberton, who mixed the first Coca-Cola) that permanently altered the business landscape. The pioneers who create new industries or new product categories, whether soft drinks or personal computers, comprise a kind of royalty, and certain perquisites come with that exalted status.

The perk I have in mind here, as you might guess, is the prerogative to charge high prices. In effect, you have a monopoly; you have a one-of-a-kind product. You don't have competitors forcing you into a price war. Your product is filling a need (or fulfilling a desire) in a way that no other product has done before, so you can charge what you want. Consequently, you build your cost structure based on a high-margin business.

Your costs are high anyway. You're building an infrastructure, hiring personnel. You need everything. It's like building your own house. It seems like you'll never stop writing checks. Plus, your capacity is limited, so your per-unit costs are also unusually high. But all this is okay because your margins are even higher.

What happens? As the industry you created begins to mature, here comes the competition, undercutting your price. You're forced to bring down your own prices and make up for it in increased volume. You expand your capacity (in effect becoming your own competitor since capacity determines price). But expansion itself is costly, and you find that your costs are not declining as rapidly as the price of your product in the marketplace. Your margins are collapsing while your cost structure remains relatively high.

Ultimately, you have to face a new truth: you are not in a high-margin business anymore. In the beginning, when you were the pioneer, the monopolist, your cost structure made sense. But your industry has grown up around you, and now you're being squeezed. This is often the fate of the pioneer firm. Once again, success breeds failure. It's a tough situation to confront. You're the creator. You want to assert some proprietary rights. It's hard to admit that you no longer have any. For a great illustration of this scenario, consider IBM's PC business.

IBM VERSUS LENOVO

When IBM introduced its "Personal Computer" model in 1981, it was a revolutionary machine. It also proved to be a runaway hit with businesses, which were eager to take advantage of its unprecedented mix of power, features, and affordability. The IBM Personal Computer was a financial boon to IBM, which sold 500,000 of the machines in the first two years at a substantial profit margin. Since then, of course, PC margins have collapsed. IBM licensed the PC architecture to the world ("IBM-compatible"), and alternative manufacturers have come in. The interesting thing is, despite capacity expansion and presumed economies of scale, costs have not dramatically declined. A study conducted by Boston Consulting Group tells us why. It turns out that in the operations of three industry leaders—IBM, Compaq, and HP—the total value added in the factory was only 11%, 89% of costs came from procurement, and of that 89%, 79% went to two vendors, Intel and Microsoft. There's no way that the meager 11% of value could create enough margin to support the business. It's way below the threshold of survival.

The assumption was that the more downstream work you do—in assembly or manufacturing—the more value you add, and the more margin you create. In this case, with Intel and Microsoft laughing all the way to the bank, that assumption proved false. Now we understand why IBM, the pioneer, finally waved the white flag.

In fact, when IBM finalized the $1.75 billion sale of its PC unit to China's Lenovo in early 2005, a startling fact came to light. The IBM unit had been losing money at least since 2001, with the red ink totaling $965 million over the three years prior to the sale. Again, this was the pioneer, the company credited with creating the corporate market for the personal computer. But when the margins collapse in your high-margin business, you're out of business.

The question is not why IBM sold, but rather why Lenovo would be tempted to buy. Well, to get IBM's name (for five years); to get IBM's customer base, and thus to catapult itself into IBM's place as the world's No. 3 PC maker; and to gain the cachet of being a global player. But the tough question still exists: if IBM couldn't make money in the PC business, why will Lenovo be able to? The company's investors clearly had their doubts. Worried that the IBM acquisition would drag down Lenovo's performance, they sold enough shares to send the stock price down 24% over the two months after the deal was announced.

The answer is actually simple: Lenovo won't be running the race with IBM's bloated cost structure saddled on its back.

Similarly, to escape Microsoft's stranglehold, Lenovo will likely move to the nonproprietary, open-source world of Linux software. Affordability will be the key issue in the emerging markets Lenovo will serve, not brand name, and adopting the free Linux platform will be another way to wring out substantial costs.

The third reason is simply a difference in attitude between West and East. Asian companies have their origins in trading cultures, where margins—as well as costs—have historically been low. There was no inventor class, nor any high-margin mindset. Margins that are unacceptable to Westerners look good to Asians. It's the Chinese restaurant again, where high volume and hard work drive success in a low-margin business.

I'm not saying it will be easy. Lenovo will have plenty of challenges. Founded in 1984 by researchers at China's Academy of Sciences and still majority-owned by the government, the young company has already had a few hiccups. But it got on track when it designed a circuit board that would allow IBM PCs to process Chinese characters, and by 1990 it was assembling PCs under its own Legend brand. (Unable to export that brand to America because of a trademark conflict with the Acura Legend, it changed its name to Lenovo in 1994.) Its business plan—tailoring products to Asian markets and keeping inventories and costs down—appears to be working. Before the acquisition of IBM's unit, it had become China's biggest PC supplier and has remained steadily, if marginally, profitable in a very tough industry.

Will Lenovo leverage IBM's assets and shed its liabilities? I believe so. In fact, I believe Lenovo's cost structure is so advantageous and its business philosophy so adaptable that the company will not only make money now but will actually increase its margins over time.

The IBM story is by no means unique. Think of the consumer electronics industry or the textile industry. Here again, U.S. companies were the pioneers—with appropriately high cost structures and margins. In both cases, margins collapsed (thanks primarily to foreign competition) while costs remained too high. Now both industries have fled from these shores. The generalization holds: when you pioneer an industry, you want to command a high-margin business. You structure your costs with the assumption that the business will remain high-margin. But as your industry matures, margins come down more than costs do, and you are trapped.

THE FAST-GROWTH PHENOM

Since the mortality rate for new businesses is so high, it's not surprising that those that do survive begin to feel good about themselves. Now it's time to take on the world; it's time to grow, quickly. In addition to overconfidence, there's a kind of logic here. Companies in this position may fear that those they've left behind may catch up again, may overtake them. Or (lending credence to "the Rule of Three") they may believe that to ensure their survival, they have to overtake the company ahead of them by acquiring and consolidating smaller companies.

In any case, fast expansion and increased capacity are at the top of the agenda. The expansion may be geographic, such as building new facilities and pushing the company product into new territories at home or abroad. Or the company might grow the business by capturing new customer segments. The computer industry, for example, expanded its customer base from the government to corporations to consumers. And that industry is typical in that its customer expansion moved from highest-margin customers to lowest. This is one of the inherent dangers of expanding into new customer markets—especially when that growth is uncontrolled. Growth opportunities are almost always in the lower-margin sectors, and companies that fail to adjust to lower margins can wind up in trouble.

New product lines also tend to be lower-margin, as the computer industry once again illustrates. The progression was from mainframes to minicomputers to PCs as the industry sought products that were affordable to a wider customer base. There's nothing wrong with the logic here, but you've already seen what happened to IBM's PC business. Fast-growing companies, in particular, need to be wary of their shrinking margins. Expanding business virtually guarantees higher revenues, but it's the bottom line that counts.

Yet another caveat is that growth requires capital—fast growth even more capital. To raise a lot of money in a hurry, the company decides to go public. Once you've sold yourself through an initial public offering (IPO), however, you're no longer the master of your fate. You're now driven by the harsh dictates of Wall Street. Like a fox on the run, you're chased by analysts and investors who howl, "Show me the growth, or I'll drop your price." Now you're under immense pressure to grow even faster. In too many cases, as the trap begins to close, company leaders decide that the only way to buy a little more time is to begin fudging the numbers.

This unhappy but often predictable trajectory is nicely illustrated by the rise and fall of Krispy Kreme.

GLAZED AND DAZED

In possession of a few dollars and a secret recipe a French chef had sold to his uncle, Vernon Rudolph founded Krispy Kreme in 1937 in Winston-Salem, North Carolina. It was a wholesale business at first, with Rudolph selling his doughnuts to local grocery stores. But—according to company legend—people walking past the original Ivy Avenue plant were so transported by the aroma they began pounding on the door and demanding to buy direct. Rudolph cut a hole in the factory wall, and all of a sudden he was running a retail operation.

Rudolph began to expand, but slowly. Every store made its own fresh doughnuts, from 50-pound bags of the special mix produced at the Ivy Avenue plant. The yeast-risen, confection-glazed treats enjoyed a growing renown. They were delicious, after all, and customers were willing to pay for them. Nevertheless, when Rudolph died in 1973, there were still fewer than 50 stores, most of them spread throughout the Southeast. But three years later, in 1976, Beatrice Foods bought the little chain and started to grow it. Beatrice also tried to change it—selling soups and sandwiches during midday when demand for coffee lulled, and then cutting costs by using cheaper ingredients in the doughnuts: Both initiatives failed miserably, and in 1982 a group of early franchisees bought back the company for ***\$22*** million. The original recipe was quickly restored, some of the stores Beatrice had created were closed, and, thanks to debt incurred by the leveraged buyout (LBO), plans for expansion were indefinitely tabled.

As the company struggled to get back on its feet, it devised a couple of marketing concepts that enhanced its cult image and embellished its word-of-mouth reputation. First, CEO Mack McAleer, son of the franchisee who put together the LBO, came up with the idea of "doughnut theater." In so-called "factory stores," patrons could watch the whole doughnut-making process—the 115 seconds of cooking in 365-degree vegetable oil, the shower of glaze, and then the conveyance of the delectable product straight to the service counter, where customers could gobble them up as soon as they were cool enough to touch. The decided preference for still-warm doughnuts led to the second innovation: the now-iconic "HOT DOUGHNUTS NOW" signs that light up when a fresh batch comes off the line. Begun in the early 1980s by a store in Chattanooga (where sales had subsequently exploded), the sign was quickly implemented company-wide.

After the company pulled out of debt in 1989, Krispy Kreme's ambitions began to escalate. Slow but steady expansion throughout the early 1990s gave way to aggressive franchising in 1995. Opening stores in the Midwest and Southwest, it quickly grew from roughly 60 (mostly company-owned) Southeastern stores to more than twice that many. Then, in 1998, it announced a big push into California, where it planned to open another 80 franchise stores over the next few years.

In 2000, CEO Scott Livengood, who had worked his way up the ranks over a 25-year career, took Krispy Kreme public. Conforming to the pattern just outlined, the company at the same time announced plans to open 500 new stores over the next four years, along with a large-scale expansion into Canada. The timing appeared to be perfect. As the dot-com bubble burst, the little doughnut company soared. While the stock market headed south over the next two years, Krispy Kreme showered its magic glaze over the jaundiced eyes of Wall Street.

In July 1993, ***Fortune*** magazine put Krispy Kreme on its cover and positively reveled in the company's unlikely triumph. By that point it had expanded to 292 stores, which in 2002 had earned $33 million on 492 million in sales. The stock price had quadrupled (from ***$9*** to ***$37,*** adjusted for splits) since the 2000 IPO. Same-store sales were growing by 11% annually. Total revenues, including sales by franchises, were expected to top ***$1*** billion in 2003.

Things looked pretty good on the operations level, too. In 2002, the original Ivy Avenue plant, where one of those 50-pound sacks gets filled with mix every seven seconds, was running 24 hours a day at 110% capacity. But after the opening of a new plant in Illinois, where a bag gets filled every three seconds, the Ivy Avenue plant was able to cut back, to 18 hours a day.

CEO Livengood was taking it all in stride. "Running a public company growing like this—that's nothing," he told ***Fortune***, "I'm enjoying myself." Erskine Bowles, the North Carolina banker and former Clinton chief of staff who had recently joined Krispy Kreme's board, was effervescent. "I've got to tell you. I've never seen another company like it. It's clean, it's conservative, and I love the margins."

Fortune conceded that there had been some glitches, some off-balance sheet financing (relating to that new plant in Illinois), and some governance problems—all of which had been rectified. Also some people were raising their eyebrows at a doughnut company with a price/earnings ratio up in the heavens. But the magazine disagreed with the naysayers and declared that unless the "fat police run riot across this land, Krispy Kreme is here to stay." The company had a 66-year history and sold a product that people loved and understood. ***Fortune*** asked, "Is the American dream still alive? Is Krispy Kreme for real?" and then confidently answered its own question: "Don't bet against it."

That advice remained sound for about a month. Krispy Kreme stock hit an all-time high of $49.74 in August 2003. Anybody who sold then, or at ***$37,*** or even at ***$27*** is patting himself or herself on the back today. A cold undercurrent of uncertainty accompanied the company's 2003 fourth-quarter numbers. Profits were still up, sales were up, and the company said it would continue to expand aggressively. It had added 100 stores in 2003, planned to open another 120 in 2004, and intended to reach 1,000 (including stores in Canada, Mexico, and Britain) by the end of the decade. But average weekly same-store sales were off close to 10%, and that news knocked a four-dollar chunk off the stock price. The party was beginning to end. In July 2004, the ***Washington Post*** reported that Krispy Kreme was the subject of an informal inquiry by the Securities and Exchange Commission. According to the company, the

Commission was looking into its repurchasing of franchises and its announcement back in May that it was sharply cutting its earnings forecast. That same announcement brought the news that Krispy Kreme had lost money for the first time since going public—news that sent the stock into a 29% nosedive. Word of the inquiry knocked it down another 16%. Less than a year after its high, Krispy Kreme shares were trading at just under ***$16,*** constituting a precipitous 70% decline. The flight of investors along with the SEC inquiry had analysts speculating that the company "might be falling prey to problems stemming from too-rapid expansion."

In the process of chasing new markets and growing market share, Krispy Kreme did more than open new stores. Not content to be the premier purveyor of hot doughnuts, the company cannibalized itself and vitiated the Krispy Kreme brand by pushing into supermarket chains, convenience stores, and retail giants like Walmart and Costco. Again, the result was increased sales but with plenty of additional costs (trucks, facilities, logistics, people) to make them happen. Plus, all these retailers had to make their profit. In other words, not much margin was left. In explaining to investors why earnings in the second quarter of 2004 continued to disappoint (and why Kroger stores were dropping Krispy Kreme from their product line), CEO Livengood seemed to admit his business strategy had been shortsighted. "Our focus has been on sales and growth, and less on the day-to-day profits. We have not gotten the job done to get the sales to the bottom line."

Before the woeful year could end, a stockholder lawsuit alleged padded sales figures, and Krispy Kreme was forced to restate its fiscal 2004 earnings. At the same time, it warned investors that it might have to default on a $150 million line of credit. In January 2005, the stock price fell to a new low of ***$8.72.*** In one of the wheel of fortune's typically dramatic turns, Livengood, the erstwhile darling of Wall Street, was not only ousted by the board, he was also named by ***Business Week*** magazine as one of the worst managers of 2004.

How did such a feel-good story so quickly become a nightmare? Clearly, the company grew too big too fast, and pressure from Wall Street after the IPO no doubt played its part. An internal investigation into the company's financial irregularities, led by two independent board members, laid the blame squarely on Livengood and COO John Tate, who created a corporate culture "driven by a narrowly focused goal of exceeding projected earnings by a penny each quarter."

Finally, we should note that an essential component in Krispy Kreme's formula for failure was its willingness to use franchising as the means to rapid growth. It's tempting. You get your franchisee to put in all the sweat equity and some of the capital, and ***voila***—you're adding stores, on the cheap. But it's risky, and part of Krispy Kreme's troubles have stemmed from having to buy back franchises that didn't work out. Compare to Starbucks, which had never dealt with franchisees until it bought Seattle's Best Coffee in 2003. Even today, Magic Johnson is the only U.S. franchisee of Starbucks branded stores. McDonald's, too, as we've noted, has always franchised with extreme caution, screening potential franchisees carefully and strictly limiting the number of stores any one franchisee can operate.

Maybe Krispy Kreme can stage a successful comeback. In the meantime, too-rapid growth, fueled by an IPO and undisciplined franchising, has at least temporarily taken the yeast out of the once-heavenly snack food.

THE PARADOX OF SCALE

We like to talk about economies of scale, but the concept isn't quite as simple as it sounds. We understand that in our industry, even if we were the pioneer, competition will ultimately bring our prices down, and we plan to counterbalance that decline by reducing our costs through scale. Unfortunately, those cost savings may not materialize. As economists know, scale is a "step" function.

Let's say you want to get into the ceiling-fan business. You've spotted the trend—fuel conservation—and are sure there will be an upswing in demand, so you build a manufacturing plant. You have enormous start-up costs—building the plant and the back-office infrastructure, creating the supply chain, hiring and training personnel, everything. Yes, over time these costs do come down, and to the extent that increasingly efficient operations at this original plant allow you to produce more and more ceiling fans, your per-unit costs decline, and you begin enjoying economies of scale.

However, when you decide to pursue ***real*** economies of scale by means of a major expansion of capacity, you suddenly jack those costs back up. Why? Because you are starting all over again: new plant, new infrastructure, new IT, new people. Furthermore, those new people need ***their*** people—secretaries, administrative personnel, quality and safety inspectors, janitorial. And if your expansion takes place overseas, you're likely to create mini-czars—managers who need their own entourage. These support costs are not mitigated by increased capacity, so suddenly your costs are very high again, even as your capacity is expanding. Each new expansion incurs these same very high initial costs. This is the step: As you get the new business or factory up and running, costs gradually decline, but with every expansion they shoot back up again. Meanwhile, price continues to decline with more capacity, so if you are not planning carefully and operating efficiently, you can expand yourself right out of business.

This problem comes into even sharper relief when we examine it from the demand side. Our ceiling-fan factory is running at full capacity, but as we expected, demand is slowly, steadily (linearly) increasing. We reach the point where there's more demand than our factory can supply. We build a new factory, and, along with costs, supply also goes straight up in one big step. The result is that now there is too much supply, and we face the additional costs of inventory management, warehousing, and so on. Since capacity goes up in steps while demand rises linearly, there is always a gap between the two. Managing that gap is a cost we may not have prepared for.

This problem arises in traditional "heavy" manufacturing industries like paper mills, mining, and steel-making. In industries like these, capacity expansion is no small thing. Your costs are huge, the added capacity will be huge, and the gap (at least temporarily) between the new supply and demand will be huge. By the way, this situation is what creates the spot market, where you end up selling your excess capacity to your competitor.

A more contemporary—and more dramatic—example is the semiconductor industry, with big players like Intel and Motorola. The drama is supplied thanks to Moore's Law, which predicts that the number of transistors on a microprocessor chip will double every 18 months. (Intel cofounder Gordon Moore swears that he originally predicted that the number would double every two years, not 18 months, but his law is apparently no longer subject to his own legislation.) In any case, the point remains that for chip manufacturers, their products are almost obsolete as soon as they come off the line. This means an almost constant need to redesign, retool, or build new facilities. A new semiconductor factory can cost upwards of $3 billion. And that's just the capital costs. Then you add in operating costs—maintenance, people—and you find yourself committed to spending a lot of money. At the same time, all your customers are still using your old chip (Pentium III instead of Pentium IV, for instance), so you have tremendous excess capacity. By the time all your customers catch up with you, it will be time for a new factory to manufacture a more advanced chip—or your competitors will beat you to it. Now you understand why the semiconductor industry is considered a feast-or-famine business: there is always a mismatch between supply and demand. In fact, companies often have to enter into joint ventures with their competitors to build these facilities.

THE BALL AND CHAIN OF UNINTENDED OBLIGATIONS

It's often difficult to foresee how the obligations we incur today, when the sky is blue and our margins are high, will affect our cost structure 50 years down the road. But virtually all successful companies make such obligations—with their employees as well as with their communities—and often they prove difficult to fulfill.

Take the manufacturing concern of looking for a place to build a new factory. It will be besieged by incentive packages from state and local governments far and wide—tax breaks, amenities, access to natural resources, pollution allowances. In all likelihood, it will build the new facility where it gets the best deal (as Dell did in accepting a $318 million package to build its new plant in Raleigh, North Carolina). But these "freebies" are not really free. When the company begins to prosper, the community comes knocking. The company is expected to "give back" by supporting community initiatives—that is, by making large donations to local charities and other worthwhile causes. What's more, the company's executives will be expected to chair the local United Way or stadium authority or museum foundation. Such commitments take time (sometimes a year or more), and time—especially that of high-ranking corporate officers—is money. The successful company can count on an increasing number of such non–business-related activities, hidden costs that are difficult to calculate in advance.

That's not all. Fifteen or 20 years later, it may be time to move on. This old factory with its' outdated technology is no longer cost-effective or competitive, so it's time to build a new one—probably in Eastern Europe. But it's not that easy. Despite all your community involvement, you find you still have obligations. You have exit problems. You've polluted the river, which was fine as long as you were employing half the town's citizens, but it's not fine now that you want to leave and lay off all those people. This huge plant you built, not to mention the brown space around it—what will happen to those? You might have to clean up the river. You might have to turn your ugly property into an upscale retail center. In other words, it will cost you to get out—a cost that will be particularly painful now that your margins are not what they used to be.

Even if that debt to the community turns into a big number, it will be small potatoes compared to what you will owe your retiring employees. Who could see the future? Who could predict that, thanks to automation and integration, you would have fewer and fewer current employees funding the benefits packages of an ever-widening pool of retirees? Who could have foreseen that people today would be living 10 years longer than they were 40 years ago, when your actuaries were fingering their abacuses? Who had any idea that the birth rate would decline as it has? Fifty years ago, nobody was talking about the "aging of the population." What happens is, you pick up obligations under one set of assumptions, only to watch those assumptions lose their validity.

Moreover, while automation and integration are eating away at current employment rolls, so is the outsourcing phenomenon. Outsourcing absolutely makes sense—whether we're talking about call centers in Bangalore or data processing in Peoria, Illinois. If it's cheaper to get somebody else to do it, get somebody else to do it. You're driving your costs down, and you should. But less visibly, you're increasing another cost "because your company is left with fewer employees to contribute to the retirement system. That cost will come back to haunt you.

Funny how the solution to one problem aggravates another problem. One way to control costs as your margins decline is to break up your vertically integrated company and jettison any units that you find to be inefficient or unprofitable. Indeed, we'll recommend this strategy at the end of this chapter, and GM, to take one example, has implemented it by divesting Delphi, but here's the caveat, especially for companies like GM: Once again you are reducing the number of your current employees and thereby decreasing the contributions to your company's pension fund.

These unforeseen obligations, willingly entered into when one set of assumptions prevailed, now, under vastly changed circumstances, constitute a potentially ruinous cost.

UNCLE SAM'S CUT

The costs we've looked at so far—whether operating or nonoperating, whether payable now or later—are those we ourselves have incurred, more or less willingly, to get our business up and running and to keep it headed in the right direction. Now we come to costs imposed from without, by local, state, and, especially, federal government. True, such costs are not the result of our own volume obsession, but still they are costs, sometimes hidden or unexpected, and they have to be covered. They can't be ignored.

Local taxes, business licenses, and operating permits are where such costs begin. But quickly we run into the larger net of government regulations: OSHA guidelines, employee hiring and termination rules (like Affirmative Action), handicapped accessibility building design, and dozens of others. The bigger you get, it seems, the more interested the government gets, and these hidden costs of doing business continue to escalate.

This problem is compounded by the fact that government regulations continue to change, and the stroke of a pen on Capitol Hill can cost you millions. The EPA is a great example. Today nobody regrets that the federal government has taken some responsibility for protecting the environment. In fact, lots of people wish that the EPA had more teeth. But 50 years ago neither corporations nor the government nor society as a whole had much awareness of the dangers of pollution, and it's not surprising that corporations operated without keen environmental consciousness.

Even more expensive, if more mundane, are the traditional nonoperating costs imposed by the government: interest rates (or the cost of capital) and corporate taxes. It was GE's Reginald Jones, perhaps more than anyone else, who called attention to the fact that these costs were rendering American business uncompetitive at the global level. GE, under Jones, had high enough costs anyway, with some 60 businesses and a strategie planning committee of some 150 executives. But when that strategic committee investigated why U.S. corporations were falling behind their global competitors, Jones became devoted to the cause of reducing the excessive costs added by Uncle Sam.

When Ronald Reagan came into office in 1981, corporate taxes in the U.S. topped out at 46 percent. Such a rate was absurdly counterproductive on the face of it. Rather than paying a reasonable rate to the government and then plowing the tax savings back into their businesses, companies spent time on shell games, dummy corporations, and other tax-avoidance sehemes or on figuring out how companies under their banner could ***lose*** money and be used as writeoffs. Thanks to lobbying by GE and others, Reagan reduced the rate to 34%, but GE believed anything higher than 10 percent would continue to shackle American business. After all, competitors like Japan's Mitsubishi and Franee's Snecma (the jet engine manufacturer) were paying zero.

In this case, then, even though we may run our business efficiently, high costs imposed by the government may be our undoing—especially when we face global competition. Given little relief by the government, Reginald Jones planned a vast restructuring of GE's businesses to bring his costs in line. Continued by "neutron" Jack Welch and current CEO Jeff Immelt, the process has been largely suceessful, and the number of GE's business units has been slashed from 60 to roughly half a dozen. But not all companies have both the wisdom and fortitude to take such drastic measures.

By the way, the issue of eontrolling nonoperating costs has led to a new approach to shareholder value, called "economic value added" (EVA). Financial analysts now advise against investing in a business unless it generates out of its operating costs enough profit or margin to support nonoperating costs. In other words, your nonoperating costs, including taxes, dividends, and cost of capital, are now in the formula for allocating resources to divisions or business units.

The consequences of volume obsession, like overeating, are incremental. Once we're fat, we know we're fat. We don't need to be told (and often resent it when we are told). But the process of overeating—a doughnut here, a second, helping there—that results in being fat is somehow easier to overlook. The price of staying lean, like that of freedom, is constant vigilance. Here's what to look for.

GUIDELINE-FREE, AD HOC SPENDING

The problem here is that you've never really addressed the issue of controlling your costs—whether in terms of operating expenses, procurement prices, travel, capital spending, or whatever. This is not as uncommon or irresponsible as you may think. After all, in the early days of high margins and rapid growth, it's all too easy to deal with spending on an ad hoc basis. You have other things—more interesting and challenging things—to think about, so you never put the necessary spending guidelines in place. Basically, you're flying by the seat of your pants, and when it comes to costs, your "adhocracy" is in charge.

Another symptom of guideline-free spending is lavishness at the top. Add irresponsibility to adhocracy, and you've got no ceiling on your spending. You've discovered the joy of splurging; the sky's the limit. Everybody else is in coach, but you're flying first-class, literally and figuratively. Check out the furnishings in your conference room. Mahogany table? Leather-padded chairs? Of course, the most visible sign of excess is your fleet of corporate jets. RJ Reynolds built its own corporate jet terminal at Atlanta's Charlie Brown airport shortly before the company was taken over in a leveraged buyout. But many other companies are equally profligate. According to statistics, corporate jets are in the air 10% of the time and sitting idle on the ground the other 90%. If you're spending money like a drunken sailor, it's pretty clear that you're not taking care of business.

Without the appropriate guidelines in place, you're also likely to have highly decentralized discretionary budgets. In other words, you're not the only one spending too much money. You have empowered all your unit managers to do the same. This is empowerment without accountability, and you can be sure it will lead to abuse.

FUNCTIONAL-LEVEL COST CENTERS

From the beginning, your profit and loss (P&L) has been calculated at the corporate level, so your costs are aggregated, like revenues. As a result, all your functions, except sales, remain cost centers. You haven't yet reexamined this structure, although it may no longer be efficient or even sensible. It may be possible to turn some of those cost centers into revenue centers (as I'll suggest a little later).

A cost center–based structure makes sense when you're a monopoly, like the old Bell system, with the government capping your profit margin at, say, 14%. Bell was organized according to return on investment (ROI). The formula is "revenue minus cost, divided by assets." So the way to persuade the government that it's time for a rate increase is to build up the denominator, to spend money building up assets.

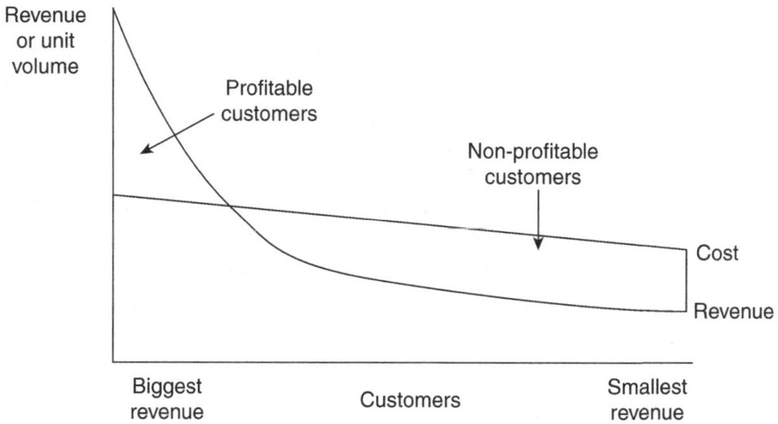

Figure 7-1 Cross-subsidized revenue

To play that game, you keep all your functions in-house, and you make them expensive. You build gorgeous buildings for training centers, state-of-the-art facilities for R&D. You gold-plate everything. In this scenario, you don't want your functions to produce revenue; you want them to be costly "assets" that you've invested in. Then, to get the necessary "return on investment," you tell the government you've got to increase revenues by bumping up the prices you charge your customers. Of course, this whole strategy was conceived in a monopoly environment. Now that the monopoly has gone away, the problem is how to wring out all these costs.

More typically, however, the cost center mind-set has been less a matter of strategy than of good old standard operating procedure. As we suggested at the outset, businesses tend to organize themselves in this way: generate revenue through sales and budget money to the various other functions to support sales. Following this logic, all other functions—R&D, manufacturing, logistics, marketing, customer service—become cost centers rather than revenue centers. Once this structure is established, human nature (or business nature) perpetuates it. The managers of every function will be sure to spend more money next year than they did this year. They all want their functions to grow, they want bigger budgets, and they want more people under them. After all, that's how their own performance is likely to be measured. As these functional costs build up over time, efficiency is seldom a consideration. Fat is accreting on the corporate body.

A CULTURE OF CROSS-SUBSIDIES

Chapter 4 examined the problem of cross-subsidizing, but it deserves further mention here. If you allow the success of one business unit to conceal the failure of another one, you're certainly not operating efficiently. As the following chart illustrates, it's not uncommon for a company's profits to be generated by 10% of its operations and for that 10% to effectively subsidize the other 90%.

Again using the Bell system as an illustration, we see how cross-subsidies are sometimes put in place by regulation. The government mandated that local service be inexpensive and also that installation and maintenance were to be free. The monopoly on long distance generated plenty of revenue to cover those costs. So, in effect, long distance subsidized local phone service, and heavy users subsidized light users. As we've seen, the end of that long-distance monopoly spelled doom for Ma Bell.

In a similar vein, when Procter & Gamble took a hard look at its operations, it discovered that out of some 1,500 accounts, it was making money on only 90. The company eliminated the problem with its customer-focused reorganization. The money Ernst & Young made from serving 200 profitable clients subsidized the costs incurred in taking care of the other 3,800. But the company didn't realize this until it looked at results from a customer-by-customer perspective. A culture of cross-subsidization encourages this kind of ignorance, confusion, and inefficiency.

TRUTH IN NUMBERS

One sure sign that you're spending too much money to make money is when your internal or external auditor tells you so. When you get on the scale at the doctor's office and you find that you've gained five pounds since your last checkup, you can't talk your way out of it. You have to face the facts. It's the same with your audit. You can say, "Yes, but..." and rationalize all you want. But if your costs are rising and your margins are falling, that's that.

Your stock price and the opinion of industry analysts are also dependable gauges of your company's health. Your own people inside the company (including your CFO and internal auditors) may have an agenda, but outside analysts can be relied on to look at your results objectively. And when they turn against you, you'll get yet another unmistakable sign of poor health: Your investors will flee. Dell, for one, has benefited from listening carefully to the cost analysis of industry experts.

Finally, be aware that benchmarks can change. In the face of all other indications to the contrary, you may yet deceive yourself into thinking you are doing well because you are succeeding according to the benchmarks you have long had in place. It may be time to throw out those benchmarks. It used to be okay if your "bad" cholesterol reading was 200. Now a reading that high gets you a prescription for Zocor. Consider global competition today.

It's now imperative that U.S. software and IT companies compare their performance to India's and that our manufacturing companies measure themselves against the new benchmark set by China. This trend is epitomized by the new global business buzzword—the "China price."

HOW TO BREAK THE VOLUME OBSESSION HABIT

Breaking the volume obsession habit requires strategic vision and a time commitment for planning and implementation activities. It can also be a painful process when the remedy involves workforce reduction. However, because volume obsession has a direct negative impact on the financial well-being of a company, it must be dealt with.

IDENTIFY WHERE YOUR COSTS ARE

This sounds self-evident, but a lot of companies still don't know how to create the appropriate revenue/cost alignment. As mentioned in the preceding chapter, Procter & Gamble, because it was organized by product, didn't realize that Walmart had become its largest customer. Once it realized it had to reorganize, P&G took three years to figure out its cost structure from the customer side. The company called it "activity-based costing" (ABC), and insiders today like to joke that their formula is more secret than Coke's.

If revenues are skewed, if 20% of customers are generating 80% of revenue, profitability is likely to be even more skewed. It may be that 10% of your customers are actually making money for you, and 90% are being subsidized. More and more companies are coming to realize that if the customer is the revenue generator, costs should align that way. The new platform is sometimes called customer relationship management (CRM). At its heart is the "customer profitability analysis"—calculating costs and revenues on a per-customer basis.

At this point you may want to ask, if customers are people who buy something from us, how can all these customers not generate any revenue? The answer: easily. In the first place, sometimes customers are people who ***might*** buy something, like the millions of bank customers who enjoy free checking. Banks provide this service (and shoulder its cost) in the hope that these customers might generate revenue through other services, like savings accounts, CDs, mortgages, or other loans. In other cases, customers are buying something, but competition has driven the price so low that sales generate losses rather than profits. If I fly from Atlanta to Washington, D.C., for ***$49***,1 doubt I'm having a positive impact on the airline's balance sheet.

The best example is AT&T Long Distance. The business has 60 million accounts, but one-third of them never make a call. They remain a cost because they're in the system, they get their statements, they're part of the accounting department's workload. In fact, the average cost of serving those customers has been calculated to be ***$6*** a month, or ***$72*** a year. Multiply that by 20 million, and these customers are costing you $1.44 billion. In years past, with its monopoly, AT&T could still make money on long distance, but now prices have collapsed in the face of competition. Declining price has to be offset by rising volume, but thanks to the cell phone phenomenon, volume is also declining. Revenue has plummeted, and profits have disappeared.

CONVERT COST CENTERS INTO REVENUE CENTERS OR PROFIT CENTERS

As noted, it's not unusual for companies to designate sales as their revenue-generating function and then define other functions as cost centers in support of sales. It doesn't have to be that way. A fresh approach can sometimes turn even strategic functions from cost centers into revenue or profit centers.

For example, when Procter & Gamble CEO Alan Lafley looked into his R&D function, he found that he had 150 PhD scientists on the staff. He knew he didn't need that many; in effect, he had idle capacity. These are brilliant people who love their work, but inside P&G there aren't enough opportunities to keep them happy and productive. Still, Lafley didn't want to fire these loyal, talented employees. His solution was to contract out research to other companies, and with that simple initiative, his cost center became a revenue center. A win-win-win: good for P&G, good for the scientists, and good for the companies to which they are contracted out.

Similarly, parts departments—or, more generally, service/maintenance functions—are evolving from cost centers into profit centers. In many consumer products categories, free repair or underwarranty repair has traditionally relegated these functions to cost centers, but now consumers find themselves purchasing "free" repair in the form of the extended warranty. As product quality has improved, the extended warranty has become a huge profit center for retailers like Best Buy. At Sears, the merchandizing group found that in the 1980s, 64% of all profits in its $24 billion business came from two places: 34% from credit card financing, and another 30% from extended warranties. The extended warranty is simply insurance, of course, and the healthier the body, the more profitable the insurance.

On a larger scale, when a manufacturer like GE builds a plant, free support—from installation to maintenance to repair—has historically been a cost. But look at what's happening now. Companies large and small are reorganizing around the "service" function, and service is becoming a critical revenue center. In addition to GE, the best examples are the big business-to-business companies like IBM, Xerox, Lucent, and many others. It used to be that after IBM sold its mainframes, it offered customers free support. It was good business in that it firmed up the relationship and encouraged customers to buy next-generation computers. But these after-sale services were a significant cost. Eventually the company saw it was missing a huge opportunity and created a new unit: IBM Global Services. Now its revenue equals that of the product business.

Note that in turning its service function from a cost center into a revenue center, IBM—and others—didn't limit themselves to charging their regular customers for a service they had been providing free. What IBM did was offer its capacity to the outside world—that is, it created a new business unit, with its own costs but with big returns.

The data services company EDS offers another illustration. When GM decided to outsource its mainframe computing, Ross Perot's EDS won the contract—with a bid of close to ***$11*** billion for the service. Some smart finance guy at GM took a second look and said, "Hey, we should just buy the company instead." In 1984, Perot agreed to sell for ***$12.5*** billion. That was a lot to pay for a business that would simply consolidate, integrate, and run all its own data processing systems, so GM eventually began selling EDS services to outside industries like cable and telecom. GM had turned a cost center—internal data processing—into a revenue center.

Admittedly, this is a woefully abbreviated version of a fascinating page in American corporate history. Commentators agree that, in purchasing EDS, GM wanted not only data processing but also the brilliant and entrepreneurial Perot himself, who was granted a seat on the GM board and considerable oversight over EDS's operations under the GM umbrella. Of course, Perot and GM's conservative Roger Smith blended like oil and water, and Perot used his seat on the board to hammer away at GM's manifest failings. The divorce came when GM paid Perot $700 million (twice what his shares were worth) to "shut up and go away." In the last analysis, though, and despite the fact that in a return to its core business GM spun off EDS in 1995, the deal had been profitable for GM. Between 1990 and 1995, EDS's revenue had doubled to more than $10 billion.

To reiterate, virtually any function—R&D, manufacturing, logistics (like shipping), customer support—can be reorganized into a revenue center. Almost all the cheese at your local supermarket, whatever the brand, is stocked by Kraft, just as most cigarette racks are owned and operated by RJ Reynolds. In this case, these two megacompanies have turned inventory management into a revenue producer. By selling excess carrying capacity, shipping firms (both ground and air) create revenue centers from the logistics function. Companies with extra capacity at their call centers can produce revenue from customer support by taking calls for other companies.

Now when you read about companies that have reorganized to make individual functions more "entrepreneurial," you know how to translate: they're transforming cost centers into moneymakers.

DECENTRALIZE PROFIT AND LOSS TO MORE AND SMALLER "BUSINESS UNITS"

If you have centralized P&L at the top, you may have poor oversight over how your individual units are doing. One corrective is to apply the EVA principle described earlier: delegate to each unit the responsibility of justifying its costs, including nonoperating costs or hidden costs. Require each unit to pay its own way, to cover even shareholder dividends, income taxes, and the cost of capital that might have been passed up to the corporate level. Let managers know that they will be supported only if they can generate more than enough revenue to cover these costs; otherwise, they will be divested.

Banks and telephone companies have pursued this strategy by dividing their huge customer bases into separate business units—industrial, small business, consumer, and so on. Decentralizing P&L into these smaller customer groups has the added benefit of discouraging cross-subsidies—except, of course, for cross-subsidies within the unit or division.

MOVE FROM VERTICAL INTEGRATION TO "VIRTUAL INTEGRATION"

Throughout the 20th century, vertical integration has been the model. Ford set the standard, making its own steel, tires, and parts; doing its own assembly; and selling the cars to consumers through its dealerships. GM followed the model, as did IBM and practically every big company; they wanted complete control over their business, from raw materials to final sale.

This model doesn't make as much sense as it used to, for a couple of reasons. First, it's difficult to have enough oversight to make sure every unit in a vertically integrated business is running with optimum efficiency. In fact, the system is likely to have some cost inefficiency because, basically, you're buying from yourself; no market mechanism is at work. (For example, Peter Drucker reported that, in the old days, the manager of Ford's giant steel mill didn't know how much the company paid for the coal he used.) And second, even if your units are efficient, there's still an excellent chance that a specialist company can do it better. The new model is "virtual integration"—concentrating on the one or two things you do best and letting others do the rest.

Blazing the trail to this new model is Cisco Systems, the dominant player in routers and switches. Cisco does two things: It develops new products, and it sells these products to customers. Everything else—manufacturing, supply, inventory control—is contracted out. Most of the time Cisco never even sees the products its customers purchase. Another good example is Nike. It is a design and branding company; it coordinates most value-added functions performed by contractors.

Thanks to communication technologies made possible through the Internet, individual companies no longer need to define themselves as manufacturers of products. Instead, members of a virtual enterprise contribute ***processes,*** and no single company is obliged to feel proprietary about the final product. In the virtual operation, seamless cooperation is the ideal, not ownership. As this model becomes more widely used, your ability to integrate your functions with those of other companies will become a critical competency.

OUTSOURCE NON-CORE FUNCTIONS

If you're not quite ready for virtual integration, you can still increase efficiency and cut costs by outsourcing non-core functions to outsiders that have appropriate economies of scale. (We also recommended outsourcing in Chapter 4 as an antidote to the bloat and sloth that characterize complacent companies.)

Many companies have seen the wisdom of outsourcing payroll to specialists such as Britain's EDP (Electronic Data Processing) or IT services to companies such as IBM, EDS, or Accenture. And the commonplace outsourcing of customer support is well known to anybody who has called for technical assistance with his or her home computer or Internet service provider. It's a sure bet that the voice on the other end of the line will be coming from India, the Philippines, or Ireland.

Today, moreover, more and more firms are beginning to outsource what used to be considered "strategic" functions. For instance, pharmaceutical companies are realizing that even some of their R&D work can be contracted out. While they concentrate on next-generation drugs, they can outsource the job of reformulating and improving older drugs whose patents might be about to expire. Much of this work is being done in India these days.

To take another example, since diapers comprise one of Procter & Gamble's essential product lines, the company long thought it necessary to own and run its own paper mills. Eventually P&G concluded that the market constituted a "reliable supply" of paper pulp and that it really didn't need to make its own. P&G's core strengths were marketing, branding, and distribution—not running paper mills—so here was a non-core function ready made for outsourcing. The move released the capital tied up in the plants, as well as the management time, and it substantially reduced costs. In this case, to put it concisely, to buy was cheaper than to make.

In fact, enough manufacturing and R&D functions are being outsourced these days to earn their own acronyms: CMO (contract manufacturing outsourcing) and CRO (contract research outsourcing). I don't mean to imply that outsourcing is always a no-brainer. As Nobel Prize–winning economist Ronald Coase and his disciple, Oliver Williamson, have pointed out, outsourcing (buying rather than making) always entails "transaction costs." Search and information costs, bargaining costs, and enforcement costs—to name a few—are always applicable when we go to the market rather than make it at home. Such transaction costs need to be calculated before we close the deal.

DOWNSIZE (OR RIGHTSIZE) THE COMPANY'S MANAGEMENT

Most companies, as they grow and prosper, start adding levels of management—in spite of Peter Drucker's timeless axiom that the best-organized corporate structure "will contain the ***least number of management levels,*** and forge the shortest possible chain of command." Drucker enjoyed pointing out that the proper economy of management levels was demonstrated by the oldest, largest, and most successful organization in the Western world—the Catholic Church. "There is only one level of authority and responsibility between the Pope and the lowliest parish priest: the bisop." Nevertheless, here comes the human resources department, organizing personnel into an infinite number of grades and levels for salary-scale purposes. This proliferation of management levels is, for Drucker, a classic symptom of "malorganization."

It's possible, and often advisable, to compress some of these management layers, as BellSouth has shown. It eliminated two layers by compressing seven into five and leveling off the hierarchical pyramid. In this scenario, fewer people at the top are given more to manage—more budget, more employees, more geography, or whatever. In fact, this "flattening" at the top that reduces management costs, alleviates bureaucratic complexity, and shortens the chain of command, which is now a trend that's bringing U.S. business closer to the more collective European model.

Consider professional services companies, which tend to offer the "flattest" paradigm. In law or accounting firms, or in IT consulting, everyone is a revenue producer. The partner who runs the shop is called the managing director or managing partner, but he's not a full-time bureaucrat with a hierarchy of managers under him. He spends half his time as a manager or coordinator and the other half earning money doing the same work the other firm members do.

REENGINEER YOUR PROCESSES

Borrowing from Michael Hammer's concept of reengineering the corporation. Chapter 4 suggested reengineering as a way to break the habit of complacency. Let's elaborate just a bit.

One key process to examine is what's known as "factory forward"—that is, the whole process centers around the factory, which must be kept running at full capacity. In simplest terms, the system is this: raw materials come into the factory and have value added as they're made into finished products. These go out into the pipeline, and then to the store, and finally are bought by the consumer. The problem in this scenario is all the "holding time." Since the factory can't be kept waiting, an oversupply of raw materials is held at the gate. Since the factory never stops, the value-added products constantly streaming out need to be warehoused until they can move into the distribution pipeline. The pipeline holds the goods until shelf space is available, and goods languish on the shelf until the consumer comes along. In packaged-goods companies, for example, your costs rise as much as 40% for every year your finished products spend in the distribution pipeline or on the shelf before purchase. There goes your margin.

The question becomes, why "factory forward"? Why not "customer backward" into the factory? This kind of process reengineering wrings out all the costs caused by inefficient inventory management. As you've seen, "customer-backward" or "demand-driven" operation is the model Dell has incorporated with such success. But notice, too, that in our increasingly services-oriented economy, services generally are demand-driven, not supply-driven. You have to sit in the chair before the barber can begin cutting your hair. You have to show up at your doctor's office before you undergo a physical. What's happening now is that the demand-driven model is being recognized as viable for manufacturing operations as well.

(I should note that the "automation and integration" recommended in the following chapter as a corrective to the habit of territoriality also exemplifies reengineering in the name of cost efficiency.)

MOVE TOWARD "MASS CUSTOMIZATION"

Demand-driven manufacturing leads naturally to the next phase of reengineering: "mass customization." This seeming oxymoron—also known as "agile production"—essentially means producing customized products with the cost economy of the assembly line. Not surprisingly, as Joseph Pine pointed out in his book ***Mass Customization,*** the concept was pioneered by Toyota, which sought to capture the Japanese market by producing a greater variety of cars at lower volumes. This meant reengineering the presses used to stamp out steel auto parts, thereby drastically reducing press setup times. The new process, part of Toyota's fabled "lean operations" that also includes just-in-time delivery and zealous quality control, enabled the company to produce a greater variety of models (customization) without any forfeit of speed and precision.

The point is not so much "lower volume," but rather volume on demand, or a demand/supply alignment that creates zero inventory. Motorola brought mass customization to the U.S. pager industry when it came under attack by the Japanese in the early 1980s. Combining its architecture of six manufacturing variables (shape, size, color, functions, features, guts) with computerized ordering direct from customers, Motorola created a "build-on-demand" process that reduced assembly time from four hours to four minutes. Plus, the build-on-demand system allowed customers to get exactly the pagers they wanted direct from the factory.

Over the past decade, as consumers have become more demanding and markets have splintered, mass customization has swept through industries as diverse as carmaking, consumer electronics, clothing, retailing, and fast food.

IMPLEMENT TARGET COSTING

In U.S. business, the standard practice (born during the beginnings of the Industrial Age) has been to price our products based on what it costs us to make them. We don't really know what a new product will cost until we've finished making it. At that point we add up all the bills we've had to pay (design, procurement, manufacturing), add in a couple more (distribution, marketing, sales) to get the product to the marketplace, decide how much margin we need, and—presto!—we affix the price.

It was the Japanese, again, who recognized the fallacy in this model and inverted the process. They understood that the manufacturer cannot control the price. The competitive market determines the price. But what the manufacturer ***can*** control is costs. In other words, price doesn't come out at the end of the formula; it goes in at the beginning. The real formula is market price minus target return equals target cost. The Japanese went a step further, observing that the market price typically declines. In a noninflationary economy, as competition comes in, a reasonable working figure is a decline of 5% a year, or 15% over three years. So forget ratcheting up the price to cover volume obsession spending. Our task is to nail down costs from the beginning—from initial design all the way through the process—and hold them there, or reduce them, to be assured of a return. Target costing is a "price-minus" calculation, rather than "cost-plus."

Caterpillar learned this lesson in the mid-1980s when it was getting clobbered by Komatsu (and losing $1 billion over three years). While Caterpillar's accountants studied Komatsu's financials to figure out its cost structure, Cat's engineers tore apart Komatsu's products to study its manufacturing processes. The work yielded the predictable, if unwelcome, results: Caterpillar's costs were 30% higher than Komatsu's. To its credit, Caterpillar swallowed the medicine and got up off the sickbed. It invested $1.8 billion in plant modernization, eliminated non–value-added processes, adopted just-in-time inventory control, and reduced the number of parts used in its products. By the early 1990s, it had returned to profitability.

BECOME A WORLD-CLASS CUSTOMER

Driven by standards of customer satisfaction, and coveting approval from JD Power and Malcolm Baldridge, companies strive for excellence as producers and marketers. At the other end of the line, however, companies are often lousy customers.

Remember that for most companies procurement is the biggest cost—often 65 to 70 percent of the total. You've already seen what procurement means to IBM in its dealings with Intel and Microsoft. In the steel industry, iron is the biggest cost. In retailing, the cost of goods sold comes to 65%. So pursuing excellence in procurement can be a critical cost-reduction mechanism.

How? Not by strong-arming your suppliers into reducing their price, but by nurturing them and making them emotionally loyal to you. Just as you have your own best customers, those you enjoy doing business with the most, so you need to be that kind of customer for your suppliers. If you treat your suppliers with as much respect as you do your customers, they will want to do business with you. Strive to create a mutual-appreciation society. That way, you won't have to bargain when you order (a game you will lose anyway). Your supplier will offer you the price that will benefit both sides, and that will guarantee the health of the long-term relationship.

As noted in Chapter 5, British clothier Marks and Spencer set the standard for nurturing its suppliers—even to the point of insisting on good working conditions for its suppliers' employees. Japanese carmakers have followed this practice, as have U.S. companies such as McDonald's and Starbucks.

In all likelihood, your emphasis traditionally has been on selling, not buying. But smart companies need to be excellent buyers as well—not by squeezing suppliers, but by making them lifelong partners.

To "go lean" is a tough request in this world of ours. It runs counter to the archetype of success: spending, consuming, growing "fat and happy." This archetype is deeply ingrained—in society as well as in business. When Jimmy Carter asked us to tighten our belts in 1978, he accomplished little except abetting his own political demise.

But the plethora of best-selling diet books these days coincides with an epidemic of obesity in America's grand-old companies like automakers and airlines and textile manufacturers and consumer electronics firms. The story across industries has the same general outline: In the face of increasing competition (often global), prices are falling, but cost structures, full of fat like clogged arteries, remain high, and margins inevitably collapse.

The current wave of restructuring suggests that a lifelong habit of volume obsession has pushed many U.S. corporations against the wall. Many, at the eleventh hour, are taking measures like those just outlined. Others, more likely to survive, will take these steps as precautions, rather than as desperate remedies.

VOLUME OBSESSION

Things that lead to volume obsession:

- The high-margin pioneer
- The fast-growth phenom
- The paradox of scale
- The ball and chain of unintended obligations

The warning signs of volume obsession:

- **Guideline-free, ad hoc spending:** You have other more interesting and challenging things to think about than controlling your costs.
- **Functional-level cost centers:** You've always calculated profit and loss at the corporate level, even though it may no longer be efficient or even sensible.
- **A culture of cross-subsidies:** You allow the success of one business unit to conceal the failure of another one.
- **Truth in numbers:** Your auditors, your stock price, or industry analysts are telling you that the numbers are not in your favor.

How to break the volume obsession habit:

- **Identify where your costs are:** Create an appropriate revenue/cost alignment.
- **Convert cost centers into revenue centers or profit centers:** Virtually any function can be reorganized into a revenue or profit center.
- **Move from vertical integration to "virtual integration":** Concentrate on the one or two things you do best, and let others do the rest.
- **Outsource non-core functions:** You can increase efficiency and cut costs by outsourcing non-core functions to outsiders who have appropriate economies of scale.
- **Reengineer to automate your processes:** Automate and integrate to improve cost efficiency.
- **Implement target costing:** Nail down costs from the beginning, and hold them there, or reduce them, to be assured of a return.
- **Become a world-class customer:** Smart companies need to be excellent buyers as well—not by squeezing suppliers, but by making them life-long partners.

CHAPTER 8

THE TERRITORIAL IMPULSE: CULTURE CONFLICTS AND TURF WARS

As companies grow and become successful, they tend to organize themselves into what I call "functional silos." Growing bigger still, they add "geographic silos"—regional offices or international operations. This organizational process is usually quite necessary. The freewheeling style of the founder/entrepreneur is fine in the company's infancy, but successful growth requires rules, policies, and procedures. It requires organization. Organizing also entails a kind of breaking apart—into functions, divisions, units, regions, or whatever. What had been one, with a kind of organic, intuitive wholeness and health, now becomes many. Again, this is a rational and logical process as a company comes of age. But it has unintended consequences, and these consequences foster self-destructive habits.

To put it generally, the various units or "silos" into which a company organizes do not always get along with each other. They might seek their own autonomy, dismiss the company's larger vision, and work at cross-purposes. One functional group might disdain the others. In a high-tech company, for example, the research silo might have contempt for "the flakes" in the marketing division. Culture conflicts ensue, along with suboptimal performance.

Also, almost inevitably, the organizational process engenders turf wars, as the various functional or geographic silos seek to protect or extend their own territories. Recent research has shown that "territoriality" can lead employees "to become self-focused, taking away from their ability to connect with and focus on the goals of the organization." Focusing exclusively on your own turf, to extend the metaphor, means failing to see the forest for the trees. Again, the result is dysfunction. Culture conflicts and turf wars should have been side effects, suppressed and controlled, but have become main effects. Headaches become migraines. The engine of growth sputters and stalls.

This chapter, then, focuses on yet another "symptom" of success. For the sake of efficiency, growth necessitates organization into silos, which threaten to become factions, fiefdoms, or ***territories.*** In the absence of a strong leader who can instill his vision in the minds of the chieftains, the company is likely to find itself expending its time and resources mediating conflict among its own warring tribes. Stakeholders—including employees themselves—find themselves nonplussed and angered:

This company has so much potential. Why are we running around in circles? In his famous book of the same name, noted anthropologist Robert Ardrey called it "the territorial imperative." But we'll call this self-destructive habit "the territorial impulse."

THE CORPORATE IVORY TOWER

In getting at this syndrome, I like to use the analogy of the 50-story building. As successful companies grow, they organize themselves into a complex of 50-story office towers, connected by common areas on the bottom and the top. On the bottom is the lobby, where employees might run into each other as they hurry to their own set of elevators. On the top, of course, is the executive suite. The executives have their own private offices, but they meet freely in the conference rooms, the executive dining room, maybe even the executive washroom. In this architecture, the CEO and his top management are insulated in their ivory tower. I've always been amused to hear academics accused of living in an ivory tower. Academics are foot soldiers, in the streets with the students, investigating their areas of research. For an example of true isolation, consider the typical CEO. His whole day is precisely coordinated, and he's surrounded by gatekeepers. In the morning, he leaves home in his chauffeur-driven car, sitting in the back, reading the paper or fiddling with his Blackberry. The car pulls up to his private entrance, and he goes straight into the elevator and ascends to his top-floor office. Moreover, everybody who comes into his office is screened—not only in terms of who he or she is, but also regarding the meeting's purpose. There will be no unpleasant surprises. This is the real ivory tower—an existence completely unbuffeted by the winds of reality.

To these Roman emperor types who have no idea what's going on in the provinces, I always have one urgent recommendation: Go out into the field. Go visit customers, go visit remote locations, without the blare of trumpets, without fanfare, perhaps even incognito. Top executives need to spend at least one day a month out in the field. Jack Welch learned this lesson when as a line manager he found himself unable to fight his way through the horde of gatekeepers to get in to see Reginald Jones.

At the bottom of the office complex is the common lobby. It's Grand Central Station. It's chaotic. Between the bottom and the top, organization rules. Each office tower represents one of the company's functions—engineering, manufacturing, sales, customer support. This is as it must be, according to the time-tested laws of division of labor and specialization. This is the route to efficient operations. Moreover, as your company grows, you have to recruit talented people to come work for you, and those people will come only if they're offered the opportunity to work in their field of specialization. Organizing by function abets your efforts to recruit and retain good people. It just makes sense. It's the correct model.

Of course, organization by function requires great management, great orchestration. It requires a leader with the skills of a great chef. He has all the ingredients at his disposal, but will he combine them? Some chefs are ordinary, and nobody notices the way they prepare. But some are exceptional. They blend their ingredients brilliantly and create distinctive, memorable dishes. Patrons rave, and the chefs fame grows. Some end up celebrities, with their own shows on the Food Channel. It's a matter of unique fusion and skillful resource blending—exactly the talent required by great leaders. They wow their stakeholders with the results they serve up in the form of quarterly earnings reports. Like Coke in the early days, or Procter & Gamble with its first product, Ivory Soap, organizing by function enabled them to grow and succeed.

Again, organizing functionally is the correct method, but the erection of the 50-story silos has unlooked-for consequences. As noted, except for the common areas at the bottom and the top, the towers do not connect. And that's the source of the dysfunction. I'll have more to say on this subject later.

What's more, after the functional towers have been erected, the company continues to grow, necessitating yet more towers or silos. Nationwide expansion requires the establishment of regional offices—Southeast, West, Central, Northeast. Again, it makes sense. It's a big country. But turf wars are looming. The regional guys don't want to talk to each other, especially if growth is uneven. Regional offices enjoying the fastest growth become the darlings, while the others become whipping boys.

These kinds of problems are exacerbated when expansion goes international. But how can companies resist such great growth opportunity? U.S. and European companies are now racing into China and India for good reason. China's economy has been growing at a phenomenal 9.5% a year for the last two decades, and India's at a strong 6%. Economists predict that both will continue to grow in the 7%-to-8% range for decades. It's either get in or stand on the sidelines and watch your competitors prosper.

There are risks, of course. We don't fully understand these countries. Their accounting systems are different; they calculate profit differently. So we mitigate these risks by creating a specialized international division—that is, yet another silo. It's simple enough to begin with. We have excess capacity, so we sell it wherever there is a market. We remain an "ethnocentric" company, a domestic company with an international division for export.

Having a separate division for the international business is a sound strategy because domestic operations remain protected if the foreign investment goes south.

But growth continues, and the "ethnocentric" organization no longer suffices. The company evolves to become "polycentric"—with separate subsidiaries in each country. Like every other move along the growth arc, this one, too, makes sense. After all, each country is unique, both culturally and also in terms of business regulation. Business in India, although it's improving, is still hampered by a bewildering array of regulations. U.S. firms cannot get into the retailing business in India, for example, and in certain industries, like telecom, ownership by foreign entities is still seriously restricted. China, with its large number of state-owned enterprises, offers a different set of challenges. The solution is to form a subsidiary in India, another in China, and so on.

So, now you have 50-story office towers all over the world. Like IBM did with the old IBM trading company, and like HP and many others have done more recently, you have created a Roman empire. You are in Rome, and your provincial chieftains are in the remote corners of the world. You never see them; they never see you. Out of sight, out of mind—as long as those tax revenues keep pouring in. In fact, those chieftains are likely to be doing their own stuff, running their own increasingly autonomous enterprises. Back in Rome, you remain unaware because your financials are still fine. More silos have been created. The self-destructive habit is growing, and the side effects can't be ignored forever.

The final step on the journey comes when we put the local person in charge of the foreign subsidiary. We make the logical assumption that we'd better have a Chinese guy in charge of the China market. He knows the politics, the culture, and the language, to say nothing of the complicated business environment. This, we believe, is a no-brainer. In fact, it's the worst mistake we can make. The reason is that the local honcho will be loyal to country first and company second. What's more, he has blinders on and looks upon the world from his country's viewpoint. He is the classic provincial chieftain; he is the Afghan warlord. We think we have won the war and have these guys under our control, but they spend 30% of their time doing the company's business and 70% ruling over their own clans and protecting their own territories.

What we have been describing is the more or less natural process of growth—those seemingly commonsense organizational steps that allow a company to move from one phase to the next in its evolution. We want to grow, of course. How do we get there? First we organize by function, next we expand nationally, and then we go abroad and form international subsidiaries. What's wrong with this picture? Nothing that's immediately apparent. But growth, like drug therapy, must be carefully monitored. Otherwise, it may become an end in itself rather than a means to an end. It may become habit-forming. Let's look at how this happens. Let's consider some scenarios in which the natural desire to grow—***to acquire territory***—entails side effects that devolve into self-destructive habits.

WHEN GROWTH REQUIRES THE INSTITUTION OF FORMAL POLICIES AND PROCEDURES

The free and easy entrepreneurial culture on which the company was founded works fine while the company is small, but now operations need form and structure. Organizing into functions requires clear delineation of resources and responsibilities. Employees in the 50-story building may think they are still managing the old way, but gradually, perhaps imperceptibly, each silo is losing contact with the others. The left hand doesn't always know what the right hand is doing. The bureaucracy of rules and regulations replaces human communication. Everyone starts guarding his or her turf.

Let's illustrate this process with a story that appeared in the business press some years ago. A branch bank in downtown Spokane, Washington, decided it needed to control access to its small parking lot, so it installed an automated gate. Customers pulled up, punched the button to make the gate lift, and got a ticket from the machine. If they completed a transaction inside the bank, the teller would stamp their ticket, and the 60% fee would be waived. Otherwise, they would be charged that amount on their way out of the lot.

Into the parking lot comes a man driving a pickup truck, dressed in khaki pants and a flannel shirt—a farmer or outdoorsman, perhaps. He picks up some forms available in the lobby and then asks the teller to validate his ticket. "Did you complete a transaction?" the teller asks, following procedure. "No," the man tells her, "but I'm a regular customer." She says she's sorry, but he'll-have to pay the 60 cents. The man protests that it's a ridiculous policy, that as a regular customer he shouldn't have to pay to park in the bank's lot. We might note that the teller has a computer terminal; she could look him up and confirm that he's a customer. But she has not been trained to do that. She's following policy and doesn't want to cross over into somebody else's territory.

The customer is understandably miffed. He believes he should be recognized as a regular customer in this small-town bank and should be treated as such. He seeks redress from the branch manager inside his glass booth. Surely the manager will overrule his employee, but it's not that simple. It seems that the banking company has just instituted a new performance appraisal system called "360 feedback." That is, the manager's promotion depends on how his employees—as well as his superiors—rate him, so he needs a good performance review from his tellers. Plus, he doesn't have to live with this customer, but he has to work day in and day out with his teller. He has to back her up on this. He has the authority to remedy the situation, but he's caught in the bureaucratic trap—the policies-and-procedures trap.

The man goes home and calls the bank's Seattle office. He's no longer a customer; now he's a crusader on a mission. He explains the problem. You can guess what the woman on the phone says. "That's a branch problem."

At this point the customer, who happens to be a retired telephone executive, withdraws all the money from his ***$2.5*** million account. He calls headquarters again and says, "Okay, I've completed a transaction. Now I want my 60% back."

So the bank has lost a well-heeled client, a high-net-worth guy with whom it stood to do a lucrative business for years to come. How could such a thing happen? With each person locked into his or her own piece of turf by the bureaucracy of policy and procedure, there's no connection between these managers and tellers and supervisors. The operations manual has taken over. Growth demands systems of organization, but in the 50-story building, real communication may become a casualty.

WHEN THE FOUNDER'S CULTURE IS SUBSUMED WITHIN A LARGER CORPORATE CULTURE

Sometimes, to meet its growth objectives, a company must give up private ownership and offer itself to the public. This move is likely to entail a radical change in culture because the leader is no longer autonomous but must answer to Wall Street's unforgiving demands. If the company falters, it may be forced to take shelter under somebody else's umbrella. For example, two old family-owned department stores in Atlanta, Rich's and Davison's, both became part of the national Macy's chain, which, in turn, is now part of the retail conglomerate Federated Stores. In cases like this, the culture of the original founder/entrepreneur is extinguished— whether quickly or slowly. Ownership culture—characterized by informality and spontaneity—is supplanted by management culture, and the process of bureaucratization is under way. The same thing happens when a community bank becomes part of a big bank or when the town's local drugstore sells out to Walgreens or CVS. Some of the most dramatic examples, though, take place within advertising agencies.

WIRE AND PLASTIC PRODUCTS

Maybe you didn't realize Wire and Plastic Products was the original name of the global advertising conglomerate now known as WPP Group. Maybe you also didn't know that the company's original business was making grocery baskets. All that was before former Saatchi & Saatchi executive Martin Sorrell took over the company in 1985 with the intention of remaking it into an advertising, marketing, and media consulting powerhouse.

Sorrell's first Sig move was his acquisition of J. Walter Thompson in 1987. JWT, as it's now called, got its identity 110 years earlier when James Walter Thompson bought the New York City–based Carlton & Smith ad agency in 1877. Thompson's shop dreamed up the Rock of Gibraltar to represent Prudential Insurance in 1896. Sorrell moved again in 1989, acquiring another iconic U.S. ad firm, Ogilvy & Mather. That firm had been founded in 1948 by advertising pioneer and best-selling author David Ogilvy, who had lent his creative talents to heavy-hitting clients such as American Express and IBM.

In the late 1990s, WPP entered another period of rapid growth, buying up more than two dozen companies around the world in advertising, market research, media planning, and related units. The binge culminated with the 2000 acquisition of leading U.S. rival Young & Rubicam for *4.7* billion (the largest advertising merger ever). Y&R's roots went back to 1923, when Raymond Rubicam and John Orr Young founded their Philadelphia agency by taking as their first client Presto Quick Tip Shoelaces. By the time it opened a New York office in 1926, the young firm had become known for its informal atmosphere and creative energy. With that acquisition, WPP officially became the world's biggest advertising company, but it wasn't done yet. In 2005, it made industry headlines again when it acquired the huge Grey Global Group for $75 billion. Grey was founded in 1917 when 17-year-old Larry Valenstein borrowed $100 from his mother to start up a direct-mail agency called Grey Art Studios. He and partner Arthur Fatt placed their first national ad in a 1926 issue of ***Ladies Home Journal,*** pushing the Mendoza Fur Dyeing Works. Thirty years later, working on the Greyhound Bus account, Fatt came up with "Leave the driving to us."

There, in general and broad outline, is a picture of growth-driven consolidation in the advertising/media relations industry. I noted those few details of the acquired companies' histories to make the point that most, if not all, of the firms—whether big rival ad agencies or smaller companies offering related media services—that now crowd together under the WPP umbrella at one time had their own unique, entrepreneurial cultures. Now let's take a closer look at the disruptions, the clashes, the turf wars that are bound to ensue when an advertising shop decides to mutate into the world's biggest "communications supermarket."

Already in 1988, the ***Wall Street Journal*** was editorializing about the trend among ad agencies to snap up not only each other but also PR firms, market research firms, direct-mail houses, and all kinds of related companies in their effort to become one-stop shops. They were spending a lot of time and money marketing the concept to their clients, with Young & Rubicam labeling its various endeavors "the Whole Egg" and the Ogilvy Group (about to become part of WPP) coming up with "Ogilvy Orchestration," among others.

But the clients weren't buying. According to the journal, Eastman Kodak's approach was typical. It went to WPP's J. Walter Thompson agency to create ads for Kodak film but rarely called on any of WPP's other 30-odd marketing subsidiaries. A Kodak spokesman explained this was because there was real uncertainty as to whether one agency could truly be the best at everything. Why? Because of what we have been describing as the 50-story building effect, the various subsidiary units often don't know, don't like, or don't communicate with each other. As an advertising VP for MasterCard told the journal, "[The units] don't talk to each other. You might as well go to the guy down the block."

The one-stop shopping concept has also been stymied by "internal politics and competition"—in other words, turf wars. The journal notes that in general an agency's marketing unit is judged by the amount of business it generates, which in turn often leads to fierce infighting as units battle for a bigger share of a client's budget. For example, Richardson-Vicks hired Y&R to create ads for its Tempo antacid; then, when consumer response was disappointing, the manufacturer hired Y&R's direct-marketing unit to pinpoint heavy antacid users. According to Ronald Ahrens, who was running Richardson-Vicks' consumer health-care division at the time, the unexpected result was conflict between the two units. Ahrens told the journal that sometimes one unit would disparage another and give you the impression that "if you put more money in their unit, you would be better off than putting it in the other unit. It was disappointing."

Looking back on the episode, a Y&R spokesman conceded that conflict often arises early on "when two strong institutions with separate histories merge."

Twelve years later, Young & Rubicam was "merged" into WPP, the acquisition that made WPP No. 1 in the world. Ironically, CEO Martin Sorrell decried the very "bigness" he had so avidly sought for 15 years. "It was never about bigness" he said in an interview in ***The New York Times.*** "If anything, there are diseconomies of scale in creative businesses."

Indeed, Sorrell preferred that WPP be thought of as "a group of a hundred or so tribes. What we're seeking to do is capitalize on the benefits of scale, with the heart, mind, soul and energy of a small company." WPP's health, Sorrell went on to say, "depends on the health and strength of the individual tribes." And according to Sorrell, the deeper you go into WPP's organization of 55,000 people, the stronger the level of cooperation.

Can WPP's "hundred or so tribes" really coexist independently and productively, maintaining their individual cultures, as Sorrell's vision would seem to imply? Or will there inevitably be multiplying levels of bureaucracy as WPP continues to gobble up its rivals? Apparently Y&R's clients thought something would be lost in transition. Shortly after the deal was completed, KFG, Kraft, and United Airlines all defected from the agency, and Y&R CEO Thomas Bell was soon gone as well (apparently because of tension between him and Sorrell).

The next wave of defections from Y&R included Jaguar, Sony, and Burger King. Interestingly, the No. 2 burger chain took its 350 million account to Crispin Porter & Bogusky, a still-independent "boutique" house located in Miami. This may not be a knock against Y&R, since Burger King has recently been changing agencies as frequently as women's fashions change. But it's worth noting that Burger King was impressed by Crispin Porter's innovative campaigns for clients like Ikea and the Mini Cooper. In one spot for the Mini, for example, a sport utility vehicle is seen driving around with a Mini on its roof. Maybe this is the sort of creativity you get before you become another "unit" in somebody else's 50-story building.

If swallowing Y&R caused any indigestion, Sorrell showed no ill effects, at least not based on WPP's 2005 acquisition of Grey Global, the world's seventh-largest agency. Grey's biggest client is P&G, and some of P&G's biggest rivals, like Unilever and Colgate-Palmolive, are already represented by WPP. In the months leading up to the deal, Sorrell was said to have exerted considerable effort assuring WPP's existing clients and P&G that nobody would suffer from the takeover. Maybe it's possible to have one tribe too many.

WHEN A COMPANY'S CULTURE IS DOMINATED BY ONE FUNCTIONAL SPECIALTY

At the risk of overstatement, I honestly believe that a company's functional cultures are stronger than national or ethnic cultures. That is, the cultural differences between a German, a Frenchman, and a Brit are not as divisive as the differences between an engineer, a sales guy, a designer, or whatever. Moreover, a company often has a bias (perhaps stemming from its founder's background or vision) in favor of one of those cultures. Our values are likely to have been shaped by our education and training—our specialization. To the extent that we embrace the culture of our own function or specialty within the company, we are also likely to be contemptuous of others.

Especially since the Industrial Revolution, it seems, the German bias toward science and engineering has been ascendant—especially in the world of business and industry. The hard sciences and mathematics attract the brainiest people, according to the stereotype. Liberal arts majors—though they may be brilliant in their own way—are liberal arts majors by default; that is, they made Cs in biology and calculus. Thus, within the corporation we end up with something like the Indian caste system, with scientists and inventors—the people who create knowledge—at the top, the Brahmins. Then come manufacturers, people who create tangible value. Perhaps next are designers, who turn rough manufactured goods into appealing consumer products, followed by marketing people who know how to package and promote and brand. Selling is lower, always tainted by the vulgarity of money-changing. And at the bottom of the scale are the untouchables, the customer support personnel—installation, service, and repair people with their ***n*** high school educations and blue-collar identities.

Again, the idea is that as a company organizes into functions, it is likely to engender a kind of cultural warfare. Which function really drives the company and provides its vision? Which produces the most revenue? Which should get the most support? All are valuable, even essential, but you won't find many companies where the various functions agree that they are all ***equally*** valuable. Given the Western bias as we've described it, it's not surprising that many of today's splashiest companies are engineering-driven, and it's not hard to find examples of companies whose engineering culture has been dominant to an unhealthy degree.

But first, let's return to the metaphor of the 50-story complex, within which each function inhabits its own tower. The lack of communication and coordination inherent in this architecture is exacerbated by cultural conflict. Dysfunction grows. Each function gripes about the others and tries to take its complaints to the 50th floor. In the common lobby on the bottom floor, the atmosphere is poisoned by politics and gossip.

When management feels itself besieged by too many people trying to come up the elevators with all their problems, its typical response is to build a temporary bridge linking the various towers. This is the "task force." It's a great idea in theory, but in practice it often just brings covert conflict into the open. Now the engineers, the sales guys, the designers, and all the others have to look one another in the eye: The manufacturing guy looks at the sales guy and says, "I can't trust him. Look how slick he is. He'll overpromise, and I'll have to deliver." The sales guy looks at the engineer and says, "What a nerd. Still wearing his pocket protector. I'll have to dress him up before I can show him to a customer." Honestly, you can put Muslims, Christians, and atheists into a room and have a better chance of productive dialog than if you bring together representatives of the various company functions. What's more, each person on the task force has been charged by his boss to defend the function's territory, to represent the functional interest. The last thing you want to do is surrender any functional autonomy. So you have an advocacy environment in which agreement and cooperation are in short supply. Instead of visionary decision-making, you have compromise. On the task force battlefield, functional loyalties are likely to become fiercer than ever. Think of it; a scientist can talk to another scientist anywhere in the world, but he doesn't want to have anything to do with the marketing people in his own company.

BRAINY MOTOROLA

To find an example of a company where one functional culture dominates to the detriment of the others (and of the company as a whole), let's return to the Motorola story. In Chapter 3, I accused Motorola of arrogance; at this point let me add that the company's arrogance stems from the "smarter than you" attitude fostered by its strong engineering culture.

From the first two-way radios to integrated circuits to satellites, the company's successes have been remarkable. In the early 1990s, Motorola was the "nimble giant" that led the world in cell phones, pagers, two-way radios, and microchips used in devices other than computers. In the mid-1990s, Motorola enjoyed 33% of the global cell phone market. But five years later its share was 14%. Over the same period, rival Nokia's share increased from 22% to 35%, and the Finland-based company has led the world ever since. What happened?

Nokia seems to have understood that it's not all about engineering. Things like sales, design, and keeping customers happy are also essential functions. While Motorola played the role of the "bossy, know-it-all supplier," even telling wireless carriers how to display its phones in their stores, Nokia was busy forging mutually fruitful alliances with companies like Verizon and Cingular. Frank Boyer, a Cingular vice president, told the ***Wall Street Journal*** that it was always tough to get the attention of Motorola's top executives; "It was difficult to know if you were really reaching the influencer or decision-maker within Motorola." On the other hand, said Boyer, he talked to Nokia's head of U.S. sales every month.

Nokia has made an art of listening and responding to its customers. When' the risks of talking on cell phones while driving became an issue, SBC (new Cingular) asked its suppliers to come up with a line of phones that displayed "Safety is your most important call" when first turned on. Nokia responded in 24 hours. Motorola in two weeks. Showing a little marketing savvy, Nokia created a series of faceplates for the phones it sold to Alltel featuring the colors and logos of college sports teams in Alltel's coverage area—teams like Duke, Alabama, and Arkansas. Sales of those phones surged 20% or more. Alltel didn't even approach Motorola about a similar program because, according to an Alltel spokesman, "We knew they didn't have the capability to do it."

Also while Motorola and other suppliers have sought to cut costs by outsourcing manufacturing operations, Nokia has insisted on keeping manufacturing under its own roof. Chairman Jorma Ollila told ***Business Week*** that producing its own phones is yet another way Nokia stays in front of its rivals and that doing so keeps it immediately responsive to customers. And saving money on manufacturing, noted ***Business Week,*** will not solve Motorola's problems. More important in this fast-changing market are snazzy design, powerful marketing, and a sure feel for consumer tastes non-engineering functions that Motorola has failed to emphasize. As one analyst told the magazine, "If they make ugly phones that no one wants, lower costs won't help much."

As Motorola took its lumps at the turn of the millennium, with its stock price losing three-fourths of its value between mid-2000 and mid-2001, CEO Chris Galvin (grandson of founder Paul Galvin) appeared to see the need to change his company's elitist engineering culture. "It's all about the customer," he told the business press. "The customer pays the bills." But two years later, Galvin was gone, and, still floundering, the company brought in outsider Edward Zander, formerly president of Sun Microsystems.

Zander, a top-notch salesman with a ready smile and a working-class Brooklyn background, might have known intuitively what Galvin learned the hard way: It was time for Motorola to focus on the customer. We can't give Zander all the credit for the quick and dramatic turnaround in Motorola's numbers in the first two quarters of 2004 (67% increase in cell phone sales, revenue up 41% from a year earlier), but there's no doubt that he has shaken the foundations of Motorola's 50-story building. "We need to break down some of those walls" between business units, he told the press, and his first order of business was to visit key customers all over the globe.

Will Zander succeed in transforming Motorola's culture? Industry insiders think he may have a chance. Zander is "the real deal," according to RadioShack CEO Leonard Roberts. "Motorola has needed for some time not only a person who understands technology but who also understands the customer."

THE WARNING SIGNS OF THE TERRITORIAL IMPULSE

They're not hard to spot. If your company has developed this self-destructive habit, it will be harder to hide than cigarette smoke on your clothes. Look for the following symptoms.

DISSENSION

Instead of one strong general, your company has a lot of headstrong lieutenants, all of whom want to go their own way. Your head of manufacturing thinks your head of marketing doesn't know how to position your products. Your South American office is resentful because Asia is being allocated more than its share of resources. Your regional managers have become mini-czars with no use for directives from headquarters. Your CEO has failed to articulate the single vision that will galvanize all the troops, and consequently his power has been vitiated. Probably the prototype of the fragmented organization is the university, where deans have ceded power to department heads, and where faculty, notoriously independent-minded, don't want to listen to anybody anyway.

INDECISION

Since there's a leadership vacuum at the top and unit managers disagree, decision-making is an agonizing if not impossible process. The situation is exacerbated in cases where bureaucracy is ascendant, where "policies and procedures" have taken over. Instead of saying, "Do it now!" your leader sets up a task force, suggests a "new initiative," or puts together a blue-ribbon committee to study the issue. We see this syndrome regularly in government, where conflicting agendas stymie any real action, and in nonprofits, where bureaucracies are as settled as layers of rock.

But it's also easy to see in big, iconic companies like GM, IBM, and Coca-Cola mired in the status quo; such companies don't seem to be able to respond quickly to an ever-changing environment.

CONFUSION

With too little leadership and with too much autonomy among the warring chieftains, the left hand doesn't know what the right is doing. Some commentators see this kind of situation in Iraq today, with Secretary Rumsfeld offering one assessment of the insurgency, the generals on the ground offering another, and President Bush yet another. A classic case occurred recently when a delegation led by U.S. Senators Richard Lugar and Barack Obama was detained for three hours at an airport in Russia. Border officials in the Siberian city of Perm insisted on searching the U.S. plane, despite a U.S.-Russian agreement that prohibits such inspections. Senator Lugar put his finger precisely on the problem when he described the Russian government as "dysfunctional."

Closer to our immediate interests is the example noted earlier, when Young & Rubicam's creative team squabbled with Y&R's direct marketing unit over the Richardson-Vicks account. When functional silos are so obviously working at cross-purposes, it's time for somebody to yell, ***Who's in charge here?***

MALAISE

As a result of all of the preceding warning signs, nobody's happy, especially the rank and file. And why should they be? The company should be performing, but it's not. It has the potential—the products, the markets, the infrastructure—but it's not getting the results. Raises are puny. The stock in the retirement plan is losing value. Jobs are at risk.

Employees look to the top of the 50-story building, where they see executives closeted in their suites, powerless to turn the company around. They look up to their own managers, but find them snarling at each other over turf—or, worse yet, clock-watching. The once fast-moving company is paralyzed by internal conflict, and the atmosphere is poisoned. It's not a good place to come to work.

HOW TO BREAK THE TERRITORIAL HABIT

It's not easy. These remedies range from a top-to-bottom attitude adjustment to a radical reorganization of your business processes. But if you want to survive and succeed, you don't have any choice.

ENGAGE IN EFFECTIVE INTERNAL MARKETING

Simply put, the leader must bring his people together—all his people, across functions—in a common cause. He has to sell his vision with such passion that everybody wants to buy in. He must make loyalty to the vision more compelling than functional loyalty. To return to the analogy of the great chef, he must be able to blend engineering and manufacturing with marketing, positioning, service, and sales so that what the company produces and what the customer experiences become seamlessly and gratifyingly integrated. Then the 50-story building becomes a landmark, a source of pride not only for employees but also for the larger community of customers, investors, suppliers, and all stakeholders.

For a striking example of internal marketing, let's consider the world's biggest coffee chain. Part of internal marketing is giving people good reason to become true believers, and Starbucks does as good a job of that as anybody. People who work there are not employees; they are "partners" whose job it is to provide "the Starbucks experience." This means not only cultivating "enthusiastically satisfied customers" but also, according to the "guiding principles" of the Starbucks mission statement, "providing a great work environment and treating each other with respect and dignity."

Beyond the feel-good philosophy lies material reward. New hires get their first raise after a three-month trial period, and the regular raises after that are supplemented by an enticing array of benefits. Along with preferred stock options, the Registered Retirement Savings Plan (RRSP) program adds 25 cents to every 75 cents contributed by the employee. What's more, all employees and their spouses—including common-law and same-sex partners—have full medical and dental coverage.

In founder and CEO Howard Schultz's own words, "We pay much higher than the minimum wage, and in 1999, we were the first company in America to provide comprehensive health care and company stock to part-time workers as well as full-time workers. Today [1997] we're still the only company that does this." Schultz explains that such a policy is not only right but also makes good business sense because it's more expensive to train a new worker than it is to provide health benefits. By providing coverage to all employees, Starbucks reduced its turnover rate to one-fifth the retail and restaurant industry average. And giving stock to employees allows them to share in the company's growth and success. Schultz doesn't mind mentioning that his father never made more than 20,000 a year and never got family medical benefits. "I've tried to make Starbucks the kind of company I wish my dad had worked for."

Then there's Starbucks' community outreach. The company is a major contributor to CARE as well as to a variety of AIDS treatment and prevention programs. When working conditions of coffee pickers appeared on the social radar screen, Starbucks adopted a "Code of Conduct" to improve the work environment of the people harvesting its beans.

What Starbucks does well is at least ***seem*** to care about a lot of things other than the bottom line, which inspires loyalty among both employees and customers. In 1995, for example, the chain started selling CDs in its stores, but these were not the kinds of CDs that were for sale in the music stores. ***Just Passin' Thru No. 3,*** for example, was a compilation of songs from the vaults of a Washington-area FM rock station. Other offerings have coffee-pun titles like ***Blending the Blues*** and ***Hot Java Jazz.*** Of course it's good marketing, but Starbucks claims it's more than that. The discs Starbucks comes up with are "handcrafted just like our coffees and our drinks, with dedication and passion," says a Starbucks spokesman. Overstatement, perhaps, but, uniquely,

Starbucks created its own music department, with 12 people—aficionados and former music retailers—whose full-time job is to find music for upcoming CDs and to play in stores' backgrounds. Employees want to work there. Customers want to patronize the place. Investors want to own the stock. Everybody has bought in—which is the enviable result of successful internal marketing.

PUSH YOUR MANAGERS OUT OF THE IVORY TOWER

An effective way to quell turf wars and quiet cultural conflict is to rotate your people in and out of different functional or geographic silos. It's the old "walk a mile in my shoes" theory. There's no better way to understand somebody else's problems than to have to solve them yourself. Some companies—such as specialty chemicals, pharmaceuticals, or office equipment—are fortunate enough to have customer support people with engineering or technical training. But this is not the case as often as it should be. Especially for R&D and engineering people, with their tendency toward elitism, experiencing the manufacturing process, sales and marketing, or customer support is critically important.

As we noted, in the "corporate caste system," customer support people were relegated to the lowest status, but we need to remember that those people, more than anybody else in the company, have their ears to the ground. They're out in the field every day hearing what the customers say, seeing firsthand how customers' needs are being met or not being met by your product or service. Bell managers learned this important lesson when their operators went on strike and they had to take over the call centers. Managers from across functions would do well to learn the same lesson.

Perhaps because they constitute the natural nexus between the company and the customer, salespeople (like Motorola's Ed Zander) seem uniquely equipped to move from function to function and to evolve into effective general managers. Peters and Waterman talk about "the salesman as problem solver." They recall how at 3M salesmen expanded their role—and their value—by avoiding the purchasing agents and going directly to the operators on the shop floor.

What's to be avoided is the congregation of managers at the corporate level in the ivory tower. Peters and Waterman recommend "fewer administrators, more operators." They offer as a useful guideline their "rule of 100." Even the biggest companies, they suggest, seldom need more than 100 people at corporate headquarters. Intel for example, has virtually ***no*** permanent staff; all staff assignments are given to line officers on a temporary basis. Sam Walton embraced the same ideal when he said, "The key is to get into the stores and listen."

Perhaps the best example, though, is IBM, where, according to the authors, management adheres strictly to the rule of "three-year staff rotation." Staff jobs are manned not by "career staffers" but by line officers who, after their stint on the corporate staff, know that they'll be back out on the line again. What a great corrective against cultural warfare and territoriality. "If you know you are going to become a user within 36 months, you are not likely to invent an overbearing bureaucracy during your brief sojourn on the other side of the fence.

CREATE PERMANENT CROSS-FUNCTIONAL TEAMS

We're not talking about the temporary task force here, but rather permanent management teams that include representation from all functions or silos. The idea is to break down cultural competition and turf-guarding at the top of the organization and to allow the spirit of cooperation and shared vision to ripple outward and downward. Asian manufacturers have been practicing this concept for decades. It's probably exemplified nowhere better than in Toyota's famous Toyota Production System (TPS), which has set the standard for so-called lean manufacturing.

For a look at the essence of TPS, consider the experience of automotive engineer Gary Convis, who has been inside it for 20 years. With his newly minted BSME degree, Convis went to work in GM's management training program. He later switched to Ford and worked his way up through Quality, Engineering, Maintenance, and Manufacturing Management. His years at GM and Ford convinced him that the U.S. car industry was in trouble. "We were doing things the same old way," he writes, "and that way was not getting the job done." Worse yet, even though the people in the plants had an abundance of good ideas, it didn't matter because they were stifled by an organization with an entrenched legacy of inflexibility.

Convis was pulled out of this quagmire when Toyota recruited him to help start New United Motor Manufacturing, Inc. (NUMMI), Toyota's joint venture with General Motors. As a way to start building cars in the United States, Toyota wanted to reopen a GM plant in Fremont, California, that had been closed for two years.

For GM, this would mean resuming production of the cars that had been built there and re-employing the several thousand workers who had lost their jobs when the plant closed. The catch was that American workers would be supervised by Japanese managers implementing the Toyota system. Could it work? Convis says Toyota was wary, unsure that Americans could adapt to Toyota's TPS. But Convis believed that Americans could be just as productive as workers anywhere else and that TPS would give them a chance to perform up to their potential. After 15 years with NUMMI in Fremont (before being named president of Toyota's NUMMI plant in Kentucky), Convis is unequivocal in his conviction that the Toyota management and manufacturing methods were the reason that the plant saw a total turnaround.

So, what is TPS all about? Gross-functional teamwork is at its heart, as Convis makes clear in elucidating its "customer-first" philosophy. While most corporations define the customer as the person who purchases the final product at the end of the process, TPS takes a very different view. It looks at each preceding process, workstation, or department as "the supplier" and the next operation downstream as "the customer." At a Toyota plant, all team members and departments have a dual role as customer and supplier.

Here's the crux. For the system to flourish, no artificial barriers can separate one area or one department from another. Instead, problems are shared by the entire organization, and everyone works together to find solutions. Every manager has to be on board, has to support the system, and has to actively seek solutions to problems, even if they are not directly in his or her scope of control. This "all-hands-on-deck attitude," says Convis, is the essential component in the TPS environment.

We have suggested that the skilled leader blends a company's various functions much as a great chef blends his ingredients into a successful recipe. Convis offers an equally apt metaphor. He likens the productive TPS environment to a greenhouse, "where just the right combination of soil, light, temperature, humidity, water, and nutrients allows plants to grow and flourish. If any one of these elements is removed, the plants will weaken and eventually die."

In fact, at Toyota you can see not only the value of cross-functional teamwork but also an appreciation of the well-rounded manager who is at home in any of the company's silos. In a ***Fortune*** magazine profile, Hiroshi Okuda, who ran the company in the late 1990s before taking the chairmanship, described himself as "a specialist at being a generalist." Though an accountant by training, on his way to the presidency Okuda managed nearly every one of Toyota's major functions: domestic and international sales, finance, purchasing, public relations, and new business, as well as accounting. With such a broad-based leader at the top, it's difficult for factionalism and cultural warfare to flourish.

REORGANIZE AROUND CUSTOMERS OR PRODUCTS, RATHER THAN AROUND FUNCTION OR GEOGRAPHY

This kind of reorganization quells internecine conflict among functional and geographic silos by relocating your profit-and-loss centers. Rather than a geographic P&L (how is the Southeast Region performing?) or a functional P&L (how is manufacturing doing?), try putting in place a product P&L (how are printers doing?) or a customer-based P&L (how are we doing with Walmart?). Quite a few companies, when their functional or geographic units have become too turf-conscious, have shifted their P&L focus to product categories. Packaged-goods companies have largely succeeded with this strategy, although it's not without pitfalls. It's possible for brand managers to become every bit as territorial as functional or geographic units. When that happens, a further shift to a customer-based P&L may be the solution. Let's look at a couple of examples.

Back in the 1980s, BP Exploration, the oil giant's exploration and production business, had a typical regional/functional organization. The heads of the various regional operating companies, each covering a geographic area, joined a group of functional directors (finance, human resources, etc.) on a global management committee. Left pretty much out of the equation were the managers of the individual oil fields, who had little to say about how their operations were run. John Browne, whose success in revamping Exploration would help elevate him to BP CEO in 1995, restructured to put the emphasis back on the product—the oil coming from the fields. First, he sold off the smaller fields and kept the larger ones, where BP had scale advantages. Then he began evaluating the performance of the individual fields themselves, bypassing the bureaucratic "regional" layer.

When the limited experiment proved clearly successful, the new structure was implemented across BP Exploration. The regional operating companies were dismantled, replaced by some 40 separate business units, each representing a single large field or a collection of smaller ones. The unwieldy "global management committee" was also jettisoned. The managers of the separate business units reported directly to a streamlined committee consisting of Browne and two other officers. Here is a simple case of shifting from a geographic to a product-based structure—with positive results.

The case of Lucent Technologies is not quite so simple. Spun off from AT&T in 1996, Lucent became a Wall Street darling during the dot-com boom days. During that heady era, to quote the ***Washington Post,*** telecom equipment makers were "the pick and shovel salesmen in a modern-day gold rush." The company grew fast, but it also grew wrong. To meet and anticipate what seemed like inexhaustible demand, it developed too many product lines, built too much production capacity, hired too many marketing people, and stocked its shelves with more equipment than it could sell.

Not surprisingly, many of its customers were dot-com start-ups, to whom it sold its wares by extending credit, booking the sales as revenue. When the bubble burst, a lot of those customers went under, without paying their Lucent bill, leaving the company in the embarrassing position of having to restate its earnings time after time. Investors took flight.

Henry Schacht, who returned to Lucent in 2000 to stop the bleeding and turn the company around, explained that Lucent had made the mistake of organizing into 11 "hot little businesses"—a structure that caused duplication and increased expenses as each separate business unit strove for its own growth and revenue. By the time of his arrival, the situation was dire. The company reported a loss of $1 billion for the last quarter of 2000, and the company's once high-flying stock had lost three-quarters of its value.

Schacht immediately announced a restructuring plan that would "centralize operations," reduce expenses by $2 billion a year, and cut 10,000 people from the payroll.

At the heart of the reorganization, though, was a winnowing of unprofitable product lines and unreliable customers. No more dealings with shaky start-ups. A leaner Lucent would develop products and services with its top 30 customers in view, a group representing 75% of its sales. Patricia Russo, who replaced Schacht as CEO in early 2002, has continued the program—with a vengeance. The once-bloated workforce of 106,000 has been slashed to 39,000. Instead of 11 businesses, there are three: wireless networks, wire-line networks, and network services. The company continues to concentrate its sales and marketing efforts on only its biggest customers—the Bell companies and national carriers.

Competition in the telecom industry remains fierce, and the future is uncertain. It's worth noting that with its customer-focused structure, Lucent returned to profitability in 2004—its first year in the black since 2000.

For a company that's customer-centric, though, you can't do better than Procter & Gamble, and the customer it's focused on is, of course, Walmart. As noted earlier, packaged-goods companies pioneered the idea of organizing around product categories, and P&G, with its 300-plus brands, led the way in this type of organization. Then it met Walmart. Or, more accurately, Walmart got big enough to begin to make some demands.

It wasn't always that way. Lou Pritchett, the P&G sales executive who canoed down Arkansas' Spring River with Sam Walton for two days in the summer of 1987, recalls that before that time there hadn't been much of a relationship between the two companies. "We shipped them products and they sent us a check back," says Pritchett. "It was: We sell. You buy. Good-bye." When Walmart named P&G its supplier of the year, P&G didn't bother to show up to receive its award.

That was how P&G operated with all its customers. Like the typical big supplier, P&G relied on a traditional sales force with a heavy in-store presence that kept the company abreast of retail conditions such as pricing and out-of-stock updates, haggled over proper placement of P&G products on the shelves, and personally introduced new products. Then Walton pointed out something that P&G, with its brand organization, hadn't realized: Walmart had become P&G's biggest customer. As such, it demanded special treatment. Lured by Walmart's carrot and threatened by its stick, P&G reorganized. Now it relies on multifunctional customer teams at headquarters to take care of major accounts.

Or, in the case of Walmart, it relies on cross-functional teams at its "satellite" headquarters in Bentonville, Arkansas. These days about 300 people work in P&G's Arkansas office, overseeing sales of its brands to Walmart and devising cross-marketing and other tie-ins. Why the army? Because 17% of P&G's sales, $8.7 billion worth, comes from Walmart's 5,100 stores worldwide. In fact, the relationship between the two companies has become so intimate that P&G prefers not to let its managers stay on the account for more than a few years. As a former veteran of the Walmart account explains, if they don't get out in time, the P&G people start to identify as much with Walmart's needs as with P&G's.

"It's a lot like a marriage," says Pritchett. "Sometimes you want to slice each other's throats, and there are other times when it's a **love-in."**

Actually, despite the immense reward each company derives from the other, there must be plenty of days when the marriage appears to be on the rocks—or, more particularly, when P&G feels like an abused spouse. For instance, how is P&G supposed to react when Walmart decides to sell private-label diapers or detergent? With the resurgence of private labels since the early 1990s, purveyors of national brands have been seriously pinched. An executive at BBDO Worldwide told ***Fortune*** magazine that only the top two brands plus a private label in a category have a chance for success. "Anything below that will get squeezed right off the shelf." The pressure this puts on manufacturers was aptly summed up by P&G's then-CEO Edwin Artzt: "We're not banking on things getting better with time. We're banking on us getting better."

They have ties with a seemingly insatiable partner like Walmart. The retailing behemoth makes money by moving product, and it's quick to abandon brands—no matter how famous—that sit on its shelves. In other words, to stay competitive, manufacturers like P&G have to keep prices low, quality high, and innovation fresh. Even then, can they retain market share? "The answer is solely in the hands of the national-brand manufacturers," said former Walmart CEO David Glass with a touch of smugness. "If they can contain their costs and deliver a well-known brand at a competitive price, the consumers will buy them."

Ouch! Is Walmart's cavalier attitude toward its most faithful partner behind P&G's $52 billion purchase of Gillette? Is P&G seeking more leverage against Walmart? P&G CEO A.G. Lafley says no. When asked if the balance of power has shifted to suppliers, he likes to reply, "The power has shifted to the consumer."

But the consumer meets the product on the clean, wide aisles of Walmart. P&G knows that. That's why the packaged-goods giant changed how it did business at the bidding of its biggest customer.

Any number of other examples could be cited to illustrate the shift away from functional or geographic organization. Hewlett-Packard reorganized around product lines. HSBC is now in the process of changing from a geographic-based organization to one based around its five major customer groups. It might be useful to think of four buckets that can be filled or emptied: function, geography, product, and customer. One or the other might have become too full or too heavy, throwing the company out of balance. Restoring that balance might be the key to revitalizing a corporate culture that's been paralyzed by internal conflict.

AUTOMATE AND INTEGRATE

We're witnessing this evolution right now. Functional silos are becoming integrated. Geographic silos are coming online. It's the only way big global companies can manage their bureaucracies.

Automation proceeds from back office operations to front office, or customer interface (moving left to right on the chart). Integration begins internally and then moves to external, or supplier management (bottom to top on the chart). Internal integration of the back office is called enterprise resource planning (ERP). It's handled by companies like SAP and Oracle, which coordinate disparate databases to bring together information. It's also sometimes called work automation—a more general term than factory automation or office automation.

Then we move up the matrix to external integration, or supply chain management (SCM). "Just-in-time" inventory management is a good example, wherein suppliers ship raw materials or products on an optimum schedule. This is tremendously important to retailers (like Walmart), of course.

Both ERP and SCM are columned under "back office" on the matrix. Now move horizontally to "front office." At bottom right you see customer relationship management (CRM) platforms and technology. Airlines' computerized reservation

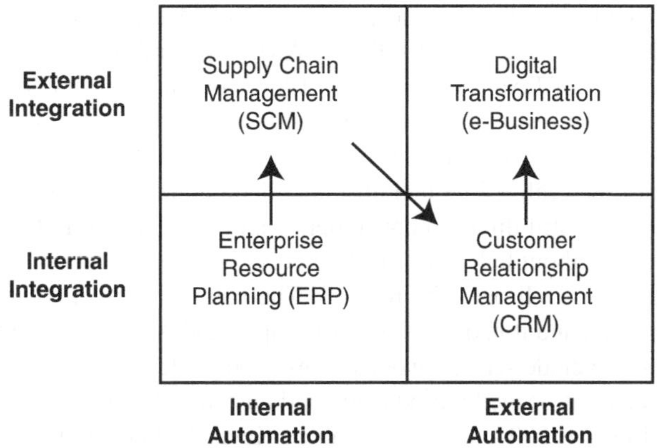

Figure 8-1 Automation and integration

systems provide a good example. After you make your reservation, it is accessible worldwide. For a more concrete example, P&G again stands out. With 300 brands and customers all over the globe the company decided to hire Siebel to construct a global integrated CRM platform that could also be configured for specific markets. Begun in 2000, the initiative required five years for full implementation.

At top right on the matrix is complete online automation and integration, or e-business. External integration and front-office automation come together on the Internet. Companies used to depend on mainframe computers linked by telephone lines or satellites. Then came client/server architecture, in which intelligence/information came from a single server and each desk was a client. Travel agencies operated this way with their Sabre reservation systems. Now all this information management is going to the Internet, and the Internet has become the common standard—as opposed to proprietary standards from IBM or HP or whoever. Companies like SAP specialize in integrating disparate standards, and they charge high fees to perform these integration upgrades. For example, a company like Coke, burdened with the traditional organization of functions and territories, will spend nearly $1 billion for a complete SAP upgrade.

Hotel phone systems are an obvious target for automation and integration upgrades. In the old days, even internal calls (to housekeeping, for example) had to be routed out of the building through the central switch of the public telephone company. Consequently, inside the hotel, the left hand didn't know what the right hand was doing. Today's PBX (private branch exchange) systems have brought the switch inside the business. Now when you call from your room, you come up on the automated system, and everybody knows who you are and what room you're in. High-tech companies like Cisco and Nortel provide the hardware for such systems.

The one company that best exemplifies the integration and automation revolution is Dell. The company that sells more PCs than anybody else in the world, ***without any retail presence,*** must know something about the latest in business processes.

But let's begin with the obvious question: How did Michael Dell do it? Always an entrepreneur, Michael Dell started selling RAM chips and disk drives for IBM PCs out of his University of Texas dorm room in 1984. He bought overstocked goods from IBM dealers and then resold the items through newspapers and computer magazines at prices 10%-to-15% below retail. When his dorm-room business was doing about $80,000 a month, he realized he had all the college education he needed. He started selling IBM clones—still direct to consumers—and by eliminating the retail markup, he kept his prices at about half what an IBM cost.

In almost no time, Dell blew the roof off. The company began adding international sales offices in 1987, and it had subsidiaries in Japan and Australia in 1993. It expanded its product lines to include servers, workstations, storage devices, Ethernet switches, and handheld computers. It opened a production and customer facility in China in 1998 and added a second one in 2004. Current president Kevin Rollins predicts that 2004-2005 revenues of roughly $50 billion will increase to $80 billion by 2008.

At the heart of Dell's success was a radical business model built on innovative supply-chain management. Instead of the conventional model—buy supplies, build your product, and then sell it—Dell sold first and then ordered the materials to build his computers. In other words, no inventory. Or, in the words of Mike Gray, Dell's supply chain guru, "inventory velocity." In effect, suppliers do all the warehousing, and Dell's facilities are manufacturing centers, not places to store finished goods. This fully automated (computerized) supply chain management, says Gray, has allowed Dell to grow to a $50 billion company in just 20 years.

Dell is at the forefront of the automation and integration revolution in other areas as well. To streamline support of its 35,000 server customers around the globe, Dell rolled out Microsoft's Systems Management Server (SMS) 2003. The upgrade to SMS 2003 allowed Dell to consolidate five geographically separate SMS hierarchies into one, with significant cost savings. Its new patch-management features provide hot fixes and updates continually, saving hundreds of man-hours annually. And its support capabilities have enabled Dell to bring thousands of remote systems into its global SMS hierarchy.

Yet another initiative on the CRM side has Dell partnering with Intuit to help small and medium-sized enterprises (SMEs) integrate their own business processes. The bundle includes a Dell OptiPlex computer, Intuit's QuickBooks Point of Sale software, and a complete set of retail hardware, including a receipt printer, a bar code scanner, a credit card reader, and a cash drawer. As the head of Dell's SME division explains, "Our independent retail customers are telling us that they want affordable technology systems to help automate their day-to-day operations so they can spend more time generating sales." One satisfied customer, a gift store owner in Austin, Texas, reported that it was "an easy, seamless experience to deploy the system."

With its history of direct selling—much of it Internet-based—it's not surprising to find Dell at home on the frontiers of e-business, where automation and integration come together. We won't claim that Dell has had none of the growth-related problems we've described in this chapter, or none of the squabbles among functional or geographic silos. But, after all, Dell was born in the computer age and spent its adolescence online. Maybe it was blessed with enough high-tech savvy to keep those four buckets—function, geography, product, and customer—in proper balance. Maybe the self-destructive habits associated with culture conflicts and turf wars never had a chance to develop.

Growth, for a business, is as difficult as growing up is for human beings. That's why child psychologists stay as busy as business consultants. It's hard to arrive at that point, that level of maturity, where self-interest becomes "enlightened." It's natural to be selfish, to be protective of what's "ours," to want more. As the fun of starting up a business (like the fun of childhood) gives way to the imperatives of discipline and organization, corporate behavior is not always everything it should be. CEOs are as fallible as parents; sometimes they are slow to see self-destructive habits developing in the corporate family; sometimes they are powerless to correct them.

But the wise CEO understands that the company is not an end in itself. He or she has the vision to see its larger purpose, and the essence of his or her leadership is to share that vision. When that happens—when the whole family sees what the leader sees and believes what the leader believes—adolescent squabbles come to an end. No more culture conflicts. No more turf wars. No more sibling rivalry. The company can grow without divisiveness or factionalism. It can take its place in the grown-up world.

THE TERRITORIAL IMPULSE

Things that lead to territorial impulse:

- The corporate ivory tower
- Growth requires the institution of formal policies and procedures
- The founder's culture is subsumed within a larger corporate culture
- A company's culture is dominated by one functional specialty

Warning signs of territorial impulse:

- **Dissension:** Instead of one strong general, your company has a lot of headstrong lieutenants.
- **Indecision:** Decision-making is an agonizing or even impossible process.
- **Confusion:** The left hand doesn't know what the right hand is doing.
- **Malaise:** Nobody's happy, especially the rank and file.

How to break the territorial habit:

- **Engage in effective internal marketing:** The leader must bring his people together—all his people, across functions—in a common cause.
- **Push your managers out of the ivory tower:** Rotate your people in and out of different functional or geographic silos.
- **Create permanent cross-functional teams:** Organize permanent management teams that include representation from all functions or silos.
- **Reorganize around customers or products, rather than around function or geography:** Quell internecine conflict among functional and geographic silos by relocating your profit-and-loss centers.

CHAPTER 9

THE BEST CURE IS NO CURE AT ALL

In dissecting the problems that ail corporations under the rubric of "self-destructive habits," we are, of course, anthropomorphizing. After all, comparing corporate behavior to human behavior is instructive, and it works.

- The kind of denial that caused the collapse of Digital and the decline of Xerox is not foreign to our personal experience. Who doesn't know someone—a friend, perhaps, or spouse—who refuses to acknowledge that he or she "has a problem"? Perhaps we ourselves have needed an occasional "reality check."
- Why do we cheer for the upstart Google? Because everybody, at one point or another, has been victimized by the kind of arrogance that Microsoft exhibited. Everybody wants to see the schoolyard bully get his comeuppance.
- Whenever we're treated indifferently by a penpushing bureaucrat who knows his job is a lifetime sinecure, we're staring at complacency. When airlines suddenly had to face real-world competition, and many proved unable to, it was hard to feel a lot of sympathy.
- While we're criticizing Singer and Encyclopaedia Britannica for competency dependence, let's not forget all the people in the world who know how to do one thing only. (Now that I think about it, university professors—like me—might be the most competency-dependent people in the world.)
- The competitive myopia that Coke exhibits when it obsesses about Pepsi is everyday fodder in the sports pages, where it's called "looking ahead." The undefeated football team starts anticipating the end-of-season matchup against its highly ranked archrival, only to find itself upset by the nonconference patsy that it should have beaten by four touchdowns.
- If you can't relate volume obsession to your own human experience, you probably need to go shopping.
- As for the territorial impulse, the kind of turf battles we documented at WPP are recapitulated in every family that has more than one child—or, for that matter, in every family that has more than one pet.

The analogy continues, at least to this extent: breaking these self-destructive habits, for corporations as well as for human beings, begins with awareness. It begins, as we have put it in each chapter, with recognizing the "signs" and saying, "Okay, that's me."

So, if companies can develop awareness as a basis for correcting self-destructive habits, why not use this cognizance to ***prevent*** a self-destructive habit from happening in the first place? As I pointed out in Chapter 1, the more you practice "anticipatory management"—as opposed to "status-quo management"—the less time you spend resorting to "crisis management." To carry our anthropomorphizing further, "An ounce of prevention is worth a pound of cure" applies just as aptly to the business "body" as it does to the human body.

The overwhelming consensus among the medical profession is that correcting diseases, injuries, and addictions is more expensive and more difficult to accomplish and has more consequences than taking steps to prevent the problem in the first place. Even when medical intervention is deemed successful in rectifying an affliction, the intervention process itself often has mild to serious consequences. For example, the surgical process carries unintentional risks—such as bacterial infection, reactions to anesthesia, and surgeon error—that are unrelated to the problem being corrected. Even after surgery, the patient may be better in some ways, but other problems may develop as the shock filters through the body's complicated and interrelated systems. And even if the surgery is successful, it doesn't keep the patient from repeating the behavior that caused the problem in the first place.

Prescription drugs are another case in point. Without a doubt, numerous drugs have made an important contribution to society's overall medical well-being. But all too often they are expensive and lifelong corrective measures with their own negative side effects. Instead of having to put patients with high levels of cholesterol on a lifelong regimen of Lipitor or Mevacor, wouldn't it be better to prevent the cholesterol in the first place through a healthy diet and exercise?

Kicking some unhealthy habits is a more difficult process than having something removed or taking a pill. According to the Centers for Disease Control and Prevention (CDC), in 2004 there were 44.5 million adult tobacco smokers in the U.S. An estimated 70% of these smokers said they wanted to quit. It is possible to quit smoking, and millions of people have done so; however, for many, the first cigarette is the beginning of a lifelong habit that has harmful and expensive fallout. The best solution is to avoid that initial cigarette.

As in human health, corporate health is better served if self-destructive habits never have a chance to get a foothold. Just as with humans, if the self-destructive habit forms, it may be too addictive to stop. Or it may be allowed to go on until irreversible damage occurs. Or the cure may be so invasive that the company suffers additional negative consequences or never recovers. And the cure may be expensive and require lifelong maintenance. It would be much better, as we know from human health care, to encourage wellness instead of treating illnesses.

In business, prevention of self-destructive habits is a much more visionary and continuous process than a cure. You can't wait until a self-destructive habit has had time to infest itself in the company's body. Waiting until there is a groundswell of customer or employee discontent—or, worse yet, a crippling financial hit—does not constitute a prevention program. Successful prevention involves having systems or processes in place that frequently monitor your present situation and anticipate the future so that warning flags can be detected at the earliest possible moment. Prevention also involves having up-to-date methods in place to automatically correct the company's course to avoid the self-destructive habit.

So what can companies do to prevent the self-destructive habits from developing in the first place?

DENIAL

The best way to prevent denial from becoming a habit is to have systems in place that constantly challenge business assumptions and orthodoxies. An easy way to do this is to put into place a periodic or continuous process of "scenario planning." Scenario planning is a strategic method of flexible, long-term planning. The basic process involves having a group of analysts generate what-if scenarios for decision makers that combine known facts about the future with possible trends. Using the six drivers of change identified in an article I coauthored with Dr. Rajendra S. Sisodia—technology, regulation, globalization, competition, customers, and capital markets—as a framework would be particularly helpful. By institutionalizing this process of watching trends, especially external trends that drive the company and the market, management is reminded of the potential competitive threats that exist. This keeps decision makers from falling into the comforting trap of ignoring or avoiding the existence of competitors, competitive technologies, or events that could harm the company. In this case, a little bit of paranoia is good for your business condition!

In the oil industry, dramatic, one-time events such as the damage caused by Hurricane Katrina to refineries and the resulting disruption of the nation's oil and gas supplies, or more complicated scenarios such as the historical political and military conflicts of the Middle East, cry out for a need to understand and anticipate the future. Royal Dutch/Shell is a pioneer in the use of scenario planning for this purpose. Its Global Business Environment (GBE) unit is tasked with differentiating between "what's inevitable [and] what's unknowable."

In the 1970s, what was Shell Company at that time employed the services of an eccentric Belgian and French oil executive, Pierre Wack. He was certain that with the right mixture of "deep perception and intellectual rigor" you could make a fairly accurate prediction about the future. Wack developed this into what was essentially a method of storytelling that links the knowns (the ***tendances lourdes,*** as Wack called them) and unknowns about the future to the decisions that must be made today.

One of the first scenarios that Wack and his team pondered was the Middle East. The scenario that unfolded was one of a group of oil-rich nations that were too small to absorb the wealth that was flowing their way. They would find no bank asset or piece of real estate that would appreciate as quickly as the oil in the ground, especially if the oil stayed in the ground. With this scenario in mind, Wack and his team perceived that an effort to control the flow of oil would be initiated (OPEC) and that rising oil prices would be the ***tendances lourdes*** "that would drive the global system for the next 10 years."

Your past and current achievements may be useful as plaques in the boardroom or as a way to impress golfing buddies, but if they become a diversion to what is around the corner, you're setting yourself up for an unpleasant surprise. Regardless of the specific tools or how the internal process is set up, the key is to develop a corporate mind-set of skepticism about the assumptions you have made and continue to make about the future and to take proactive measures accordingly. As innovative leadership consultant and author Michael J. Gelb puts it, "The best way to forecast the future is to create it!"

I do have a caveat for all of this: that you should keep one eye (not both) on your competitors and competing technologies. There is a real danger that if you become too focused on "the other guys" you will develop an obsession or full-blown paranoia. This happened to Microsoft when it became fixated on the threat posed by Netscape to the Internet Explorer Internet browser and, more threateningly, the near-monopoly control of the Windows operating system on the PC market. This resulted in ethically and legally questionable actions and a subsequent lengthy and expensive court case. Having a healthy suspicion shouldn't blind you to a wider view of the competitive landscape.

In addition to having a role in preventing arrogance, a hands-on leadership institute can serve as a way to teach managers how to focus on the future. GE's "Workout," "Action Learning" with Noel Tichy, and Motorola's Participatory Management Process (PMP) help tear down barriers between middle and senior management. They are also excellent programs for allowing participants to challenge prevailing assumptions about how things have always been done and to come up with recommendations for improvements in organizational processes. If you require all managers to take part, the institute will create a common language and become embedded in the decision-making process.

ARROGANCE

Arrogance is harder to prevent because it's often a result of unintentional and external forces. As pointed out in Chapter 3, most successes occur by accident, and there is a tendency for someone to take credit for that success. The media contributes to this by hyping CEOs and other top business leaders and giving them a larger-than-life persona (e.g., Ken Lay of Enron) for its own self-interests of selling magazines, newspapers, and books or boosting television ratings. As humans, we have an innate attraction to being singled out as successful or in charge, so it's easy to see why a CEO would develop a self-perception that he has done everything and is all-powerful—and why this would then lead to a bad case of arrogance. However, the path to arrogance isn't always traced back to outside or uncontrollable factors. Powerful positions are very tempting, but optional opportunities to flaunt success and get away with abusive behavior. In this case it's more a matter of resisting the choice.

A good way to prevent arrogance is to have an advisor or executive coach who constantly reminds you of the pitfalls of arrogance and alerts you when you begin to head down that route. Although the trusted advisor role could be filled by a spouse or coworker, I strongly recommend that you have someone outside your company, and outside your profession, who can act as a confidential sounding board, detached observer, and objective advice-giver. Someone who will actively watch or observe you and be what Harvard Business School professor Thomas DeLong calls a "truth speaker." An enthusiastic supporter of this process of career oversight is David Pottruck, CEO of Eos Airlines, who credits former IBM executive Terry Pearce with "transforming him from a sharp-elbowed despot into a sensitive consensus-builder." ***Clients for Life,*** a book I coauthored with Andrew Sobel, contains numerous examples of extraordinary advisors throughout history, from Aristotle to Peter Drucker.

Although it was once regarded as pop psychobabble, in recent years executive coaching has become a respected and widely used resource for shaping leadership behavior. The International Coach Federation, a membership-driven organization that developed an accreditation process and provides continuing education opportunities, has more than 10,000 members in 80 countries. IBM is an active supporter and utilizer of this profession and has more than 60 certified coaches among its ranks.

A second approach for preventing arrogance is to limit personal publicity. Because publicity shapes your identity, it is better not to spend too much time in the limelight. Do it in a more subtle or silent way instead of flaunting yourself. It's one thing to be the "face" of the company to stockholders, employees, customers, suppliers, and the community to promote the company as a worthwhile investment and a good corporate citizen. It's another when this steps over into a personal branding campaign or the executive's personal life becomes fodder for gossip columns. This is doubly important in the wake of high-profile scandals at Enron, WorldCom, and Tyco, which have left an impression in stakeholders' minds that a self-promoting, egotistical leader is a warning sign of impending corporate disaster.

Finally, make sure that company processes of checks and balances are in place so that no one individual has absolute power. That way the institution doesn't allow you or anyone else to become arrogant. This concept has worked remarkably well throughout the history of the U.S. government.

COMPLACENCY

The first step in preventing complacency is to develop strong metrics—preferably numerical metrics—that give you a quantitative method of constantly judging the company's level of complacency. If we go back to the health analog, it's comparable to being connected to a heart monitoring machine. If any aberrations occur, you know it's time to take a more thorough and more serious look at the company's health.

Another prevention measure is to institute performance-based compensation. Often complacency arises when employees assume their job is guaranteed and they will have automatic annual raises, regardless of how the company performs. This is also true for top management and board members. Having a certain amount of compensation tied to company performance encourages everyone to innovate and excel. You should develop a set of performance measures (such as business growth, profit growth, employee retention, customer loyalty, stock price) that are in alignment with your company's strategic goals.

One company that has taken this approach to the highest levels of governance is The Coca-Cola Company, which announced a new Board of Directors compensation plan in April 2006 that consisted entirely of equity-based remuneration, payable only when the company met defined performance targets. "Shareowners understand that they are only rewarded when the company performs," said James D. Robinson III, chairman of the Company's Committee on Directors and Corporate Governance. "The Coca-Cola Company Board will hold itself to the same standard." This sent a clear message that a business-as-usual attitude has financial consequences, not only for Coca-Cola but also for those who are guiding its growth.

A third approach for preventing complacency is rotating leaders from function to function. If you rotate people, they don't have time to develop complacency in any one job. Instead, they constantly energize themselves, learn new things, and see the company from different perspectives.

COMPETENCY DEPENDENCE

This is a very hard habit to prevent. The reason is that we are firm believers in specialization. Most of the education system after high school tends to focus on becoming specialized. By occupation you are specialized, and the function you fill in a company, especially large companies, is specialized. This has benefits for the individual and the company because as you become more specialized, you are more efficient and more valuable in your role. But this specialization becomes very comfortable (similar to a monopoly), and you tend to lose the ability to develop alternative ways of looking at products, technologies, customers, markets, opportunities, competitive threats, and so on.

So how do we prevent this habit? The first mechanism is to be in a constant state of proactive migration from the current technology to the next-generation technology. This system has no upper limit on performance or improvement, so you don't become too dependent on any single competency. Nike is a company that practices this very successfully. It constantly improves athletic shoes. It is in various stages of development on several new generations of shoe technology, even as the latest and greatest product hits store shelves.

Proactive migration has been a cornerstone of Intel's success. It has an almost religious adherence to a prediction made in 1965 by Gordon Moore, who also happens to be Intel's cofounder. Now known as Moore's Law, the original prognostication of how long it would take for the number of transistors on a chip to double now has a more popularized interpretation that computer processing speed doubles every 18 months. To take advantage of this prediction, Intel has built its business around taking products from initial design to the sales channel in 18 to 24 months, which is a tremendous feat considering that in most industries this is a two-to-five-year process. The constant pressure to meet the standard of Moore's Law keeps Intel running hard. And as long as the company continues to successfully meet its production goals, the best the rest of the industry can hope for is to temporarily pull even.

Another approach for prevention is to expand your core technology into other products and markets. In other words, diversify your competency so that it can do other things. So instead of allowing your competency to have a narrow focus and become a dependency, you institute a regimen of continually looking for ways to apply it to other technologies, products, services, markets, or market segments. You still have the competency, but can you manage it so that it doesn't become a dependency? For example, to produce petroleum products, you have to be very competent in specialty chemicals and chemical engineering. This expertise and experience in specialty chemicals and chemical engineering can also be used to develop agricultural or pharmaceutical products. As noted in Chapter 5, Church & Dwight has been particularly adept at keeping Arm & Hammer baking soda in American households for more than 155 years by incessantly searching for and promoting alternative uses of the bicarbonate soda "technology." The product's website reinforces this by offering "solutions for the home, the family, and the body," a "daily solution," and contests that reward customers who come up with their own cretive uses for Arm & Hammer baking soda.

You can also diversify your competency into different markets or market segments. Let's say you are primarily a defense company. There is nothing that says you can't adapt your competency into products or services for industrial customers. Or you are primarily an industrial company and you offer your competency to a consumer market. Or you are a consumer company focused on high-wealth customers in developed economies, but now you apply your competency to the bottom of the pyramid market.

Avon now has separate lines for younger and older women, and even one that is marketed directly to the highly groomed urban male, or "metrosexual." More importantly, the company has enthusiastically expanded its operations outside the U.S., most successfully in East and Central Europe, Latin America, and Asia, where the culture is still more home-oriented and income-earning opportunities for women are less plentiful. As a result, more than 60% of the company's sales now come from outside the U.S., and the typical Avon representative is just as likely to be Hungarian, Brazilian, or Indonesian.

The last approach to prevent competency dependence is to have a strategy for growing through acquisition and integration. The advantage of acquisition and integration is that you bring in outside perspectives and outside talent, even if the acquired company is in your same product space. You have one set of specialists who know your competency. Buying a competing company can open up new ways of looking at that competency and new ways to expand its capabilities and opportunities for growth.

Cisco is a company that has made a regular practice of acquiring and integrating companies to expand its technological competency. The November 2005 purchase of Scientific-Atlanta was Cisco's 105th acquisition in its relatively short history and the 18th acquisition in that year alone. This was an important move for Cisco because it gives the company a boost in the increasingly important area of video technology.

COMPETITIVE MYOPIA

To prevent competitive myopia, one relatively easy solution is to organize a stand-alone competitive intelligence team. This needs to be a corporate staff function whose sole job is to track competitors and to frequently analyze and disseminate information about changes in the competitive landscape. This is not something that day-to-day managers should do because they most likely already have competitive myopia themselves.

One of the best evaluation frameworks for this intelligence unit is Michael Porter's Five Forces of Competition model. It takes an expanded, outside-in view of sources of competition and provides a method for positioning your company so that it can maximize opportunities and minimize threats. To this end, Porter identified five competitive forces that shape every industry and market and that are the source of opportunities and threats: the bargaining power of customers, bargaining power of suppliers, threat of new entrants, threat of substitute products, and rivalry among existing competitors.

Another framework that is helpful is to track, analyze, and assess disruptive technologies for their potential impact. This is especially important in fast-changing industries such as computers and communications. However, in a world that is in the throes of globalization and hyper-innovation, there are few industries where disruptive technologies are not popping up somewhere on the horizon. The works of Clayton Christensen ***(The Innovator's Dilemma, The Innovator's Solution,*** and ***Seeing What's Next)*** provide excellent methods for this type of strategic exercise.

Making stand-alone, independent investments in alternative competing technologies that are independent of the core business is another way to prevent competitive myopia. This way you can have an insider view of an emerging technology's development. These are not disruptive technologies; they are gradual substitutes that will likely become next-generation technologies. For example, telephone companies have invested in mobile telephones because they are a substitute technology for wired communications. Kodak's move into digital photography is another case. The company began a transition toward digital imaging while its traditional film business was still strong. As the demand for film cameras, film, and film processing began to shift to digital cameras and digital processing, the company used its revenues from the old technology to make major investments into the substitute technology. The transition has been a mammoth undertaking, and the race to shift revenues from film to digital is a delicate balancing act. However, if Kodak had not taken a proactive role in avoiding competitive myopia, it would certainly have suffered a rapid and painful death.

Competitive myopia can also be prevented by regularly scouting out and acquiring peripheral or niche companies that are potential paradigm shifters (new entrepreneurs with disruptive technologies). This is an effective way to give you time to recover investment in a core technology. Or your motive may be to have control over when the disruptive competency is introduced, to allow your current technology to exit after it has produced positive ROI. This is commonplace in Silicon Valley, especially in the application software industry.

You can also target an emerging market where future eompetition is likely to come from. If you are a company focused on the automobile, automotive parts, appliance, and consumer electronics industries in advanced economies, you should be looking at your counterparts in China and India because this is where future competitors are most likely to come from. You should enter those markets now to learn how to compete against your potential adversaries on their home turf, rather than worrying about having to first engage them on your turf. If you can successfully compete with them in their home market, you will have an advantage when the time comes to compete with them in your own. This is also a way to keep your rising competitors busy defending their base and delaying their entry into yours.

VOLUME OBSESSION

Since the fundamental problem of volume obsession is margin erosion, the first thing you should do to prevent volume obsession is set up a reward system for your sales force that is based on account profitability. This is especially important in the largest accounts or largest key accounts, where margins are often surrendered for the sake of protecting revenues. In essence, you empower each salesperson to be a mini-CEO who is responsible for the company's growth and profitability instead of just growth: bottom-line and top-line. Volume obsession grows your top line but at the expense of the bottom line. To prevent that from happening, you give your people incentive on both the quantity and quality of the revenue.

It's also important to make procurement a strategic function instead of an administrative one. What often happens is that you become a volume-driven company, and your economies of scale move from inside the company to outside the company. Your value-add is generally about 30% of your product or service. The other 70 percent resides in outside procurement. The end result is that your suppliers end up making a lot of money from your product! This is even more extreme with high-volume, low-margin products such as PCs. According to the Boston Consulting Group, the sellers (such as Lenovo, HP, and Compaq) add only about 11% value, with 89% going to suppliers (such as Microsoft and Intel).

For a multiproduct company, an important component of a volume obsession prevention program is to have a consistent and aggressive campaign of adding new, higher-margin products to your portfolio. It is imperative that this not be a spontaneous and haphazard activity; it must be carefully planned with a unified strategy in mind. With this approach, you can avoid being caught in the trap of relying on volume to stay afloat when a margin collapse occurs in your core products or business. Essentially you are creating a portfolio around margins. P&G does this very well. As margins for its food products (such as Grisco and Jif) began to collapse, P&G divested those less profitable businesses. But before that P&G began to invest in higher-margin product lines such as beauty care (including Giorgio, Oil of Olay, Clairol, and Wella).

TERRITORIAL IMPULSE

A transparent and predictable method of succession planning can go a long way in preventing the territorial impulse. Usually, it's best not to associate succession with any one functional silo. You don't want to instill an expectation that top-level management will always come from production or manufacturing or engineering silos. You create a separate system in which anyone who rises to the corporate leadership level has to have cross-functional experience. You can do this by rotating managers through functional silos or by creating a separate track that encompasses all the silos.

The packaged-goods industry uses brand management for this purpose. Managers in a brand management system don't have a lot of people reporting to them, unlike typical functional heads, who base their power on how many people report to them (headcount) and the budget they own. With a brand management system, your influence is limited mostly to budget power. You use your buying power to get the functional people working for you, something akin to an internal buying system. With a brand management system, power more distributed and is not tied to a particular silo. Another way to keep the territorial impulse at bay is to create a culture in which no one function is treated as "superior" to another. Southwest Airlines is the largest U.S. airline in terms of domestic passengers carried and is a profitable rarity in an industry awash in red ink. Southwest has a program called "Walk a Mile," in which any employee can do another employee's job for a day. A baggage handler cannot fly a plane, but pilots can—and do—work as baggage handlers. 75% of Southwest's 20,000 employees have participated in this job-swapping program. "It's an administrative nightmare, but one of the best tools I know for building understanding and collaboration," says Southwest CEO Herb Kelleher.

You can also lessen the likelihood of territorial impulse by having the company focus on an external driver as a way to have employees operate as a coalition with a common goal. For example, you could reorganize the company around key accounts and make it customer-centric. If the company's focus is customer-centric, there's less of an internal battle over which function comes out on top (production vs. marketing vs. engineering, etc.). Instead, everyone's energy is directed toward an external focus—the customer.

Dell Computer became the world's number-one direct-sales computer vendor by creating its entire organization around customer satisfaction. This driving interest in the customer led to the creation of a Customer Experience Council, which consists of a representative from each corporate functional area (finance, sales, product development, manufacturing, corporate communications, and IT). The council tracks data on customer issues such as product reliability, time to resolve customer support issues, and customer satisfaction surveys. Employees' bonuses and profit sharing are determined by whether the results measure up to yearly goals. And when the goals are not met—in other words, the customers should have received better service—everyone takes a hit.

If your company has a culture that is necessarily dominant, as scientists are in a pharmaceutical company, you can prevent the territorial impulse by rotating the dominant culture among the various functional silos. Scientists are a necessary element in a pharmaceutical company's success, but they have value other than in developing new drugs. They also have the potential to move into other positions within drug development (managing laboratories, people, budgets, assets) or into other functions such as sales or customer support. By shifting them among other functions, you have the benefit of their knowledge in the new function. They also are less likely to get into a turf war with other areas, such as drug development, because they have a commonality.

FINAL THOUGHTS

It's interesting to contemplate that even as human life expectancy is increasing, corporate life expectancy is decreasing (as mentioned in the Preface). Health news, on the consumer or individual level, is often upbeat; drug abuse is down, teen pregnancy is down, medications are new and improved. When a new health risk appears on the cultural radar screen such as obesity—the nation's resources are mobilized, and suddenly a hundred diet books vie for space on the best-seller lists.

But then we turn to the business page, where we find the wreckage of once-iconic companies littering the landscape, or one-time giants now teetering toward collapse. To return to where we began, here are but a few of the megacompanies whose fortunes have shifted dramatically since Peters and Waterman awarded them their imprimatur of "excellence" in 1982: Digital, Xerox, Kodak, Delta, Merck, Kmart, and GM. Shall we conclude that it's more difficult for corporations to break or prevent self-destructive habits than it is for people?

That probably is a safe conclusion. After all, businesses are institutions—layered, bureaucratic, self-protective, resistant. Companies are not amenable to public service campaigns or warnings from the Surgeon General. We all know lifelong smokers who quit cold turkey. Can companies change their identity, their culture, their business philosophy overnight?

No. But they can change. And when push comes to shove, they often do. We've seen several that have broken their self-destructive habits and—like IBM, GE, and DeBeers—have positioned themselves for a healthy future. We've seen others that have recognized their self-destructive habits (Motorola, Kodak) and are trying mightily to find the road to recovery.

Recognition is the key. Not merely recognition that what we used to do no longer works. That should be the easy part. Declining market share, net losses, and plummeting stock price should tell us that much. The harder but more critical part is recognizing that what works today may not work tomorrow. This is where recognition is no longer just a means to a cure but a proactive prevention measure.

Such recognition, such vision, has to come from the top, from exceptional leaders like Lou Gerstner and Jack Welch—leaders who prepare for the future by practicing "anticipatory management." Habits are seductive and resist change. A habit, by definition, is doing the same thing repeatedly. The leader who embraces change, whose very philosophy is based on predicting and preparing for tomorrow's world, will not only shake his company out of yesterday's self-destructive habits but will also escape the shackles of tomorrow's.

WAYS TO PREVENT THE SELF-DESTRUCTIVE HABITS

DENIAL

- Have systems in place that constantly challenge business assumptions and orthodoxies.
- Create a hands-on leadership institute that enables managers to focus on the future.
- Arrogance
- Have a professional executive coach who constantly reminds you of the pitfalls of arrogance.
- Limit personal publicity.
- Make sure that company processes of checks and balances are in place so that no one individual has absolute power.

COMPLACENCY

- Develop strong metrics—preferably numerical metrics—that will give you a quantitative method for constantly judging the company's level of complacency.
- Institute performance-based compensation.
- Rotate leaders from function to function.

COMPETENCY DEPENDENCE

- Be in a constant state of proactive migration from current technology to next-generation technology.
- Expand your core technology into other products and markets.
- Diversify your competency into different markets or market segments.
- Have a strategy for growing through acquisition and integration.

COMPETITIVE MYOPIA

- Organize a stand-alone competitive business intelligence team.
- Make stand-alone, independent investments in alternative competing technologies.
- Regularly scout out and acquire peripheral or niche companies that are potential paradigm shifters.
- Target an emerging market where future competition is likely to come from.

VOLUME OBSESSION

- Set up a reward system for your sales force that is based on account profitability.
- Make procurement a strategic function instead of an administrative function.
- For a multiproduct company, have a consistent and aggressive campaign of adding new, higher-margin products to your portfolio.

TERRITORIAL IMPULSE

- Implement a transparent and predictable method for succession planning.
- Create a culture in which no one function is treated as "superior" to another.
- Focus on an external driver as a way to have functions operate as a coalition with a common goal.
- If your company has a culture that is necessarily dominant, rotate people from that culture among the various functional silos.

INDEX

V

W

X

Z